JUST SAY NO TO MICROSOFT

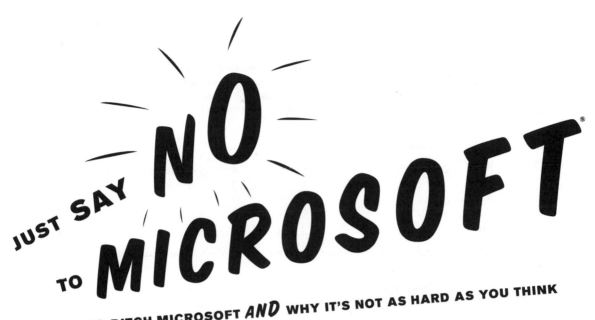

JUST SAY NO TO MICROSOFT

HOW TO DITCH MICROSOFT *AND* WHY IT'S NOT AS HARD AS YOU THINK

TONY **BOVE**

NO STARCH
PRESS

SAN FRANCISCO

Publisher: William Pollock
Production Manager: Elizabeth Campbell
Cover Design: Octopod Studios
Developmental Editor: Patricia Witkin
Copyeditor: Sarah Lemaire
Compositor: Riley Hoffman
Proofreader: Nancy Riddiough
Indexer: Ted Laux

For information on book distributors or translations, please contact No Starch Press, Inc. directly:

No Starch Press, Inc.
555 De Haro Street, Suite 250, San Francisco, CA 94107
phone: 415.863.9900; fax: 415.863.9950; info@nostarch.com; www.nostarch.com

Library of Congress Cataloging-in-Publication Data

Bove, Tony, 1955-
  Just say no to Microsoft : how to ditch Microsoft and why it's not as hard as you think / Tony Bove.
      p. cm.
  Includes bibliographical references.
  ISBN 1-59327-064-X
 1. Microsoft Windows (Computer file) 2. Operating systems (Computers) 3. Microsoft Corporation.
4. Computer software industry--United States. I. Title.
  QA76.76.063B682 2005
  005.4'46--dc22
                                                    2005023276

To the memory of Gary Kildall, founder of Digital Research and the true father of the personal computer operating system

ACKNOWLEDGMENTS

Many people contributed ideas for this book, and I thank all of them; however, some deserve special mention. John Paul Bove and James Eric Bove contributed technical expertise and allowed me to connect their Windows PCs to the Internet like guinea pigs; the PCs were promptly compromised by viruses, worms, spyware, and adware. Thanks, guys, and I'll get to eradicating all that malware as soon as I can finish these acknowledgments.

I also want to thank my No Starch Press cohorts, Bill Pollock, Susan Berge, Elizabeth Campbell, Patricia Witkin, Christina Samuell, and Riley Hoffman, for editing and improving this book immensely. A book this timely places a considerable burden on a publisher's production team, and I thank the production crew at No Starch for diligence beyond the call of reason.

I owe thanks and a happy hour or three to Carole McLendon at Waterside, my agent. And I have Kathy P. to thank for helping me come up with the title. Finally, my heartfelt thanks to my supportive family, and to members of my band, the Flying Other Brothers.

BRIEF CONTENTS

CONTENTS IN DETAIL

PART II
REHAB FOR YOUR MICROSOFT ADDICTION

4
SLAY THE WORD AND YOU'LL BE FREE 67

5
DE-MICROSOFT YOUR OFFICE 93

6
MEDIA LIB: MICROSOFT-FREE MUSIC AND VIDEO 111

PART III
THE WHOLE NETWORK IS WATCHING

7
THE MESSAGE IS THE MEDIUM FOR INFECTIONS   141

8
THIS LAN IS YOUR LAN   161

9
BROWSERS AND YOUR OWN PRIVATE IDENTITY   175

PART IV
GETTING ON WITH YOUR COMPUTER LIFE

10
TWELVE STEPS TO FREEDOM FROM MICROSOFT   197

11
WHERE DO YOU WANT TO GO TOMORROW?   211

APPENDIX
THE TRUTH IS OUT THERE   223

CITATIONS   233

INDEX   235

FOREWORD

You are about to read one of the most interesting over-
views of modern desktop computing history that's ever
been written. And that isn't to say there haven't been
a lot of good books on the subject. This one, however,
rearranges the picture in a way that properly frames
the importance (in both the good and bad senses of the
word) of Microsoft. It's hard to discuss computing today or the history of
desktop computing since 1976 without putting Microsoft into the middle of
the story. With that in mind, Tony Bove takes apart the scene with an axe and
chops away at the monolith that is Microsoft. Nobody has ever done it as well
as Bove does it here. As someone who has always been labeled a Microsoft
basher, I have mixed feelings about this. For their part, Apple users call me
an Apple basher and a Microsoft stooge. You just can't win. In fact, I like and
admire Microsoft and consider Bill Gates to be the greatest businessperson
of our generation. Our Henry Ford or even John D. Rockefeller. Others at
the company get the same praise from me and this includes Steve Ballmer,
Jeff Raikes, Carl Stork and others.

I'm also of the firm opinion that many Microsoft competitors would have done better if they were run according to the Microsoft mentality. While analysts and business schools and hotshots here and there like to say that Business is war, few companies actually take it to any extreme, short of assassinating the competition's CEO. Microsoft played hard and rough and never let up. Of course, it's now a moot point, as things have changed so drastically over the last decade that Microsoft has become a sort of latter-day IBM. More stodgy than before and with its flaws more exposed than ever. No longer is it the shark swimming forward. Personally, as with IBM, I think what we have here with Microsoft now is a dead shark bobbing around on the surface like bloated bait.

The company was once a young paranoid operation that actually enjoyed being the bad guy. They could yell and scream about it. For years I would give keynotes at various conferences and make a snide joke or two about Microsoft and you could see the Microsoft people actually relishing negative attention in a sort of defiant, "Yeah—we bad!" posture, always with a smirk. It was only within recent memory, about three or four years ago perhaps—when Bill settled into his new mansion with its heated driveway and bulletproof-glass picture window—that the company lost its edge. Maybe it began when Gates first broke 100 in his golf game. It's hard to pin down.

Maybe they got sick of the commentary or just couldn't keep their collective energy up. But all I know is that now when I make the snide remarks about Microsoft, the employees in the audience no longer seem proud; they seem defensive and they complain about it. Apparently they are not so tough anymore. The newer, more sensitive Microsoft is almost too easy to pick on. I don't like to do it. And I'm disappointed because it used to be fun all around.

The Microsoft influence on the entire computer scene is impressive, however. You run into all sorts of talented people who are running all sorts of little companies in a modified Microsoft way with emphasis on hard work and producing a good product. Even though a book like this may deride the company thoroughly, Microsoft talked a big game about producing good products and whether they did or not is not the question. The fact is employees were convinced and those employees have since taken that positive attitude elsewhere. This is actually the untold legacy of Microsoft.

Unfortunately for Microsoft, the people who stayed behind are the less ambitious corporate types who decided to work their way up the ladder internally. The nature of big companies like this always tends to reward the guy or gal who is easy to get along with and who doesn't make a lot of waves while being supportive. This tends to involve being supportive of bad ideas too. So, you end up with a company full of sensitive and supportive happy campers and yes-men. This is just a fact of corporate America. Microsoft has it worse since it is peopled by a lot of technical folks who often are not very gregarious or people-oriented. Most of them have moved into middle manager positions to which they are unsuited. Anyone at Microsoft with gumption or creativity has done whatever's necessary to gravitate to the Xbox and gaming teams—

the only areas where any real action is left. The rest of the company is represented by that dead shark. Many of the leftovers can be described one way: incredibly dull people.

This situation is not peculiar to Microsoft, but we can't keep seeing the company in the same light as we did 10 years ago. Steve Ballmer supposedly talked a big game about how Microsoft will crush Google, for example. Nobody thinks it's even possible. Microsoft has turned into the cartoon character Montgomery Burns of *The Simpsons.* Filthy rich and nasty but with no punching power. Besides, as anyone knows, to find what you are looking for within the huge Microsoft website, you need to use Google.

Whatever the case with Microsoft, it still continues to dominate in both the operating system and the Office suite spaces, two of the most lucrative and profitable businesses in the world. This dominance is not going to end any time soon, but when it does it will be interesting to see Microsoft's reaction. In fact, if someone wanted to avoid Microsoft products completely and have the same relative power on their desktop, it can be easily accomplished. And it can even be done with software that is free. Microsoft has managed to maintain market share despite this reality. This book offers up some of the possibilities to wean a user away from the expense of a Microsoft license and its limitations. Whether large numbers of people ever flock to an alternative is hard to predict.

Microsoft's problem is that the Office suite has been cloned over and over by various competitors and the OS is under constant attack from Linux and, eventually, Mac OS X too. Microsoft is not fighting back with much enthusiasm. If I personally had a choice between using Microsoft software and OpenOffice, for example, I'd choose Microsoft. But much of the decision stems from familiarity and habit. That and the fact that there are various annoying idiosyncrasies with OpenOffice that I simply do not like. But if someone was starting from scratch with OpenOffice, they may react similarly and resist switching to Microsoft Office. There are still plenty of people who religiously stick with WordPerfect, a product I could never warm up to.

But perhaps the most interesting aspect of this particular tome is the fact that it was written in the first place. During the Microsoft heyday, there was so much activity that Microsoft was not an easy target to attack. They were on the move and they were doing a great job of servicing the media. No matter how the company acted generally, their responsiveness to media questions and their proactive relationship with writers such as Bove (and everyone else for that matter) was exemplary.

I remember the days, for example, when I'd get almost every product Microsoft produced the day after its release. If I needed something else, it would arrive fast. Nowadays the only people at Microsoft who are regularly in touch with me are those involved with pad-based computing and that's only because I made it clear to them that I was getting more interested in the topic. If I read a press release from the company, I read it off the company website. I don't think I've actually been sent one by mail or email for the last five years. Not that I'm complaining. It's just an observation. But Microsoft simply isn't as aggressive with the media anymore. It's actually amazing to watch this corporate lethargy creep throughout the company.

Then again, with the company essentially banking a billion dollars a month with little effort, it's hard to justify hard work. You have to wonder whether the company could ever kick it back into high gear if it needed to. I personally don't know, but it seems unlikely.

That's what makes this book interesting. It's possibly a watershed event. In other words—a great read for anyone with a desktop computer.

John C. Dvorak

INTRODUCTION

Rings shall vanish from our noses,
And the harness from our back,
Bit and spur shall rust forever,
Cruel whips no more shall crack.

—"Beasts of England"[*]

Losing My Religion

When I first downloaded the free OpenOffice.org package, I felt a strange new sense of elation. There were no restrictions—I could copy the software to any of my computers or my family's computers. I could give copies to my friends. I had already given up on Microsoft Windows and switched to using Apple Macintosh computers. Suddenly, I no longer needed to depend on Microsoft Word, Excel, or PowerPoint.

OpenOffice.org is *open source* free software, and it runs on my PowerBook with Apple's Mac OS X. Not a piece of Microsoft code in sight. And yet, if a client were to send me a Word doc or PowerPoint file, I'm ready for it. The OpenOffice.org package includes the source code, too. Not that I know what to do with source code, because I'm not a software engineer, but it's comforting to know that nothing in the application is hidden, nothing is

---

[*] Orwell, George. *Animal Farm.* Harcourt Brace & Company. New York, NY. 1946.

secret. The source code is right there, and thousands of programmers have already pored over it, looking for bugs.

Why was my first OpenOffice.org moment so pivotal? Consider that the Mac version of Microsoft Office, which includes Word, PowerPoint, Excel, and several other programs I don't use, costs around $200 for the home or educational version—the professional version costs twice as much. With two Macs of my own and several Macs and PCs in my family, I save a bundle by going with open source software. All these computers can run OpenOffice.org for free.

But there are other important reasons for switching to OpenOffice.org. While everyone knows that most software products suck, there is anecdotal evidence that Microsoft products suck *a bit more*. My colleagues and I used to joke around with other technical journalists that Microsoft software was never truly ready for the public until version 3. No matter what the program, don't buy it until version 3. Windows versions 1 and 2 were unstable; versions of Word and Excel earlier than version 3 were worthless. Other software companies can't get away with this, but Microsoft virtually runs the industry with its near-monopoly power (or whatever the legal eagles want to call it). Millions of people place a great deal of trust in Microsoft. Could they be wrong?

One thing is certain: You need to get out from under the trees to see the forest. You need, at the very least, to try alternatives to be sure you're getting what you want from your software.

The Highway Is for Gamblers

The highway is for gamblers, better use your sense. Take what you have gathered from coincidence. —Bob Dylan, "It's All Over Now, Baby Blue" (Dylan)

Migrating away from Microsoft software seems a bit like choosing to be eccentric in a world that prizes conformity. Freeways were built to carry traffic quickly across vast distances, but I prefer to travel the back roads. Fast food is available everywhere, but I go out of my way to eat in a better class of restaurant when I travel.

I'm originally from Philadelphia, so forgive me this analogy, but Microsoft is like the toll road known as the Pennsylvania Turnpike. It looks convenient on paper, if you're coming from New Jersey and want to bypass Philly on your way across the state. Considering the traffic in Philly, it *should* be convenient. But once you get on the turnpike, you can't get off unless you pay exorbitant tolls. The rest stops are overcrowded, and the service monopolies overcharge. The fast food is terrible, and the restrooms are disgusting. It's a form of highway robbery—for most of the turnpike's length, you are stuck with two lanes and surrounded by speeding trucks, and nearly half of it seems to be always under construction.

So, are you supposed to take the back roads exclusively? Not exactly (unless you want to). There are other interstate highways, freeways, and traffic-free roads that will get you across the state in about the same amount of time, give or take an hour or two. You can get on and off them at will, without paying anything, and you can sample the local restaurants and shops, and take in the local scenery. It's a much more pleasant drive than the turnpike and is certainly more predictable in duration due to less traffic and fewer accidents. But most people won't even consider trying alternate routes. Why? Because you need to get out a map and plan the route yourself.

This book is your map.

This book is for you if you *think for yourself*. If you don't buy the party line. If you recognize the necessity of functioning in this Microsoft-dominated world but are willing to try alternatives. At the very least, I'll show you how to minimize your likelihood of being a victim of Microsoft dominance, and perhaps become even more productive with Microsoft software by making it crash less.

Chances are, you already use Microsoft software and still have some of the green-logo'd shrink-wrapped boxes of old Microsoft software—bundled with the computer but never used. And you think you have little or no choice but to use the software supplied by the not-so-jolly green giant from Redmond, Washington. But you can wean yourself off this unsafe habit and even save a few bucks in the process. You can live in the Microsoft-dominated world, work with others who use Microsoft software, participate in Microsoft-based networks, and even share Microsoft-related resources, all without having to suffer like a typical Microsoft user.

Even if you're a regular user of Windows or Microsoft Outlook, you will learn how to keep from suffering security breaches, malevolent viruses, clumsy applications, and misleading help messages by reading this book. At the very least, you'll learn how to attain some level of damage control when using Microsoft systems and software.

NOTE TO THE WISE

Don't think you are immune as a Mac or Linux user. You still have to deal with the Microsoft world—opening Microsoft Word or Excel files or Windows Media files from other people. You may have to create files for others to open with Microsoft products. You have already strayed from the Microsoft Way, but you should arm yourself with the tools you need to deal with the output from the Microsoft world.

Microsoft is everywhere and all-powerful, and you have to learn how to deal with it—either by going underground, with a Mac or Linux system, or by working within the Microsoft world. This book provides answers, alternatives, and suggestions, salted with historical (and hysterical) anecdotes, peppered with personal experiences, and cooked with considerable research and testing.

If the time is right for you to buy a new computer for travel or home use, don't automatically assume you need to use the same type of computer as the one in your office. During the two decades that PCs have ruled the industry, I've heard the same excuse time after time from people who thought they needed a Windows PC for home or travel, but would have used something else (such as a Mac) if they knew they could. Or, they thought they needed to use the same software they used at the office, which meant Microsoft Office applications (such as Word and Excel) for at least 9 out of 10 users. Even when these applications migrated to the Mac, people were wary. Then, during the last decade and a half, custom "client" applications available only for Windows appeared in many offices, locking people into using that software at home and while traveling. Microsoft's dominance grew, and the Mac lost market share. Alternative desktop systems faded away.

Living is easy with eyes closed, Misunderstanding all you see. —The Beatles, "Strawberry Fields Forever" (Lennon/McCartney)

But things have changed in just the last few years. With the Internet as the primary information carrier and the Web as its primary interface, it no longer matters which operating system you use or even which applications. All most people need is a computer that runs a browser, an email program (or just your browser with online email), and your suite of "office" applications. You can determine what works for *you* and then use what you like.

Macs work just fine, and as the market grows, Apple's share remains steady or grows. In addition, the revolutionary new model of software distribution called *open source*—in which software is given away for free and volunteers contribute to its development—is changing the dynamics of the software industry and offering the first real threat to Microsoft dominance.

You now have choices. That's what freedom and capitalism are all about, right? Let this book be your guide.

Tangled Up in Green

This book is for everyone to read, but not necessarily to follow in all ways. Only the brave might try Linux on a desktop. Many of you might switch to Macs, because it's easy to do and nearly always a rewarding experience. Still more of you will stick with Microsoft systems and software—but you can learn techniques gleaned from anecdotal experience that will help you avoid viruses and other catastrophes.

But why should you trust what I have to say? For no other reason than I *want* to say it, and I'm willing to sacrifice my "relationship" as a media person with Microsoft. I'm more than willing be left off the "A list" of analysts and editors typically invited to Redmond for early-warning non-disclosure briefings (which is no great sacrifice, since I've never been on it). Unlike many of the proponents of the nascent open source movement, I have no software to sell that competes with Microsoft. I don't have a grudge against the green giant. I once did three days of contract work for the company, and my children own some Microsoft stock (as well as Apple stock). I've used Microsoft software for decades. I still do—at least to test things. I admit that I even made money with Microsoft software. But, like a rich entertainer from Hollywood espousing the liberal agenda, I'd like to see some changes that would benefit the rest of the world.

I owe a considerable debt of gratitude to the people in the computer industry who freely exchange ideas and information. Many of these people worked at Microsoft at one time or another, and some still do.

So, to my Microsoft friends: This book contains many cheap shots, innuendos, and wisecracks about your company. If you've been with Microsoft for a long time, don't get mad—enjoy your millions and stop whining. If you just joined the company and haven't made millions yet, you have my sympathy. But this book is just one of the many irritations that Microsoft and its employees must endure in order to continue with its plan of world domination.

PART I

YOU SAY YOU WANT A REVOLUTION

1

PLAYING MONOPOLY IS NO LONGER FUN

We all know the game of Monopoly from Parker Brothers (and if you don't, go to www.monopoly.com). The object of the game is to get rich at the expense of other players by buying, renting, and selling property. In the original version set in Atlantic City, if you own Boardwalk, Park Place, Atlantic, Pacific, and Ventnor Avenues, Marvin Gardens, the four railroads, and the utilities, you pretty much own the town. The game offers a carefree attitude about business and life—you can land on Free Parking or land in Jail, depending on a roll of the dice. You can form alliances with other players to wipe out competitors. And, with a bit of luck, you could accumulate enough Get Out of Jail Free cards to rule the game.

In the late 1970s, a Harvard dropout from Seattle named Bill Gates surveyed the fledgling computer hobbyist industry and told his future Microsoft co-founder, Paul Allen, that it would be easy to monopolize. All you needed to do was control the software—the Boardwalk, Park Place, Marvin Gardens, utilities, and railroads of the computer industry. Gates was still talking about monopolizing the industry in the very early 1980s when his P.R. firm told him to stop using that word. Gates tricked the world's largest computer company, IBM, to give Microsoft that monopoly. Since then, Microsoft has tricked, bullied, or purchased its way to nearly total control over the computer industry.

NOTE *Interestingly enough, the game of Monopoly was itself stolen from its real inventor and sold to Parker Brothers the same way Gates sold his imaginary software to IBM—by tricking the game company (see "Who Invented Monopoly?" at www.adena.com/adena/ mo). The proof is that Marvin Gardens doesn't exist in Atlantic City. It's a misspelling of Marven Gardens in neighboring Margate, NJ. The charlatan inventor who tricked Parker Brothers had misspelled it when copying the board game, and the "bug" persists to this day.*

A monopoly is not illegal, nor is it unethical. Most companies strive for 100 percent market share; they just don't achieve it. It's not that Bill Gates or his company is evil; it seems somehow un-American to complain about him. But when a company becomes a monopoly, it's subject to a different set of rules, so that consumers still have some choices. Microsoft has broken those rules time and again, but it has never been entirely clear about how this has affected consumers—until now.

It is obvious now that the Microsoft monopoly, which began sometime around 1983 and culminated with its dominance of most areas of computing by 1998, has created more problems for consumers than it has solved. The result of Microsoft's monopolistic hold on the industry is the preponderance of Microsoft code. It's *everywhere*. Whether it is littered with bugs or not, the ubiquitous code is a big fat target for nefarious schemes, such as computer viruses and Internet worms that compromise your computer's security. It's as if everyone in the crowd agreed to carry their wallets in their back-right pockets to make it that much easier for pickpockets.

HOMELAND INSECURITY

You may not think that Microsoft code is so dangerous, but there's plenty of evidence to support that assertion. According to a CNET news report,[*] experts in security, technology, and economic policy agree with the Computer and Communications Industry Association (CCIA) that the reliance on a single technology, such as the Microsoft Windows operating system, by such an overwhelming majority of computer systems threatens the security of the U.S. economy and critical infrastructure.

The lack of variety makes Microsoft software a consistent target. Reliance on Microsoft software affects everyone, not just on a business or professional level, but also on a personal level. It may scare you to know that, in August 2003, the Department of Homeland Security announced that Microsoft would supply the software for the agency's 140,000 desktops. The CCIA sent an open letter asking the department to reconsider.

[*] Lemos, Robert. CNET News.com. September 24, 2003.

If you use the market-leading operating system, Windows, you are more vulnerable to attacks. That's like saying that the largest, most successful, and most heavily armed country on Earth is less secure than a third-world backwater. (Just because it's true, that doesn't make it right.)

While almost any company in America could be put under a microscope and made to look extremely hairy and ugly, the problem with Microsoft is that it *dominates the entire information technology industry*, including computer systems, applications, pocket devices, home entertainment systems, networks, and the Internet. Microsoft uses its domination to lock hardware manufacturers and consumers into using Microsoft software. That means you have no choice but hairy and ugly.

All that Microsoft code spawning more Microsoft code . . . It's like excessive in-breeding. What's next, deformed software? Bugs that reproduce tenfold? It's time to introduce new genes to the gene pool. To maintain the health of the software industry, we need an influx of code that has nothing to do with Microsoft.

The Emperor Has No Hardware

In the original gold rush of the 19th century, millions were made selling shovels and jeans. In the 1980s gold rush of the personal computer industry, software was the shovel and jeans. It was important for all personal computers to run similar software so that they could share files and applications, especially over a network. You also needed the same operating system at home if you wanted to run the programs you used at work. The Microsoft value proposition was then, and still is today, that you can use different hardware—computers, displays, and hard drives from Dell, Hewlett-Packard, etc.—while running the same system software.

Before 1983, computer folks like myself already enjoyed the relative stability of using the same operating system on different hardware—we used Digital Research's CP/M (Control Program/Monitor) on computers as diverse as the Compupro multiuser system, the portable Osborne (see Figure 1-1) and Kaypro machines, the desktop Zenith, Alspa, and Xerox computers, and the ground-breaking Processor Technology Sol machine. We even used it on Apple II with the help of a card (ironically from Microsoft) that provided CP/M compatibility.

In other words, in the beginning, we had freedom of choice in hardware, accessories, and software due to the work of Digital Research with CP/M. But this rosy scenario didn't last. Microsoft changed the industry when it made a deal with IBM in 1980 to provide the new operating system for IBM's Personal Computer (PC). Bill Gates took advantage of both Digital Research and IBM and, through sheer competitiveness and a little price-fixing, forged an entirely new industry. This industry, which took off like a rocket from 1981–1984, was based on cloning the IBM PC hardware and using Microsoft's DOS (Disk Operating System). In the name of choice, our choices as consumers were actually narrowed.

Figure 1-1: The ground-breaking Vixen portable computer from Osborne Computer Corp. ran CP/M; it was put back in the closet when Microsoft introduced DOS and Osborne went bankrupt.

Rather than encouraging a choice in computer hardware grounded in innovation, Microsoft's DOS fostered a choice grounded in copycat engineering. DOS was closely tied to the hardware configuration, which helped to solidify the IBM PC (which was made from off-the-shelf components) as a market standard, which in turn spawned an industry of IBM PC clones. Yes, you had a choice in personal computers—just like the choice Henry Ford offered with the first Model-T (you could have one in any color as long as it was black). You could choose any PC as long as it ran DOS just like IBM's PC did.

THE DREAM OF AN OPERATING SYSTEM (DOS)

The story of how Microsoft outfoxed Digital Research deserves its own book. Gary Kildall, founder of Digital Research, invented the first disk operating system for microcomputers, which he called CP/M. Its command set resembled another minicomputer system lost to history called TOPS-10. While Gates and Allen were tinkering with their first product, a programming language called Microsoft Basic, Digital Research quietly captured a considerable market share in the burgeoning microcomputer industry. More than half a million CP/M computers were sold between 1976 (when the first computer that ran CP/M—the IMSAI 8080—was introduced) and the end of 1981 (when the IBM PC was introduced).

(continued)

Kildall continued to innovate by creating a multiple-user version (MP/M) and a 16-bit version (CP/M-86), anticipating the new 16-bit computers like the IBM PC. The hallmark of CP/M and its derivatives was its loosely coupled application programming interface (API)—a software company could write applications for CP/M and know that the applications would work on all computers running it.

When IBM started working on its first PC, the company contacted Microsoft first, looking for an operating system. Bill Gates referred them to Gary Kildall and then called Gary to tell him that "a big company" was interested in his system. At that time Bill and Gary had an unofficial agreement not to step into each other's business areas—Digital Research sold operating systems, and Microsoft sold programming languages. At least that's what Gary Kildall thought.

So IBM called Digital Research to say it would be visiting the next day. Years later, rumors swirled that Gary Kildall had been out flying his plane rather than meeting with IBM. Indeed, Gary was en route from another meeting in his private plane, but he was in contact with his company when IBM showed up. No doubt the IBM reps were put off by this unruly group of programmers running a company out of a Victorian house in Pacific Grove, California. Digital Research operated more like Gary Kildall's think tank than like a business, but the company had trade secrets to protect. IBM's ironclad non-disclosure agreement gave it permission to use that information while denying Digital Research the right to disclose that the meeting had even occurred. Eventually, Kildall showed up to review the agreement (contrary to the "out flying" rumors), but another stumbling block was IBM's insistence on licensing CP/M-86 for a flat fee and renaming it. Digital Research would have lost considerable revenue and brand-name recognition and couldn't agree to that provision.

Bill Gates and his fledgling company, on the other hand, had no trouble with this stipulation because he had no trade secrets about operating systems to protect. Gates and Allen flew to Florida to meet with IBM and, in a performance that will go down as one of the most audacious in business history, sold IBM on a new operating system they didn't even have. Not only was IBM willing to pay Microsoft royalties on the new system, but in a momentary lapse of reason, IBM allowed Microsoft to retain ownership.

Gates and Allen immediately flew back to Seattle and found an operating system across town—Seattle Computer Products had developed a clone of CP/M called Q-DOS (Quick and Dirty Operating System). Paul Allen bought it outright for $75,000, and Microsoft renamed it MS-DOS. (IBM called it PC-DOS.) Kildall was not pleased. "Kildall thought it was thievery," wrote David A. Kaplan* in *The Silicon Boys*, "though it was not in his nature to sue, and the copyright law hardly would have made his case easy. . . . However, the threat of litigation was enough to bring IBM back to Pacific Grove, and this time, it seemed more accommodating." IBM would offer CP/M-86 as well as PC-DOS on its new PC. All Digital Research had to do was promise not to sue. "But the competition was rigged, and IBM's deal with Kildall was a ruse," wrote Kaplan. In reality, IBM (with help from Microsoft) fixed the pricing to make PC-DOS $200 less than CP/M-86, effectively marginalizing CP/M-86.

"At one industry forum [during that time], Gates and Kildall appeared on the same panel," wrote Kaplan. "Ever the idealist, Kildall maintained the PC market was vast enough for the both of them. Gates was more clear-eyed and prescient about the inevitability of a software monopoly. 'There's room for just one,' he replied."

---

* Kaplan, David A. *The Silicon Boys*. William Morrow. New York, NY, 1999.

Microsoft made it possible for a group of computer manufacturers to create the concept of a PC clone that used DOS and, thereby, gang up on rivals that offered proprietary systems tightly tied to proprietary hardware (such as Apple). From that point on, all PC clones basically looked and acted the same—mostly because the manufacturers relied on Microsoft for improvements to the system. Computer manufacturers that didn't make PC clones (such as pioneer portable maker Osborne Computer and award-winning, customer-oriented Compupro) went out of business, leaving Apple (see Figure 1-2) as the sole innovator to compete against Microsoft.

Figure 1-2: The newest version of the Apple Macintosh. Don't you wish we could have skipped two decades of lousy PCs and migrated from the Osborne Vixen in Figure 1-1 directly to this innovative machine?

If you were a computer manufacturer in the mid-1980s that wanted to innovate and provide an alternative to DOS—a *choice*, as in a free market—you had to roll your own, as did Apple Computer, or pay a non-discounted license for DOS. The only way to get the discount pricing for DOS was to pay what some called "the Microsoft Tax": If you offered a range of computer models in which some ran DOS and others ran the alternative, you had to pay Microsoft a fee for all your computer models, period.

Microsoft locked in the computer manufacturers that couldn't resist the lower pricing, and the rest is history. Eventually, the U.S. Justice Department's antitrust division took action, but it was many years too late. Dozens of manufacturers went out of business trying to compete on price alone, because they had no basis for innovation. They had relied on Microsoft. Today, the shakedown has advanced to the point where there are only a few computer manufacturers left.

One could go into all the reasons why Microsoft's unification of system software into one standard (DOS) was a good thing for the computer industry, especially because it led to Windows (which grew out of and then replaced DOS). Whether the good reasons outweigh the bad repercussions is someone else's debate. The question is, why do we need Microsoft's hegemony now?

SHACKLING THE PC MANUFACTURERS

In the consent decree in phase one of the U.S. Justice Department's antitrust litigation against Microsoft, worked up in July 1994, Microsoft agreed to end a set of licensing practices but without admitting any wrongdoing or suffering any penalty. A consent decree is a legal document, approved by a judge, that formalizes an agreement.

The most blatant violation was an arrangement by which PC manufacturers paid Microsoft the same royalty for shipping a computer without DOS as with DOS. As a result, manufacturers that bought a non-Microsoft operating system still had to pay Microsoft a royalty. Microsoft was "locking up the market with practices which every computer manufacturer despised and which the competitors despised," Anne K. Bingaman, assistant attorney general in charge of the Antitrust Division, said in July 1994. "To get these low prices, you had to sell your soul and never leave Microsoft." And she also said, "I hope consumers, within a short period of time, will have more choice of operating systems."

Of course, the decree was too little and too late. As James Gleick pointed out, "The practices Microsoft agreed to forgo had already served their purpose. Gates was right when he summed up the effect of the consent decree in one word: 'Nothing.'"*

*Gleick, James. "Making Microsoft Safe for Capitalism." *The New York Times Magazine.* November 5, 1995.

We don't. And as Microsoft believes in and operates according to the philosophy of survival of the fittest, it should recognize that the world no longer needs its dominance and, in fact, is stifled by it. The Internet, and hardware-neutral local area networks (LANs), provide a common way to connect computers of any kind and share files. The files themselves conform to either market-driven standards (such as JPEG or TIFF for image files and MP3 for music files) or Microsoft-driven standards from the past (such as Microsoft Word for documents). So it's not only possible but advantageous for you, the consumer, to use the operating system and hardware of your choice.

In my humble opinion, Microsoft should recognize these facts and break itself up into smaller companies that serve customers better. The breakup might even serve shareholders better than just giving them back some of their cash in dividends, as Microsoft did in 2004. Of course, I could be wrong.

You be the judge. Let's take a look at history and see how Microsoft's moves for domination affected the average computer user (me).

The Empire Strikes Back: A Thumbnail History of Microsoft

At every step of personal computer software evolution, Microsoft has either pushed out or bought out competitors and consolidated its position as a monopolist.

1980 to 1983

Microsoft rolled out DOS, a virtual copy of Digital Research's CP/M, as described in the preceding section, along with the introduction of the IBM PC. The PC clone industry was born, and nearly every manufacturer of CP/M machines went out of business.

For me, it meant that all my CP/M-based applications were useless, my third-party add-in cards for the standard S-100 bus used in CP/M computers were obsolete, and my documents and databases were locked on disks that would never be read by the new wave of PCs.

1984 to 1990

Microsoft squashed all competition by developing Windows, a virtual copy of the innovative GEM Desktop graphical user interface (GUI) by (once again) Digital Research, to run on top of DOS. The Apple Macintosh rose in opposition, its interface also loosely based on the GEM Desktop (which, in turn, was based on an interface developed at Xerox). Despite being unstable for years, Windows grew to dominate the desktop PC business, leaving the Apple Mac marginalized, while Digital Research went out of business.

For me, it meant buying a Mac to do graphics and page layout, buying a PC to maintain compatibility with clients who used PCs, and spending the next few years trying to share files between them. The Mac eventually captured most of my work because the Mac emphasized desktop publishing; to this day I can still open the files I created on early Macs.

OUR TAX DOLLARS AT WORK

The U.S. Justice Department has been investigating Microsoft since 1988 and has sued Microsoft, along with 20 state governments, at least three times. The end result of all these efforts, paid for by U.S. taxpayers? Nothing.

1991 to 1996

Microsoft released Windows 3.1, and several years later, to fix bugs in that version, they released Windows 95 to universal acclaim. Microsoft touted this version as ready and able to do desktop publishing (which it finally was) and multimedia (which it woefully wasn't—but at least it played music, a decade after the Mac started playing music). The high tech industry, dominated by high-profile investors in Windows application software companies, gave Windows 95 its vote of confidence as a standard operating system, while competitors vanished. Apple held on to its proprietary system and refused to license it, dooming the Mac to a very small minority market share.

Microsoft also took over the markets for word processing and spreadsheet applications with products that were essentially clones of WordStar and Word-Perfect (word processing) and VisiCalc and Lotus 1-2-3 (spreadsheets). All these companies, founded by ex-hippies and free thinkers, were eventually sold or went out of business, and their products are no longer on the market. All efforts to standardize document formats (including Adobe's Portable Document Format, or PDF) were sabotaged by Microsoft's inability to "print" to those formats. (Microsoft wasn't the only company to blame. The makers of QuarkXPress, the most popular page layout software for magazine publishing, were also reluctant to support them. Quark had learned a thing or two from Microsoft's marketing strategy, and locked in its publishing customers by "hard-wiring" solutions that work today but break tomorrow, forcing customers to buy upgrades.)

For me, it meant disaster if I used any word processor other than Microsoft Word. PDF remained an elusive ideal never fully realized until after the Internet hit and put Microsoft off-balance. Fortunately, Word on the Mac has been a tolerable tool set until very recently (one of the reasons I wrote this book).

1996 to Today

Microsoft owns more than 90 percent of the desktop computer system market, marginalizing the Mac as the only possible competitor. Microsoft crushed all other Internet browsers, putting innovator Netscape out of business, and moved swiftly to lock out other media players, putting pioneer RealNetworks in jeopardy. Microsoft gained considerable market share in the world of PDAs and handheld devices with a portable version of Windows, and is now moving swiftly to establish its digital rights management (DRM) technology to control access to all of the world's audio and video content. And so it goes on.

By the year 2000, I was exploring various alternatives to Microsoft software to escape virus attacks. As an employee of various technology companies over the years, I was required to use PC laptops running Windows 95, but I continued to invest in Mac technology at my home/office, because Windows 95 was not suitable for multimedia work. As my children grew up on Macs and PCs, they preferred PCs—ironically because more games and multimedia titles were available for PCs. While game developers used Macs to create and edit graphics, digital audio, and digital video, their results were coded into Windows games, because Windows owned the lion's share of the PC market.

Even I got into the act, developing and publishing a multimedia CD-ROM called *Haight-Ashbury in the Sixties.*[*] It was completely developed and programmed on a Mac, but sold to run on Windows 95 PCs. I also sold a Mac version. And I spent about 10 *hours* on PC technical support for every minute I spent on Mac technical support.

My family now uses Macs and PCs linked in a wireless Apple AirPort network (and Ethernet). We use AirPort because it works seamlessly with wireless Mac and PC laptops with no need for software installation on the PC laptops. I now use nothing but alternatives to Microsoft software on my Mac PowerBook (except for testing purposes).

---

[*] Bove, Tony and Allen Cohen. *Haight-Ashbury in the Sixties.* CD-ROM by Rockument.com. June 1996. See www.rockument.com.

With the Adobe PDF standard for documents and the service capabilities of websites and portals on the Internet, there is less of a need to use Microsoft software—even for business. It's possible to use the Web as an interface to popular enterprise applications such as SAP business packages and Oracle databases. No longer do people need to duplicate their office PC environment on a home PC. People can use whatever they want, as long as they can connect to the Web.

PUTTING BUGS INTO SOFTWARE TO THWART COMPETITORS?

It is not unusual for high-tech companies to be pursued by the Federal Trade Commission (FTC) for "deliberate incompatibilities" in products. Cases involving companies such as Eastman Kodak and IBM helped established sections of antitrust law that address issues including "non-price predation" and "predatory innovation." In 1993, the FTC investigated Microsoft about the relationship between two of Microsoft's operating systems products—Windows 3.1 and MS-DOS. In particular, the FTC's Bureau of Competition tried to determine whether Microsoft had "done something" to Windows 3.1 to deliberately keep it from running with Novell's DR DOS, which competes with MS-DOS (and was originally developed by Microsoft archrival Digital Research).

According to Andrew Schulman, a contributing editor to *Dr. Dobbs Journal*,* "If you were one of the thousands of Windows 3.1 beta testers, and if you happened to be using DR DOS rather than MS-DOS, you probably butted heads with a seemingly innocuous, yet odd, error message. . . . This message is a visible manifestation of a chunk of code whose implementation is technically slippery and evasive. While it's impossible to gauge intent, the apparent purpose of this code is to lay down arbitrary technical obstacles for DOS-workalike programs."

Schulman did some substantial system-level sleuthing to discover that the code causing the error "appears to be a wholly arbitrary test, a gratuitous gatekeeper seemingly with no purpose other than to smoke out non-Microsoft versions of DOS, tagging them with an appropriately vague 'error' message. . . . This code seems to have no technically-valid purpose, checking instead some rather unimportant aspects of DOS. In short, you can have an otherwise perfectly workable DOS, capable of running Windows, and yet not pass this test. . . . Windows beta sites that used DR DOS rather than MS-DOS might have been scared into not using DR DOS."

Of course, the section of code that performed this crucial test was the most heavily encrypted and obfuscated, resisting most attempts at decryption and disassembly. And of course, Microsoft did not comment on the report or any other accusations of misconduct, taking the position that pending investigations prevented them from responding.

So what eventually happened in the FTC investigation? In February 1993, the FTC deadlocked on a 2-2 vote and decided to take no action (our tax dollars at work). In August of that year, the U.S. Department of Justice took over the FTC investigation, which eventually led to the filing of the May 1998 antitrust suit against Microsoft. In 2000, Microsoft was found liable for maintaining an illegal monopoly in personal computer operating systems, largely due to the inclusion of Internet Explorer (IE) with Windows—but the previous allegations of misconduct regarding DR DOS were never investigated further.

---

* The programmer's magazine about languages, platforms, and tools published for more than two decades. See www.ddj.com/documents/s=1030/ddj9309d.

At the same time, all the folks using Microsoft software and Windows are targets for viruses and nearly defenseless against them, relying solely on Microsoft to address the problem. Bill Gates spoke at a trade show in early 2004 and declared that that year, Microsoft would focus on security. Thanks, Bill. Three years after September 11, and I feel as insecure as ever.

Consumers aren't the only ones left insecure by Microsoft (in this case, by Microsoft code). Businesses are also much too insecure due to Microsoft's monopolistic practices. Software entrepreneurs avoid entire areas of computing because Microsoft owns them.

No One Expects the *Microsoft* Inquisition!

In the famous Monty Python routine, representatives of the Spanish Inquisition suddenly appear and take over whatever skit is in process. Their two chief weapons are fear, surprise, and . . . No, their three chief weapons are fear, surprise, ruthless efficiency, and . . . No, their four chief weapons are fear, etc. Microsoft's chief weapons are fear, uncertainty, and doubt, which in fine Silicon Valley tradition is abbreviated FUD. As in Elmer Fudd. As in you are Elmer Fudd about to be hoodwinked again.

FEAR AND LOATHING IN THE VALLEY

Microsoft is considered the Evil Empire by so many high-level executives and well-known entrepreneurs in Silicon Valley that they are running out of metaphors to describe Gates and his company—Darth Vader, the Godfather, the Beast of Redmond, the Great Satan, the Leona Helmsley of technology, etc. Marc Andreessen, the cofounder of Netscape, referred to Microsoft as the Mafia in an interview with *The New Yorker*; Scott Cook of Intuit called Microsoft Godzilla after it tried to acquire his company; Silicon Graphics founder and Netscape cofounder Jim Clark and Scott McNealy, President and CEO of Sun Microsystems, have referred to it as the Evil Empire for so long that they started calling their respective companies (Netscape and Sun) "leaders of the Rebel Alliance." Microsoft has often been compared to the Borg in Star Trek episodes—a race of beings that assimilates entire planets and enslaves their populations. Woe unto any company that stands in its way—Microsoft will either buy you on the cheap or stomp you.

As David A. Kaplan wrote in *The Silicon Boys*,[*] "Companies define themselves in terms of Microsoft, as in 'We make software that Microsoft hasn't, doesn't, and God we hope, won't.'"

---

[*] Kaplan, David A. *The Silicon Boys: And Their Valley of Dreams*. Harper Perennial: New York, 2000.

Microsoft is not known for innovation but for copycat engineering and stifling the competition with FUD. As Jerry Kaplan points out in his book *Startup: A Silicon Valley Adventure*,[*] Microsoft became adept at identifying promising market niches with weak competitors. "It would closely study their products and tactics, then launch an attack on their position with a strong product and aggressive pricing. Sometimes, Microsoft would propose some

---

[*] Kaplan, Jerry. *Startup: A Silicon Valley Adventure*. Houghton Mifflin. Boston. 1995.

form of cooperation or joint development, to learn about the market before staging its own entry. This was the corporate version of the cheetah's hunting technique: keep a close eye on your prey, sneak up, then outrun it."

Okay, so Microsoft plays rough. Why should you care whether Microsoft stomped on the competition or locked up the market? Gushy liberals might care that small companies got stomped on, jobs were lost, the poor got poorer, and a small group of rich jerks now run everything. Libertarians might decry the lack of innovation and freedom of choice, and that a small group of rich jerks now run everything. Hard-nosed conservatives might care that Microsoft puts its multinational interests ahead of the good old U.S.A., that security is worse than ever, and that a small group of rich jerks now run everything. You should care because you're *not* one of the rich jerks that now run everything, and you're stuck with no choice but the crud put out by Microsoft, in the absence of real competition.

No competition? No choice? Sounds downright un-American. In the Sixties, we learned that in Communist Russia, you could have only one kind of car or washing machine—the kind manufactured by the state. With no competition, the state-run factories churned out products that were faulty and drab. No Calvin Klein jeans, no Guccis. Rock 'n' roll was not allowed on the radio (if you could even get a radio). Watching the PC revolution unfold in the late 1980s with cold, gray, drab PC boxes showing up on every desk, all running the same inscrutable operating system, unable even to play music the way Macs could—all I could think of was the perception back in the Sixties of Communist Russia, where you had no choices due to lack of competition.

Communist Russia and Microsoft have at least one thing in common: an agenda for world domination. Any organized effort to diminish Microsoft's power in the industry is met with overpowering force. There are numerous examples, but the case that achieved the most notoriety was the Netscape Stomp.

Microsoft's attempted conquest of Netscape in the late 1990s set a new standard for corporate arrogance. Part of Microsoft's frustration arose from being so far behind Netscape in the Internet game. When Netscape's Navigator browser first appeared on the World Wide Web, Microsoft had only a few engineers working on a browser of its own. In the summer of 1994, Netscape needed to make Navigator run properly on a new version of Windows that Microsoft was developing (Windows 95) and needed technical information just like any other company that made application software for Windows. So Netscape arranged to meet with Microsoft to talk about getting this information.

Microsoft sought first to buy the Netscape code for Windows 95. As David A. Kaplan wrote in *The Silicon Boys*,[*] "Netscape was unlikely to give up its franchise under any circumstances, but the flat fee Microsoft had in mind was a pathetic $1 million . . . During the lunch break from the meeting, the Microsoft team got on their cell phones back to Redmond—Microsoft refused to use Netscape land lines—and returned with a Microsoft vengeance. 'It was a 180-degree shift,' recalls Netscape's Todd Rulon-Miller. 'It was like Khrushchev

---

[*] Kaplan, David A. *The Silicon Boys: And Their Valley of Dreams.* Harper Perennial: New York, 2000.

at the table. They told us, "We're going to bury you. Cooperate with us and we'll consider a relationship." ' "

Indeed, the relationship Microsoft eventually proposed, in June 1995, was for Microsoft and Netscape to rig the market. Netscape CEO Jim Barksdale recalled in testimony (in the 1998 antitrust suit against Microsoft brought by the U.S. Justice Department and 20 states) that Microsoft "proposed that a 'line' be drawn between the area in which we developed products and competed and the area in which they developed products . . . They offered to allow us to continue to develop browsers for other operating systems, as long as we did not try to compete with them in developing a browser for the Windows 95 platform."

Wrote Kaplan, "It was like the mob agreeing to let honest garbage collectors have Staten Island while it controlled the busy streets of Brooklyn and Queens. Microsoft would even agree to finally give Netscape the technical data on Windows 95 it had been seeking . . . Consistent with its threat, Microsoft delayed giving Netscape technical data on Windows 95 until after the operating system hit the market. Netscape later even suggested the operating system contained booby traps to cause conflicts with Navigator." In fact, in 1996, Netscape discovered one such booby trap that prevented Navigator, the most widely used web browser at the time, to access Microsoft's home page. Imagine that.

By 1998, Navigator was overtaken by Microsoft's freely distributed Internet Explorer browser, the subject of yet another lawsuit brought by the United States against Microsoft. Internet Explorer was integrated into Windows itself, shutting out browser competition and setting the stage for other similar integrations. The Beast of Redmond sought to control the soul of computing by controlling the soul of the computer: the operating system. As James Gleick wrote in *The New York Times Magazine*,[*] "The case against Microsoft, in the eyes of its rivals, comes down to one central issue: leverage, using the operating system as a fulcrum to gain power in new markets."

By controlling the operating system and tightly integrating applications into it, Microsoft was able to shut out most of the competition, absorb anything that was innovative, and maintain its leadership. For many companies, such as Lotus, WordPerfect, and Borland, product lines and market leadership positions were lost nearly overnight as Microsoft shifted development from DOS to the Windows operating system. These companies either could not produce Windows versions fast enough or refused to do so in a timely fashion, rather than promote Windows as the new standard (which would ultimately hurt their businesses and strengthen Microsoft). Microsoft took advantage of the opportunity with Windows to integrate its Office application suite and tightly bind the suite to the Windows environment, surpassing the competition with its support for Windows—a system Microsoft could obviously support better and more quickly than its competitors because the company owned it. As the mass market caught on to the usefulness of PCs, Windows became the unofficial state religion of the high tech industry.

---

[*] Gleick, James. "Making Microsoft Safe for Capitalism." *The New York Times Magazine.* November 5, 1995.

Fear and Loathing in the Microsoft Office Suite

Anyone who has ever used Microsoft Office knows that the application package dominates desktop computing and frustrates computer users. Office includes Microsoft Word, Excel, and PowerPoint, the triumvirate of desktop business applications. Everyone knows them; they are as ubiquitous as manila folders and sticky notepads and are even available for the Mac platform. Since nearly everyone in the world needs a copy of these three applications, Microsoft imposes the equivalent of a tax on worldwide productivity with these essential but costly applications.

How did Office come to dominate desktops? Start with an operating system—Windows—that is complex, poorly documented, and not readily accessible to the competition. Microsoft has always been able to change this system at will and then preclude other companies from catching up to the new version by only releasing information very slowly. Scanning the horizon, Microsoft recognized that the emerging "office suite" packages would be the best way for the company to consolidate its leadership position in applications. Microsoft integrated its popular Word and Excel packages with a new technology called OLE (object linking and embedding) that used the operating system to allow applications to share data (such as opening a spreadsheet within a Word document). However, since Microsoft controlled OLE, it could manipulate the OLE specifications to its advantage and change them to suit its applications, leaving competitors in the dust.

Microsoft Office was already dominating the world of PC applications when Microsoft added its not–highly regarded slideshow program called PowerPoint to the mix for free. *Transform* might not be the right word to describe what the free version of PowerPoint did to the market for slideshow software. "Microsoft didn't transform the market but strangled it," said Karl Wong, director and principal analyst at research firm Dataquest in 1995.[*] The Office applications created files that couldn't be used by applications from other companies, and with the network effect of more people using Office, the need to share files with Office users helped Microsoft's market share grow exponentially.

WHAT EVIL LURKS INSIDE YOUR OFFICE DOCUMENT?

Did you know that your Office documents—Word files, Excel spreadsheets, or PowerPoint slideshows—contain hidden information, including comments and revisions? If you don't know all the tricks for stripping out or deleting this information, you are essentially compromising security every time you share an Office document. For example, if you save an Excel spreadsheet with new values in its rows and columns, the older values you deleted may still be in there, retrievable by someone who knows how.

Office stores comments, the entire revision history with multiple revisions, the document owner, links to web pages and files, hidden text, and hidden rows and columns, among other things. Microsoft now offers an Office add-in called Remove Hidden Data[*] that lets you permanently remove some of this hidden information (mostly the revisions and comments) from Word 2003/XP, Excel 2003/XP, and PowerPoint 2003/XP files.

---

[*] See www.microsoft.com/downloads/details.aspx?FamilyID=144e54ed-d43e-42ca-bc7b-5446d34e5360&displaylang=en.

By tightly integrating the applications with the operating system, Microsoft violated one of the core principles of software programming. Ordinarily, you would design loosely coupled interfaces between the system and application software, or between modules, to make maintenance easier and to upgrade different pieces at different times without having everything break. After all, why should your applications stop working, just because you upgraded the system? Microsoft employs programmers who know these principles; nevertheless, the company has discouraged the kind of modular techniques that would make computing life easier. As James Gleick pointed out in 1995, "For whatever reason, Microsoft has put aside its otherwise good practices. . . . Integration of this sort is about lock-ins through integration too tight to easily reverse, buttressed by network effects that effectively discourage even trying to resist."[†]

---

[*] Gleick, James. "Making Microsoft Safe for Capitalism." *The New York Times Magazine.* November 5, 1995.

[†] Ibid.

But you can pick this lock; you can set yourself free. You can even use software that lets you pretend you are using Microsoft Office, for the sake of your clients and associates with whom you share files, and never be imprisoned again. Chapter 4 describes alternatives to using Word as well as how to work with Word in a way that doesn't compromise your documents. Chapter 5 provides the same information about Excel and PowerPoint.

Outlook: More Viruses

Do you remember the Love Bug? Not the original Volkswagen car, but the ILOVEYOU virus, which spread quickly around the world in 2000. Security experts said the quick spread of the Love Bug was a demonstration of Microsoft software working as designed—Microsoft chose added functionality over the risk of security breaches. Microsoft's response in 2000 was to allow people to configure the software as they pleased. Of course, most people didn't understand the options or how to change them.

In May 2000, a CNET News report stated that a security hole in the open default settings for Microsoft Outlook and Outlook Express allowed email to be loaded with a destructive program that could go as far as erasing a person's hard drive. Programs that took advantage of this might not have any attachment that would make it look suspicious—the message would look like ordinary email or spam. Microsoft defended its decision to leave default settings open in the interests of convenience, noting that concerned people can change the security settings. What this means is that you have to be aware of these problems to keep your computer secure.

Microsoft Windows and Microsoft Outlook are the perfect breeding ground for virus attacks, Internet worms, Trojan Horse viruses, and spyware. Any Visual BASIC programmer with a good understanding of how Windows works can write a virus. It's amazing that these Internet security problems are continually labeled as "email viruses" or "Internet worms" rather than the more correct designation of "Windows viruses" or "Microsoft Outlook viruses."

Sun Microsystems chief executive Scott McNealy, during his keynote speech at the JavaOne trade show in June 2004, said he was surprised the market didn't share his fury at Microsoft over the security flaws that have been exploited by hosts of malicious software for many years. "Where's the outrage on viruses? I don't understand. Just in the first quarter, there were losses of $300 billion for worms and Trojan viruses. We call them worms and Trojans, but they're Microsoft viruses," McNealy said.

McNealy's estimate of $300 billion comes from analyst firms that have produced varying estimates of virus costs. Of course, these are the same firms that estimated the cost of the infamous webcast of a Victoria's Secret underwear fashion show—nearly $120 million in lost productivity, according to these guys. Who really knows? All you really know for sure is that you don't want a virus.

Security experts blame Microsoft for not moving fast enough to adapt to security threats in the Internet age. Some say the vulnerability of Outlook is evidence of fundamental flaws in many Microsoft products—rather than bugs, the problem is a flawed approach to software design. But many miss the bigger issue, which is that Microsoft considers technological innovation and perfection to be a luxury. As everyone in America knows, the "best" product is not always the bestseller. Microsoft enters a market quickly with what many believe to be an inferior product but establishes a foothold, gains market share, and eventually builds it into a standard.

NEVER BEEN A JAVA VIRUS?

In June 2004,[*] Sun Microsystems chief executive Scott McNealy reassured his audience of programmers working with Sun's Java platform that "if you write proper Java applications, we have solved Ebola, anthrax, and mad cow."

Sun's chief operating officer, Jonathan Schwartz, explained McNealy's reference to proper Java applications: "The way we architected the Java platform was on the assumption that there would be bad people out there. We needed to ensure we made it difficult for bad people and bad code to do harm to others. We haven't played this up a lot, but no one's written a virus in Java."

---

[*] CNET news report. June 29, 2004.

In some cases, rather than innovate, Microsoft creates a new product overstuffed with features that harken back to an earlier age of computing, if only to bring the trailing-edge people forward with every release. For example, according to *The Wall Street Journal*'s personal computing guru Walter S. Mossberg, Microsoft has "stubbornly insisted" that Outlook and the entire Office suite of software be programmable.[*] Mainstream users of Microsoft Office derive few benefits from this programmability, Mossberg claims, but Microsoft does not listen to mainstream users. Rather, the company listens to "techies, developers, and corporate computer departments" who love the programmability features. He suggests that Microsoft make programmability an extra option for those who want it rather than an integral part of the products.

Let's not mince words, Walt, tell us what you really think! "I don't use Outlook," he wrote in October 2002.[†] "I find it dense, ponderous, and slow. It is the most over-engineered, unnecessarily complicated program in common use today. While it has gotten a little simpler over the years, it's still overkill for most people."

I have used email and the Internet since its inception. But I have never used Outlook, and I have never been infected by an email virus. Coincidence? But don't take my word for it, at least not yet—see Chapter 7 for an entire chapter on avoiding viruses in your email.

Microsoft's Customers Sing the Blues

Microsoft is mean to its own customers. Security is the number one issue among computer users today, but if you're one of about 200 million people using older versions of Windows, Microsoft has recently reneged on its responsibility to make your computers secure. If you want the latest security enhancements to Internet Explorer, you need to upgrade to Windows XP,

---

[*] Mossberg, Walter S. "Mossberg's Mailbox." *The Wall Street Journal.* May 18, 2000.

[†] Mossberg, Walter S. *The Wall Street Journal.* October 22, 2002.

which, as of this writing, costs $199. "We do not have plans to deliver Windows XP Service Pack 2 enhancements for Windows 2000 or other older versions of Windows," the company said in a statement on September 23, 2004. "The most secure version of Windows today is Windows XP with SP2. We recommend that customers upgrade to XP and Service Pack 2 (SP2) as quickly as possible." The Windows XP SP2 enhancements provide patches, bug fixes, and security features for Windows XP and Internet Explorer.

According to the researchers at the Internet Storm Center, an unpatched Windows PC connected to the Internet will last for only about 20 minutes on average before it's compromised by a worm or virus. That figure is down from around 40 minutes, the group's estimate in 2003.[*]

The drop from 40 minutes to 20 minutes is worrisome, because it means the average survival time is not long enough for you to download the very patches that would protect your PC from Internet threats—a catch-22. In a guide to patching a new Windows system,[†] the Internet Storm Center recommends that users turn off Windows filesharing and enable the Internet Connection Firewall. Although Microsoft's latest security update, Windows XP Service Pack 2, will set such a configuration for you, you have to go online to get the update, opening yourself up to attack.

Microsoft has promised "ongoing security updates" for all supported versions of Windows and IE. But these security updates don't include the more robust and substantial security fixes that come with SP2, which is what everyone wants. At this point, more than half of the Windows customers in the world will not have access to these security features unless they upgrade to Windows XP with SP2.

One reason the security problem is getting worse is that corporate network administrators rely on employees to patch their own systems. Everyone from the low-level secretaries to the high-level executives have to remember to do it. If their Windows XP systems are configured to download the updates automatically, all they have to do is click the Add button when the Updates message pops up—like OS X on the Mac, it offers system updates like a butler offering tea and cookies. Of course, you have to be connected to the Internet and willing to download very large files when you update; you also have to be using Windows XP rather than earlier versions of Windows to stay current with bug fixes and worm blockers.

Due to the ubiquity of earlier versions of Windows in the typical corporate office, corporate network administrators can never really be sure if their networks are secure. Speaking in the summer of 2004 at the Microsoft TechEd developer conference in Amsterdam, Microsoft security consultant Fred Baumhardt said the day is likely to come when a virus or worm brings down everything. "Nobody will have time to detect it," he said. "Nobody will have time to issue patches or virus definitions and get them out there. This shows that patch management is not the be-all and end-all." Baumhardt compared the situation to the human immune system: "If the human body did patch management the way (companies do), we'd all be dead."

---

[*] Loney, Matt and Robert Lemos. "Study: Unpatched PCs compromised in 20 minutes." CNET News.com. August 17, 2004.

[†] See http://dw.com.com/redir?destUrl=http%3A%2F%2Fisc.sans.org%2Fsurvivalhistory .php&siteId=3&oId=2100-7349-5313402&ontId=1009&lop=nl_ex.

And, folks, this situation is never going to end. On October 12, 2004, Microsoft published 10 software security advisories, warning Windows users and corporate administrators of 22 new flaws. The advisories and patches range from an "important" flaw, affecting only Microsoft Windows NT Server, to a collection of eight security holes, including three rated "critical," that leave Internet Explorer open to attack. "Critical" is Microsoft's highest severity rating.

IN GATES WE STILL TRUST?

In January 2002, Bill Gates sent an important memo to Microsoft employees about trustworthiness. Gates typically uses such memos to indicate major changes in direction—such as when he kicked off the company's .Net initiative in 2000 and its push to be more Internet-centric in 1995.

"Today, in the developed world, we do not worry about electricity and water services being available," Gates wrote in the 2002 memo. "With telephony, we rely both on its availability and its security for conducting highly confidential business transactions without worrying that information about who we call or what we say will be compromised. Computing falls well short of this."

Indeed. Several years after calling for Microsoft to make its products more "trustworthy," the products are still as bug-ridden as mattresses in a flophouse, with more security holes than it would take to fill Albert Hall. Perhaps it takes more than just a few rocket scientists to make Microsoft software trustworthy. "We said that Trustworthy Computing is a 10-year project, sort of like (President) Kennedy sending people to the moon," said Scott Charney, chief security strategist for Microsoft, to a CNET reporter in January 2003, one year after Gates' memo.[*] That means the race to be trustworthy will probably spawn an entirely new security industry that will take until 2012 to make trustworthiness affordable. It's a brilliant strategy that actually profits from bugs and security breaches.

To its credit, Microsoft has made a considerable effort to clean up the Windows code, spending close to $100 million. But solutions for reliability and business integrity are largely in the planning stages, and privacy is a thorny issue. In August 2002, Microsoft signed a consent decree with the Federal Trade Commission dealing with possible violations of privacy policy in its Passport authentication service. And since no one is actively complaining against the privacy controls in Windows Media Player (except cranks like me), Microsoft seems to be getting a free ride on this initiative as well.

[*] Lemos, Robert. "One year on, is Microsoft 'trustworthy'?" CNET News.com. January 16, 2003. See http://news.com.com/2100-1001-981015.html.

Imagine There's No Microsoft . . .

I wonder if you can / No longer forced to use Windows or Office, / and everything works on a LAN.

Ever wonder how, in Star Trek, the Klingon ship's computer could easily grab data from the Enterprise's computer? Did you think they both used Microsoft software? Star Trek is not a frivolous comparison—real-world cell phones, handheld PDAs, CD-ROMs, and many other high tech gizmos were modeled after Star Trek devices. All you need to do to imagine a world without Microsoft is watch Star Trek or any of its spinoff shows, and see how it easy it will be in the future to share information between intelligent devices and systems from different planets. Don't count on Microsoft to lead us all into that utopian future.

The company means well, but it has grown too large and too powerful. As e-commerce expert Dana Blankenhorn writes in the influential newsletter *A-Clue*, "Microsoft became a defensive company with the new Millenium." According to Blankenhorn, the ultimate price of great success is moving from playing offense to playing defense. "Offense is the natural stance of a growing business, defense the stance of an institution. Competition always favors the offense, but those playing defense can stay on top by changing the rules of the game, guaranteeing their success by stopping the process that gave them success." This is why, according to Blankenhorn, "Bill Gates no longer thinks in terms of rapid growth. He thinks in terms of maintaining his advantages as long as possible."[*]

WE'D HAVE $60 BILLION TO PLAY WITH

Novell is a company that would know what to do if there were no Microsoft. At BrainShare Europe, Novell's annual conference in Barcelona in September 2004,[*] Novell CEO Jack Messman told customers and partners, "I am of the opinion that innovation has been slowed because of Microsoft. It has sucked $60 billion out of our industry that could have been used for innovation." He referred to Microsoft's exhaustive license fees for Windows, which have prevented independent software developers from directing cash into more innovative software.

The solution, according to the Novell boss, will come through the open source software movement, which will force the further commoditization of operating systems. That, in turn, will enable companies to spend more on high-level development without having to worry about compatibility with versions of operating systems. "Novell is keen to position itself as a software maker able to offer a complete alternative to Microsoft's products."

[*] Donoghue, Andrew. "Novell: Microsoft 'sucked $60 billion' out of IT." CNET News.com. September 13, 2004.

The few software companies that have survived Microsoft's onslaught (mostly by not competing head on) can imagine a world without Microsoft. Many have embraced the nascent open source movement (see Chapter 3) in an effort to simply ignore the Beast of Redmond. Others work with Microsoft at arm's length in an effort to keep Microsoft from moving into their markets, but even these companies understand that Microsoft's predatory practices guarantee that if there's money to be made in a high-tech market, Microsoft will move in.

Imagine a world in which there were at least four or five operating systems with roughly equal market share. Virus makers would have to create four or five versions of their viruses, or make them far more sophisticated to be able to work with different systems. You could choose a Mac-like system, run it on a cheap PC, connect it to any LAN or wireless network, and run applications pre-configured to run for your system.

And there'd be lots of new applications to choose from, without Microsoft Office around acting like a bully in the playground.

[*] Blankenhorn, Dana. *A-Clue*, September 13, 2004. See www.a-clue.com.

2

ALL YOU NEED IS A MAC

For a single, one-stop-shop alternative to using Microsoft software, you can't go wrong with an Apple Macintosh. From the ground up, the Mac system has no Microsoft code, and although you can run Microsoft's applications (such as Office) on a Mac, you certainly don't have to.

Some people really like the Mac because it offers a better computing experience. That's because Apple controls the hardware *and* the software, and tightly integrates them so that they work well together. Apple puts extra effort into designing its products with style, and charges a bit more for it to pay for extra R&D, but as a result, the company can offer a sexier, more innovative computing experience that makes a Windows PC look like a bucket of bolts and screws.

It's not entirely Microsoft's fault that Windows PC hardware is clunky, although Microsoft specifies to some degree how the hardware should be designed. With the exception of the popular Microsoft Mouse and some prototypes for manufacturers to copy, Microsoft doesn't make hardware. It offers an inexpensive system that other manufacturers can incorporate into their products—manufacturers such as Dell and Gateway. Blame *them* for your PC's clunkiness. By comparison, Apple markets its products as if they were meant for the fringes of the mainstream, where quality seems to matter more than cost.

Apple sells proprietary technology at a higher price. But there is very little public outcry over the ironclad control of its products or its arrogance toward companies that want to build upon its products—because Apple does not have a monopoly. (There is some outcry over Apple's near-monopoly of online music sales—see Chapter 6 for details about the iPod and iTunes.) In a better world, there would be three or four Apples, each with more than five percent market share, and you'd have choices that are truly different. The Microsoft monopoly prevents other Apples from existing.

Microsoft Windows may seem more democratic, providing more freedom of choice because it runs on less expensive hardware. But while the commonality of Windows running on all these different hardware offerings does guarantee choice, it also guarantees that there are *too many* choices with no real differentiation among them. To make a better machine, a manufacturer would have to charge almost as much as a Mac; and yet, the machine would not be as good as a Mac because Windows is too generic.

The Quickest Route to Freedom from Microsoft

So if you don't mind the extra cost, throw away that clunky Windows PC and get a Mac. In one step you can be free not only of Windows but also of hardware that relies on Windows yet is not supported by Microsoft. You have one source for support—Apple—and less finger-pointing when something goes wrong.

Acknowledging the market's demand for more affordable computers, Apple now offers a model that lets you neatly replace your PC chassis but keep your old display, keyboard, and mouse—just attach those suckers to a small, handsome, quiet Mac mini and save money. With a Mac or Mac mini (see Figure 2-1), you have a brand new computer that is immune to nearly all viruses, spyware, and other annoyances.

My primary laptop is a Mac PowerBook. I've been unhappy with Apple and some of its products more than a few times over the last three decades. Still, whenever anyone asks for a recommendation of the best desktop or notebook computer, I invariably recommend a Mac.

I'm not alone in this recommendation. Many folks use a PC at work and a Mac at home, because the Mac is more useful as a home computer and fits into the home environment better. (It's almost never the reverse—a Mac at work and a PC at home.) Highly productive people leave Microsoft Office for Windows back at the office and work on Macs at home. They may need to look at work-related documents and spreadsheets at home now and then, but Microsoft Word is available for the Mac, and there are other alternatives as well. (See Chapter 4, for alternatives to Word, and see Chapter 5, for alternatives to Excel and PowerPoint.)

Figure 2-1: The Mac mini lets you use your existing keyboard and display; just replace the guts of your old PC with this baby!

The Mac even *looks* good in the home. The very first Mac (now known as the Mac Classic) was designed to be an "information appliance" to go next to your juicer and toaster. Throughout the 1980s and early 1990s, PCs didn't look good in kitchens. Windows PCs were designed for the world of cubicles and offices. The harsh, machine-shopped desktop computers resembled the electronic typewriters and word processors they replaced. Early PC portables were no better—they looked like sewing machines from the 1950s.

Today's Windows PCs look better, but the software is still as clunky as ever—thanks to Microsoft. Windows provides just the right mix of security and obscurity to make it possible for two or more people to share the same computer and not know a damn thing about what the others are doing. "Rather than working from a theory or philosophy of system design," wrote Stewart Alsop in *Fortune* magazine, "Microsoft created Windows over time to respond to different competitive threats. So each succeeding version of the software has focused on solving a different set of problems. Commercially, this strategy has been very successful, but it is a less than artful way to make an operating system that works smoothly and intuitively. Worse, Windows must work with a plethora of hardware, each device made by a company fighting to differentiate itself, often without regard to what would make Windows run better."[*]

It's not that PC laptops and notebook computers can't ever look cool and work well as hardware devices. It's just that the office-oriented Windows software makes them inconvenient as personal devices. You've seen the befuddled look people have as they watch Windows start up and display all those inscrutable messages, wondering whether the system is okay. Windows

---

[*] Alsop, Stewart. "Just How Bad Is Windows 95?" *Fortune*. November 11, 1996. See http://208.234 .7.168/arnspub/old/Macintosh/Apple/Just-How-Bad-W95.html.

and Microsoft Office take a long time to load and run, using up your battery if you're not connected to power. And sleep mode is not much more convenient, because it still takes a while to wake up. It is difficult to figure out the power-related and battery-related controls, because they are different from one PC to the next. And the system keeps reminding you of missing devices and software updates while you are trying to get some work done in an airplane seat.

Why is the Mac recognized as a clearly superior machine to any PC on the market? "Style" is what most people think. "Grace under pressure" is what I think, and what I've experienced after two decades of using desktop and portable Macs.

So what is it about a Mac that just makes it a better experience? Is it the more intuitive menu setup that makes it easy to learn and use? How is it that the Mac can mask so much complexity behind a simple interface and provide an excellent computing experience the way BMW provides an excellent driving experience, while Microsoft Windows seems only to expose complexity at every step, like a car with its hood permanently off? You just can't put your finger on it.

Or maybe you can. This test never fails. Grab hold of a mouse connected to a PC running Windows and launch Adobe Photoshop, Adobe Illustrator, or some other graphics program. Try drawing something with it freehand. Now, do the same thing on a Mac. You can feel the difference in mouse action the same way you can feel the difference between driving a Porsche and a Camry.

So go ahead, get a Mac mini, a fully featured iMac, an iBook, or a Power-Book. You can even start wearing chino pants, floral shirts, and Birkenstocks, and make the pilgrimage to Macworld Expo in San Francisco every January. Or not.

Keep Your Identity Safe and Your System Virus-Proof

One reason for getting a Mac, and perhaps the *most* important reason for beginning computer users, is that it is less susceptible to viruses and other nasty security breaches that can reveal your identity, your Social Security number, and the password to your bank account. You can keep your digital life safe with a Mac.

The Mac represents less than 5 percent of the entire installed base of computers, as of this writing. That means it is *not* a big fat target for evil hackers like the standard PC running Windows, which has about 95 percent of the installed base. It is a fact that most viruses, worms, spyware, and other surprises of the Internet kind are designed to infect or invade Windows PCs, not Macs.

After all, if you were an evil hacker bent on getting vicarious thrills from harming others, which would you choose? More specifically, if you were launching a spam program that hunted for other people's idle computers and turned them into spam machines, you'd go looking for the large herd, not the tiny, insignificant one.

The Mac is a sanctuary, an environment safe from the slings and arrows of viruses, worms, and spyware. I have used Macs for two decades without ever getting attacked successfully. While I always follow the "rules of engagement" when encountering email—don't open strange messages and never click on attachments you don't already know are safe—I don't use any anti-virus programs and don't need any spyware protection. Why not? I use a Mac.

According to Walt Mossberg of *The Wall Street Journal*, the single most effective way to avoid viruses and spyware is to "simply chuck Windows altogether and buy an Apple Macintosh."

That's because, as Mossberg explained in his column of September 16, 2004, "there has never been a successful virus written for Mac OS X, and there is almost no spyware that targets the Mac. Plus, the Mac is invulnerable to viruses and spyware written for Windows. Not only is it more secure, but the Mac operating system is more capable, more modern, and more attractive than Windows XP, and just as stable."[*]

WHY MACS ARE SAFER THAN WINDOWS PCS

It's mainly because the Mac user base is not nearly as big a target as the Windows user base, and virus authors like big targets. But there are other, more technical reasons why Macs are safer, including these three obstacles to the installation and dissemination of viruses that Windows XP lacks:

1. Installer programs for Mac OS X require authentication to run, while installers for Windows XP don't. Authentication stops the installation process to get your password. If something starts to install itself on your Mac, you'll know because it will ask for your password.

2. Even as the sole user (a.k.a. *administrator*) of a Mac OS X system, you don't get access to system-critical files (known as *root* access in the language of system administrators). Administrators in Windows XP do, thereby allowing applications such as viruses access to those files too.

3. Security experts say the automation features in Windows make it a potential breeding ground for viruses, and that Microsoft often ships software with settings at the least secure positions. For example, Mac OS X starts out with filesharing and related services turned off—you have to turn them on to use them. Windows XP starts with these services on, assuming you want to immediately share files with other computers on the network.

While there are at least 50 known viruses written for the older Mac "classic" operating system (version 9 and earlier), there are no known OS X viruses.

A Day in the iLife

While it seems logical to compare the Mac system—specifically Mac OS X—to Windows, that comparison doesn't reflect how the entire Mac experience is more than the sum of its parts. Nothing demonstrates the Mac's superiority over Windows better than the iLife package of applications—iTunes, iPhoto, iDVD, iMovie, and GarageBand—that comes with every modern Mac.

---

[*] Mossberg, Walter S. "Personal Technology" column. *The Wall Street Journal*. September 16, 2004.

And no one describes the benefits better than Bill Gates, wistfully speaking about what may happen some day to Windows. In a *Newsweek* interview with Steven Levy in November 2003,[*] Bill Gates talked about the next big thing in Microsoft system software. "We're getting rid of a lot of specialized systems that have grown up on the PC that make it just a lot harder to work with. And then we're saying, hey, the photos will be there, so the way that you navigate photos and the way you navigate music will all be very rich and very common. . . . And that is probably the most ambitious, the most shocking advance that we've got in the system. You can find your stuff, search your stuff, share your stuff, and once people have gotten used to that, they won't want to go back to the fragmented, fairly simple world that they have right now."

Bill was talking about a future version of Windows, but he could have been talking about iLife. Mac users have it now—why wait? With every Mac you get all five applications in the iLife suite:

- iTunes for bringing songs into your Mac, organizing your music library, burning CDs, and updating your iPod.

- iPhoto for transferring photos from digital cameras, organizing your photo library, making slideshows and photo books, and sharing photos on the Internet.

- iMovie for transferring video from digital video camcorders, organizing video clips, making movies, and preparing movies for distribution on DVD or the Internet.

- iDVD for organizing media elements (music, photos, and videos) into an interactive presentation and burning DVDs.

- GarageBand for creating songs using prerecorded loops and by recording built-in software instruments and real instruments.

The closest Microsoft has come to providing these kinds of functions is the Windows XP Media Center Edition, an entertainment-oriented version of Windows XP. It works with Media Center extenders—devices that allow television shows recorded on a Media Center PC to be watched on a television in another room. At closer inspection, the operating system works just like the current version of Windows XP, but with a separate interface designed to be viewed on a television and controlled from a distance by remote control. To assemble a complete Windows-based home media entertainment center, you have to find a way to integrate other devices such as DVD burners, broadband Internet cable modems, and portable music players with this system, and then you have to figure out what software you can use to redirect the video stream to a disk file so that you can use video clips with your next digital video project. (Good luck with that.)

The Mac is already a home media entertainment center, without even trying to be one. (You can see the integration of iTunes and iMovie in Figure 2-2.) To bring in content, you can connect cameras, camcorders, a shared broadband Internet connection (using Ethernet or a wireless AirPort LAN,

---

[*] Levy, Steven. "Twilight of the PC Era?" *Newsweek.* November 24, 2003.

as described in Chapter 8), and even an audio interface for musical instruments. Combine media elements with iLife and burn your own DVDs and CDs. iLife is the hub of your Mac activities, offering functions that make use of the operating system and other applications to email photos, transfer music and video files to other computers, or keep your calendar and contacts on your iPod.

Figure 2-2: The Mac system architecture makes it easy to share media files—you can see how simple it is to choose a song from iTunes for a soundtrack while making an iMovie.

Filling iPod Softly with Your Songs

Another example of how Apple gets it right is the iTunes software and music store and the iPod for playing iTunes music. The iPod and iPod mini digital music players have become Apple's hottest-selling products. The company shipped more than 2 million iPods during the fourth quarter of 2004 alone. You can easily say no to Microsoft's new online music store and to Windows Media Player by using iTunes and an iPod. The iPod is one of the very few portable music players on the market that runs without Microsoft code—most competing players use Microsoft code for playing Windows Media Player streams (such as web radio broadcasts) and music from subscription services. The iPod steers clear of the digital rights management technology in subscription services (much of which is controlled by Microsoft, as you'll read about in Chapter 6). You can even use your iPod with Windows PCs, because the iTunes software can run on Windows, so you can share music with others stuck with the Microsoft addiction.

THE HUB OF YOUR ILIFE

So, what kind of Mac does it take to do everything iLife can do, and what more do you need to get the most out of it? Start with what you need: the latest version of OS X (10.3.4, known as Tiger, as of this writing). As a rule, get the most powerful Mac with the most amount of hard disk space that you can afford. Get a large display (17 inches or even larger) if you are serious about using iMovie.

GarageBand is the most power-hungry application in the bunch, with iDVD a close second—if you have enough to run these, you can run the rest. To run GarageBand, you need a 600 Mhz PowerPC G3 processor or higher (such as a G4 or G5), but to use software instruments, you need a G4 or G5 processor. To use iDVD, you need a 733 Mhz G4 processor or higher (G5). To use iDVD to burn DVDs, you need the SuperDrive. Many Mac models already come with a SuperDrive, which can burn CD-Rs (audio), MP3 CD-Rs, CD-ROMs, and DVD-Rs.

Older Macs can run iTunes, iPhoto, and even iMovie. I use a range of Macs, including an old iBook—six years old, in fact—that can't display higher resolutions than 800 x 600 pixels, and so it can't run iMovie or GarageBand; it also doesn't have a SuperDrive, so it can't run iDVD. But, surprise! That old iBook runs everything else.

While you absolutely need at least 4.3 gigabytes of disk space to install everything, you need far more disk space than you think, mostly to accommodate video clips, which are by far the fattest of all media types. Digital video in iMovie occupies about 3.6 MB of storage space per second—roughly 7 GB for 30 minutes. Your music and photo libraries will also take up considerable space. You can also use external portable hard disks for temporary project backup, while using a combination of CD-Rs, DVD-Rs, DV cassettes, and the .Mac service.

The bucks don't stop there. You may also need the following gear to make iLife come to life:

Audio gear

You may want to augment your Mac's speakers with headphones and portable speakers or cables to connect the Mac to your home stereo. Whether or not you have an iPod, your Mac is now a music player, so check out the listening gear in the iPod accessory areas of the Apple Store.

Digital camera

Get a digital camera for iPhoto. Your camera must be compatible with the USB (Universal Serial Bus) or FireWire (IEEE-1394) connectors on your Mac.

DV camcorder

Get a digital video (DV) camcorder that connects by FireWire to your Mac to record your video footage and to convert older footage and other video sources to the digital format with iMovie. DV cassettes can also be used to back up your video clips and final movie.

iPod

Get an iPod, of course, to play your iTunes library on the road.

The iPod is, essentially, a hard drive and a digital music player in one device, but that device is such a thing of beauty and style and so highly recognizable by now that all Apple needs to do in an advertisement is show it all by itself. The 40 GB iPod model can hold around 10,000 songs. That's more than 21 days of nonstop music. You can put enough music on a 40 GB iPod to last three weeks if played continuously, around the clock—or about one new song a day for the next 20 years.

The convenience of the iPod is really the convenience of *iTunes*. An iPod without iTunes is like a CD player without CDs. iTunes gives you access to the vast online iTunes Music Store, and it's excellent for managing music on your computer and synchronizing your music library with your iPod. Compared to Windows Media Player and other Windows-based software for organizing music, described in more detail in Chapter 6, iTunes is light-years ahead. Once people get a taste of personal music management with iTunes on Windows, they take a serious look at iTunes and the rest of the Mac software as it runs on Macs.

NOTE *About 6 percent of iPod users have already switched from PCs to Macs, and another 7 percent said they are planning to switch to a Mac within the next 12 months, according to a Piper Jaffray & Co. survey in October 2004.*

ADVENTURES IN HI-FI

To get high-quality sound from an iMac, PowerBook, other Macs, or iPods, you can connect them to your home stereo equipment. All you need is a hi-fi stereo that lets you connect a source device into its preamp/amplifier/tuner. Most stereos allow you to connect an "input" or "source" device using RCA-type cables—one (typically marked red) for the right channel and one for the left channel. All you need is a cable with a stereo mini-plug on one end and RCA-type connectors on the other.

If you get a loud buzzing sound, that means your stereo about to blow up. (Not really!) You probably mistakenly plugged your computer into the "phono-in" or "phono source" (for phonograph input) on your stereo. That connection is for phonographs (turntables)—it is not properly matched for other kinds of input devices.

The Musician's Choice: Kick Out the Jams

Making music has been part of the Mac culture since day one, when Steve Jobs introduced the original Mac—the first personal computer with built-in sound—to an audience and used it to play simple tones. Jazz great Herbie Hancock jumped on the Mac bandwagon early, using it to control synthesizers and compose music, as did electronic music godfather Vladimir Ussachevsky and pop/rock icon Todd Rundgren. Today, the Mac is the dominant platform in professional music and audio recording, and Mac software has won awards in the music industry. Digidesign's Pro Tools for the Mac even won an Oscar.

GarageBand brings the lofty capabilities inherited from a legacy of innovative music software down to the level of us amateurs. Like the name implies, this program can kick out the jams and record studio-quality music in your garage, home, or wherever you want. It turns even a notebook Mac into a portable recording studio with built-in instruments, special effects, thousands of prerecorded loops, and the wisdom of at least one or two recording engineers. You can use royalty-free loops in your songs (see Figure 2-3), play the synthesized instruments supplied with GarageBand (and add more from extra instrument packs), and even plug in a real guitar and use GarageBand's built-in amplifier simulators.

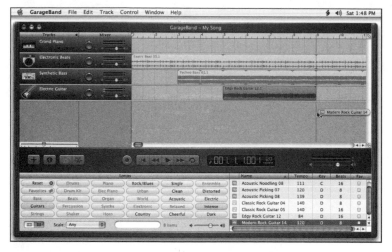

Figure 2-3: GarageBand on the Mac lets you make your own music with prerecorded loops and your own performances on keyboards and other instruments.

So you don't want to be a rock and roll star? GarageBand has other important uses, such as learning how to play previously recorded songs. You can start a song in iTunes and then switch to GarageBand and play along with it. Use it professionally to create jingles and music for advertising spots and videos. Maverick directors need music for their independent under-funded movie projects—why pay exorbitant licensing fees? The music you make in GarageBand with prerecorded loops is yours to distribute and copy as you wish.

NEVER A DULL MOMENT WITH GARAGEBAND

In his 34 years as a musician, Pete Sears has played keyboards and bass guitar with a wide variety of artists, including Rod Stewart on his classic albums *Gasoline Alley*, *Every Picture Tells a Story*, *Never a Dull Moment*, and *Smiler*. He uses GarageBand and has this to say about it: "Composing music is experimental by its nature. If you can experiment with sounds, chord progressions, and rhythm tracks whenever the moment strikes you—a professional musician could be incredibly more productive just in getting sounds and melodies together, composing bits and pieces, and then playing them back. GarageBand is a very powerful tool for pulling ideas together. . . . Not only that, GarageBand is particularly useful on the road in a laptop. You could sit in an airplane with headphones and compose music, right on your laptop keyboard, which is quite useful for a traveling musician."[*]

_____

[*] Bove, Tony. *The GarageBand Book*. Wiley: New Jersey, 2004.

.Mac the Knife

Apple has a way of cutting through all the technological bullshit and offering a way to do things that is not only easy but stylin'. The .Mac service is a perfect example: It lets you use the Internet to share media with other folks in a simple, flawless, reliable, and utterly Mac-like way.

Here's what a .Mac account gives you:

- A free email account with a cool address (membername@mac.com).

- Your own virtual Internet hard disk. Your personal iDisk is a volume that Apple hosts on its own servers and that you can access from any Mac, anywhere on the Internet. It also has a Public folder of its own, so when you toss files onto that special space on your iDisk, you can publish them to the world.

- The ability to share photos and display slideshows created in iPhoto.

- The ability to publish a custom web page of photos from iPhoto and movies from iMovie.

- Your own .Mac web page. Apple gives you slick tools that make it easy to create a personal web presence that anyone can visit and download large files from.

- A .Mac Address Book that can be synchronized with your personal address book and your browser bookmarks, so that you can retrieve contact information and browse your bookmarks anywhere, using any computer (even a Windows PC at an Internet café).

- Apple also makes plenty of special offers to .Mac users, in the form of free tutorial files and valuable commercial utilities.

Your first encounter with .Mac is when you install Mac OS X, at which time you can opt to use the service later (as many do, ignoring the many benefits it offers). You can sign up immediately, take advantage of the free trial period to get real use out of it, and then decide whether to pay to continue using it. At the moment, .Mac costs $100 a year, and that's enough to give many people pause. But when you start using it, you fall in love with it. It's incredibly convenient. There's no easier way to share photos—click a photo album in iPhoto, click another button, and shazam! It's on the Internet. You can also use iPhoto to order prints of your photos, and with a .Mac account, you can complete the transaction right away without having to enter any more information.

NOTE *Incidentally, Steve Jobs has his own .Mac account. Check out his homepage (http://homepage.mac.com/steve).*

The iDisk part of the .Mac service is a secure file server on the Internet with your own personal space already set aside for use. Your iDisk home directory appears on your desktop just like any other hard disk (see Figure 2-4). You can then drag and drop files and folders onto iDisk and know they are secure, because Apple periodically backs up its file servers and never loses anything. The files are also kept private, of course. You can then retrieve your files from your iDisk using any type of computer connected to the Internet— even a Windows PC in an Internet café. You can also copy files to your iDisk *from* any type of computer.

The real power of the Mac and the iLife suite of applications isn't just that you can collect all of your movies, photos, and songs for your own personal amusement. It's that it makes it so easy to share them with others.

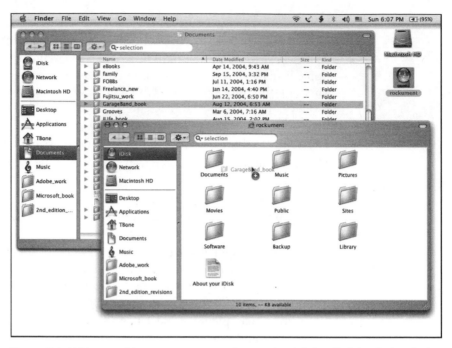

Figure 2-4: With every Mac, you can use an Internet hard disk called the iDisk, which is part of the .Mac service. Use it to back up important files or place files there for other computers to grab.

Even if you live like a hermit and can't be bothered with sharing photos, you might want to start a real estate agency out there in Hermitville. Lo and behold, the Mac makes it easy to conduct business, especially if that business involves photos, graphics, sounds, videos, and websites.

System versus System

The heart and soul of a computer is its operating system. Comparing Macs to Windows machines invariably means comparing the Mac OS X operating system to Windows XP. If you choose a PC, your choice of operating systems is either Windows XP (or some other relative of Windows) or Linux, described in Chapter 3, If you choose a Mac, the operating system that comes with it is OS X, though versions of it go by the names of Jaguar, Panther, and Tiger.

As something you spend a lot of time with and use every day, possibly more than your spouse and your car combined, an operating system is part of your life. You use it to launch applications, manage files and hard disks, and copy information from one disk to another or from one application to another. The applications rely on it to perform all sorts of functions—from saving information in a file on disk to accessing the Internet. This is why applications are designed to work with specific operating systems, and why there are at least two versions of Microsoft Word—Windows and Mac.

NOTE   *For a far more thorough feature-by-feature comparison, visit the website Mac OS X vs. Windows XP (www.XvsXP.com).*

Comparing it to Windows XP, you find that Mac OS X has many of the same functions. OS X just does many of them better. For example:

OS X is more flexible.

Both are fast, high-performance systems capable of running multiple applications at once. The Mac OS X graphical interface hides its industrial-strength, BSD-based Unix underpinnings, which offer similar memory protection and pre-emptive multitasking features as Windows XP. But OS X is more flexible than Windows in providing compatibility with older (Mac OS 9.*x*) applications, thanks to a "classic" compatibility environment. That means you can still run those older Mac programs and games rather than having to buy new versions. For example, I've successfully run Microsoft Word and Microsoft Excel applications designed for Mac OS 9.*x* or older versions of the Mac system for several years on my up-to-date PowerBook G4 with OS X version 10.3.5. I saved hundreds of dollars not having to buy new versions of these applications. On the other hand, my son's Windows XP computer cannot run versions of these same applications designed for Windows 95 or Windows 98.

OS X provides better feedback.

Mac OS X gives you immediate feedback that an application is launching after you've clicked it—the application's icon bounces up and down in the Dock. When you click something inside an application, such as the Save button in a dialog box, OS X tells you something is happening by displaying a status pinwheel. Windows doesn't give you a clue in either case, unless you try to do something else while the operation is happening.

OS X is easier to use.

Mac OS X menu items are easier to find and use. OS X adheres more closely to a design principle known as *Fitts' Law*. Virtually all application menus in OS X are attached to the top of the screen, rather than to the applications' windows (see Figure 2-5). This simultaneously adheres to Fitts' Law while reducing screen clutter. This is why selecting an OS X pull-down menu is approximately *five times faster* than doing the same in Windows.

In Windows, application menus reside within the application window, and even when the window is maximized, an application's menu items (File, Edit, etc.) are not close enough to the edge of the screen, as you can see in Figure 2-6. Maximized windows in Windows XP can't be resized, and the ease of working between applications diminishes. Dragging and dropping something from one application window to another involves dragging it down to the corresponding button on the taskbar (even though the cursor switches to the Can't-Do-That icon), and then dragging the item back up the screen to the location you want to drop it. Not impossible, but not too practical either.

It's also much easier in OS X to use the drag-and-drop method of launching an application using a particular file. You can easily drag an image from a web page onto your desktop to save it automatically, or drag a web page address (URL) from a text file into your browser's window to automatically go to that web page.

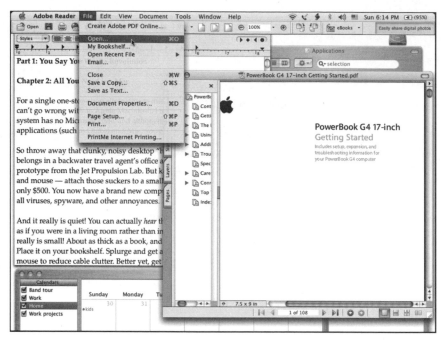

Figure 2-5: Mac OS X places application menus at the top of the screen. They change depending on which application window you select, but they are easy to find—there is always only one File menu, for example, and they are always in the same place.

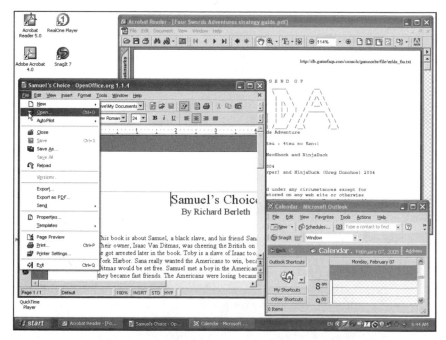

Figure 2-6: Windows XP application menus appear at the top of each window. As you can see, there are three File menus—one for each window—making it much easier to get confused.

Conversely, when you maximize a window in Windows XP, it blocks the other open windows behind it, making it harder to drag and drop content between the windows. Have you ever watched people try to resize a maximized window? You can't do it. Apple prefers windows that are not maximized to make it easier to drag and drop stuff.

Reviewers talk about "intuitive" interfaces. What they really mean is that dialogs and other messages in Mac OS X are easier to understand. Take, for example, the Save dialog box. In Windows XP, the box gives you three choices: Yes, No, and Cancel. You have to read the text in the box to understand what you're responding to. Compare that to the buttons in the Mac OS X Save dialog: Don't Save, Cancel, and Save. It's so much easier, it makes you feel warm inside.

Confusion and clutter are failures of design, not attributes of information.
—Edward R. Tufte[1]

Moving information around is also somewhat "intuitive"—we learned the principles of cutting and pasting information back in kindergarten (using those safe, thoroughly useless rounded scissors and Elmer's glue or that smelly paste). Many of us even learned how to drag and drop things in kindergarten, especially when the teacher wasn't looking. Many PC users say they prefer the cut-and-paste method of moving information rather than dragging and dropping. This is no surprise. In Windows XP, I prefer cut and paste too, not because it's an inherently superior method, but because XP's poor support for drag-and-drop has trained me avoid it altogether. But on Mac OS X—which has more thorough support for drag-and-drop—I use both methods interchangeably, according to my needs.

Though neither operating system can claim perfect intuitiveness when it comes to the drag-and-drop or cut-and-paste methods of transferring information, Mac OS X has the edge in terms of its depth of implementation, flexibility with the user, and intuitively acting as you would expect it to.

One of the most frustrating aspects of using Windows XP is installing and uninstalling applications. You can never move or rename application folders, since XP's uninstaller service relies on the exact path to the uninstaller at the moment it was installed. XP's reliance on uninstallers puts you at the mercy of application developers to make them safe and thorough. Application developers who don't want their product to be uninstalled can simply fail to provide an uninstaller, so the program stays on your computer forever. And Murphy's Law works overtime on screwing up large installations like games on Windows XP—if the system freezes during an install, it won't let you install again because it assumes you've already installed it. This catch-22 won't go away until you "clean out" the Windows Registry of any references to the application you're trying to install.

In Mac OS X, you can simply drag applications or download applications in packages to your disk or run installers that just copy a folder to your disk. Packages enable application developers to store all the various files related to the application in one place. You can move a package anywhere on the hard disk, and all the related components will go with it. Virtually all OS X applications can be uninstalled by throwing the package away and then emptying the trash.

One major advantage to drag-installations is that multiple versions of an application can be installed easily and even run simultaneously. When Microsoft Internet Explorer 5 for the Mac first came out, I often ran version 5 and version 4 simultaneously so that I could compare differences. I have also used both Microsoft Office 98 and the newer version—Office X—on my Mac. You can't do either of these things in Windows without knowing quite a few under-the-hood tricks, and who has time for that?

EVEN MICROSOFT USES MACS
(AND DOESN'T LIKE PEOPLE WHO TELL)

Microsoft fired contractor Michael Hanscom in October 2003, after he posted pictures to his weblog that he had taken of Mac G5 computers being unloaded onto the software company's campus. The blog entry, titled "Even Microsoft Wants G5s,"* got Hanscom into trouble within days of its posting. Microsoft saw the post as a security violation, because Hanscom also mentioned that he worked at the MSCopy print shop building.

Hanscom didn't think he'd done anything wrong. "The presence of Macs on the Microsoft campus isn't a secret (for everything from graphic design work to the Mac Business Unit)," he wrote in his blog *Eclectism*, "And when I took the picture, I made sure to stand with my back to the building so that nothing other than the computers and the truck would be shown—no building features, no security measures, and no Microsoft personnel. However, it obviously wasn't enough."

---

* See www.michaelhanscom.com/eclecticism/2003/10/even_microsoft_.html.

We all know how important it is to be productive with your operating system and get your job done. But coolness is a factor too. If you can use something cool—that draws you into the experience and gives you some enjoyment—you will be more productive. The Mac is not only cool, its operating system is built on a solid foundation of software that has held up for decades as reliable.

That software foundation has been tested and debugged for years by legions of the best and brightest programmers on the planet, as part of the open source software movement. While Linux grabs the headlines as the most popular piece of open source software, as you can read about in Chapter 3, Apple continues to contribute to the growth of this revolutionary software movement—the only real threat to Microsoft's hegemony.

3

LINUX: LAND OF THE FREE, HOME OF THE BRAVE

The Mac may be a nice, if pricey, alternative to using Windows and other Microsoft software, but what about all those cheap PCs, like the one your neighbor has in his garage, all dusty and stuffed with wire-wrapped circuit cards and bleeding wires all over the desktop? Your neighbor is a propeller-head engineer with years of experience in the computing industry, and every time you ask him about PC viruses, spyware, and other annoyances, he mysteriously smiles, points to his contraption in the garage, and whispers "Linux."

He's talking about the only truly free alternative to Microsoft Windows, the alternative that can run on the same hardware or other inexpensive hardware (or even Apple hardware), and operate the same devices like printers and disk drives. It's the only alternative that has a chance of unseating Microsoft from the throne of king of the business suits.

In fact, it seems like the propeller-heads are making progress competing with the business suits. On August 11, 2004, the mayor of Munich, Germany called for a bidding process to help migrate 14,000 desktop PCs from Microsoft to the Linux operating system. The competition was fierce, even though the contract was worth a modest US $35 million; Microsoft CEO Steve Ballmer interrupted his holiday in Switzerland to visit Munich and lobby the mayor. Microsoft even dropped its prices to match Linux—a remarkable feat since Linux is essentially free, and users merely purchase support services alongside it. But the Linux propeller-heads prevailed, backed by one of the biggest names in computing—IBM.

Computer history buffs must find it ironic that the roles have been reversed: the business suits are from Microsoft, and the propeller-heads are from IBM! Yes, the company known for blue-suit conservatism has come full circle over the last two decades. It has changed from a monopolistic power-house of proprietary software to a scrappy fighter promoting the ubiquitous *open source* software—software released to the public for free, accompanied by its source code.

What's going on here? Is the Microsoft monopoly slowly crumbling? Yet another European city—Bergen, Norway—opted to replace Windows and Unix machines with Linux on servers for its schools and city databases. The city chose Linux because it costs less, improves reliability, and doesn't lock the government into purchasing one company's products, said the city's chief technology officer Ole-Bjorn Tuftedal in an interview with CNET.[*] "We want great freedom from being tied to one vendor, to make the competition work better," Tuftedal said. "And it simplifies running things, if you don't need to support too many different operating systems."

Back in Munich, city officials said the decision to go with Linux was a matter of principle: the municipality wanted to control its technological destiny. Munich didn't want to place the functions of government in the hands of a commercial vendor that offered only proprietary standards and was accountable to shareholders rather than to citizens.[†]

Other countries are funding open source software initiatives outright. China, in order to be more self-sufficient, has been working on a local version of Linux for years to improve security and to avoid becoming too dependent on a single foreign supplier. Politicians in India have called on the country's vast army of programmers to develop open source products for the same reasons. Japan is collaborating with China and South Korea to develop open source alternatives to Microsoft.

The Free Software Movement

Microsoft saw it coming. Back in January 1999, at the height of the U.S. Justice Department's antitrust action against Microsoft, the company defended itself against the charge that it had used monopoly power to cut off competitors by pointing out that there were, indeed, major competitors. Microsoft's most important competitor, according to the company's own lawyers, was the open source movement, and, in particular, Linux.

---

[*] CNET News.com. June 17, 2004.
[†] "Microsoft at the power point." *The Economist*. September 11, 2003. See www.economist.com/business/displayStory.cfm?story_id=2054746.

At that time, most people thought of Linux as a system used only in the academic world of computer scientists and programmers. Today, many of the web servers of the world—the hardware and software that make Amazon.com and Google possible—are running open source software, including Linux or a distant cousin called FreeBSD. (BSD stands for Berkeley System Distribution, developed by that hotbed of radicalism, the University of California at Berkeley.) A free web server known as Apache, also part of the open source movement, controls more than half of all web servers in the universe. Open source software hums at the heart of the information technology world. In fact, the Internet could not operate without open source software such as Bind, Sendmail, or Perl.

NOTE *The Apache server was so named in the mid-1990s because the Apache was the last Native American tribe to surrender to U.S. authorities. But it turns out that the Apache server was not the open source movement's "last stand" against Microsoft—Linux, OpenOffice.org, and other open source projects are forming a united front.*

How could free software, written by refugees from the Berkeley Free Speech movement of the Sixties, challenge Microsoft for system dominance and be taken seriously by the business world? For one thing, Linux costs less than commercial software. But that's not as important as the fact that the source code is provided for free, with no legal shackles on improving it. As a result, legions of curious programmers have pounded on the code for Linux and other open source software products for years, discovering and fixing bugs. Open source software is more reliable than proprietary software produced by any single company.

Source code is the trade secret of a piece of software. It is code written in a particular programming language that you can read and understand (if you are a programmer). The source code can be changed, saved, copied, and pasted into other code because it is essentially text. The source code is then *compiled*—translated from a particular programming language into computer-readable machine code that can be executed. By providing the source code with software that is already compiled, the developer is enabling anyone to freely modify the software or incorporate the software into other software.

You might imagine that to use open source software, you need to have programming skills and plenty of time on your hands to readily fix whatever problem crops up. Not true. Linux has already been debugged and improved by a very large and energetic base of programmers who tackle just about any new problem with considerable speed—faster, in many cases, than companies that employ legions of bug fixers, and certainly faster than Microsoft. In short, you don't need to do anything but install it and run it.

Linux: The Holy Grail of Free Software

Linux was first conceived and implemented by a student programmer in Norway, and then was enhanced and refined by an enormous community of volunteer programmers communicating with each other over the Internet. As the flagship work of software representing the "open source movement," Linux has become synonymous with open source.

Conceived by a student in Norway, built up by a network of volunteers—does this sound like a system you can rely on for business applications? And yet, in very informal tests conducted by admittedly biased computer nerds whom I know and trust, Linux is more reliable than Mac OS X because it crashes less. Linux is also less vulnerable to viruses, adware, and spyware that burrow into Windows XP from the Internet.

EVERY PROGRAMMER IS A STAR

Open source is more a cultural phenomenon than a technological one. The movement started in 1984 with an Orwellian view of the corporate restructuring of the software business, which evolved from a subscription-based model that offered the source code along with the software product to a shrink-wrapped model that no longer offered any way of modifying the product. Scientists and engineers who were used to sharing source code and tinkering with software were appalled. Richard Stallman, founder of the Free Software Foundation and the GNU Project, wrote a manifesto in 1984 setting out the precepts of open source software and reminding everyone that programmers always used to share the source code and that sharing was essential for innovation.

The freedom to work with the source code is its own reward. Without any real economic motivation, the pioneers of the open source movement gave away their software and source code with one caveat: Any improvements had be incorporated back into the software and made available to everyone for free, including the source code for the improvements. Companies can build on the original source code as long as they donate their improvements back to the project.

A programmer annoyed with an open source product can "scratch the itch," as software pioneer Eric Raymond describes it (in *Free For All* by Peter Wayner)[*] and improve the software. With something as complex as an operating system, very deep, serious flaws might be hard to reproduce and identify, and it takes many more people working with the system with different hardware configurations to find these flaws. Raymond likens the difference between corporate-built software (such as Microsoft's) and open source software as the Cathedral versus the Bazaar.

In the Cathedral method of building software products, a talented architect runs a well-focused team of engineers to build the product. However, finding and fixing bugs takes months of scrutiny by the elite team, which guarantees long intervals between software releases. The Bazaar, on the other hand, acts like a free marketplace of small merchants competing with each other. Programmers around the world can use the source code to fix bugs and add new features. The best new features and bug fixes are adopted by the larger community after rigorous testing, while the worst ones fall by the wayside. New releases occur more frequently, bringing these bug fixes and features out to the public more quickly than corporate software.

Which is not to say that this undisciplined approach to system debugging produces the best code. Sometimes programmers create fixes that are just good enough for them and their specific problems. But even if a programmer fixes a problem in a way that breaks other parts of the system, the effect is to place a giant arrow on the entire problem, forcing other programmers to create better fixes.

What motivates these programmers? Many do it to show off; others use the experience to pepper their résumés with significant accomplishments. Most do it to make open source software better for themselves and, incidentally, for the rest of the world.

[*] Wayner, Peter. *Free For All.* HarperBusiness. New York, NY. 2000.

Consider the anecdotal evidence. A complete stranger sitting in the airplane seat next to me, noticing that I was reading a book about Linux, offered his own test results. "When I used a Windows laptop, I averaged about two or three crashes a day—you know, the blue screen of death," he told me. "I switched to a Mac PowerBook, and I could go for weeks without a crash, just leaving my PowerBook in sleep mode whenever I didn't use it. But this year I switched to Linux on a cheap notebook PC, and I can go for *months* without a crash."

Are there reliable, published tests and reviews that would tell us which system is better? More often than not, such comparisons try to avoid comparing Apples to oranges, so the testers assume you want to use the same software—such as running real Microsoft applications on Linux with Windows emulation and comparing that to running the same Microsoft applications on Windows. What if you did away with the Microsoft applications and Windows emulation and used free alternatives that can import and export the Microsoft file formats? Unfortunately, you're not likely to come across unbiased comparisons that take into account the change in work style.

APPLE RELIES ON OPEN SOURCE

Apple hopes the open source heritage of its operating system will spare OS X from the security woes that have dogged Microsoft. Bertrand Serlet, senior vice president of software at Apple, told CNET[*] that having a greater number of people keeping an eye on source code leads to better software security. "A lot of security problems derive from the core," he said. With open source code, "thousands of people look at the critical portions of source code and . . . check (to make sure) those portions are right. It's a major advantage to have open source code."

[*] Best, Jo. "Apple: Open-source pedigree will protect Tiger." CNET News.com. September 1, 2004. (http://news.com.com/2100-1016_3-5341689.html?tag=prntfr).

The Linux environment has to be taken at face value and in full. If you use it, don't just wade in up to your knees—dive in headfirst and use open source software as well. Windows compatibility? Fuhgeddaboutit. As in the world of web servers where specific applications don't matter (and where Linux is more popular), your world should also change so that Microsoft applications are no longer necessary.

Your computing world may also be less expensive as a result. Microsoft likes to point out that, although the software is free, support for the software can be costly. Well, yeah, but the software is *free*. This does make a difference. For one thing, the "investment" in free software doesn't lock you into buying more products from the same source, as an investment in Microsoft software does. For another, the support may be just what you wanted anyway, and you may be willing to pay for it. Commercial software also has a support price tag.

Large corporations are already discovering the lower cost advantage for large installations—it's not uncommon for a company with more than 5,000 PC users to pay more than a million dollars in license fees to Microsoft. Software vendors bidding for large installation contracts can charge much less if they provide a free operating system. Migration to Linux is a no-brainer for companies that run relatively few applications, especially if these applications are fixed-function or low-function, such as data entry, call center, or bank teller/platform automation. Office workers are using Linux on their desktops without knowing it's Linux. Microsoft is cranking up its PR machine to fight Linux because, frankly, it costs a lot less to outfit an office with Linux and a suite of free applications than it does to outfit an office with Microsoft Windows and Windows-based applications.

System Upgrades: Open Source versus Open Sores

No matter how omnipotent Microsoft is or how innovative and dedicated its talented teams are, those teams can't compete at the same level of innovation as the legions of untamed programmers in the wild. With a piece of software as complex as an operating system, there will always be bugs and upgrades to fix them; the question is how quickly you can identify and deal with bugs, and how easy it is to fold the bug fixes back into the system through upgrades.

Like just about every other software company, Microsoft tries to fix defects before shipping a new system or upgrade by providing *beta* versions—versions that include all the features and are ready to be tested in real-world situations—to power users. While that process can work for simple bugs, more complex system crashes that occur when using products from other companies (such as printers, pointing devices, network cards, etc.) are harder to detect without more widespread distribution of the beta software. And when qualified programmers outside of Microsoft find bugs, all they can do is send emails to Microsoft—they can't try to fix them, because the source code is not available to them. And, of course, Microsoft *charges you* for the "privilege" of using the buggy beta software and reporting bugs back to Microsoft. Corporations routinely pay for this privilege so that they don't get caught by these defects later, when trying to run their businesses with Microsoft software.

By comparison, open source software such as Linux is freely distributed on public websites *with* the source code. If programmers discover bugs, they can open the source code, fix them, and send the fixes immediately back to the keeper of the source code. (In the case of Linux, the keeper is its inventor, Linus Torvalds.) The programmers are license-bound to send improvements back if they intend to distribute them, so these bug fixes and improvements are rolled into new versions that become available immediately on public websites. Some improvements and fixes are hotly debated in newsgroups and emails before they become part of the new versions, and many are challenged by alternatives in a sort of competition that ensures survival of the fittest. But a lot of good code comes out of this process.

One reason why open source software such as Linux is so reliable is that it has to be—armies of programmers out in the world rely on it to make a living, and many companies have moved in to sell tools to these programmers that analyze source code and improve it. The entire source code for Linux has been analyzed and reviewed extensively.

FREE SOFTWARE HAS FEWER BUGS

An extensive review of the Linux kernel by Coverity, a company that sells a source code auditing tool, found that the core components of the operating system contain far fewer security vulnerabilities than a typical commercial software package. The *kernel* is the common set of instructions that runs in every Linux implementation.

The team at Coverity found that the Linux 2.6 kernel has 985 bugs in its 5.7 million lines of code. By way of comparison, most commercial software is generally thought to contain between 10 and 20 bugs for every 1,000 lines of code; the Linux kernel has 0.17 per 1,000 lines of code. Of the nearly 1,000 bugs that Coverity found, little more than 10 percent were actually security flaws.[*]

By comparison, one computer scientist who was not specifically looking for bugs in Windows 98 found more than 3,000 in just a small portion of the source code he was able to analyze.

Computer scientist Professor Edward Felten from Princeton University appeared as a rebuttal witness for the U.S. Department of Justice in the Microsoft trial in the early summer of 1999. Microsoft had claimed that it could not easily remove the Internet Explorer browser from the Windows 98 operating system. Felten had worked on a prototype removal program to separate Windows operating systems functions from Internet Explorer. The removal program was "proof of concept" to show that Microsoft could, indeed, remove the Internet Explorer browser from the operating system.

In court on June 10, 1999, Felten claimed that he'd found 3,000 bugs tagged by Microsoft programmers in the version of Windows 98 source code he'd looked at.[†] The code was only about one-seventh of the entire Windows 98 code. Felten had access to it under a court order so that he could produce a prototype program that demonstrated that Internet Explorer could be removed safely from Windows 98. He used the original shipping version of the source code. Presumably, Microsoft patched many of them in subsequent service packs.

---

[*] Fisher, Dennis. "Linux Kernel Review Shows Far Fewer Flaws." *eWeek*. December 14, 2004. See www.eweek.com/article2/0,1759,1741077,00.asp.

[†] Lettice, John. "DoJ expert: there are 3,000 bugs in Win98." *The Register*. June 11, 1999. See www.theregister.co.uk/1999/06/11/doj_expert_there.

LONGEST LIVING BUG IN HISTORY

In 1999, Microsoft acknowledged the existence of a bug in Windows 95 and 98 that causes your computer to crash after exactly 49 days, 17 hours, 2 minutes and 47.296 seconds of continuous operation. Every copy of the system had this bug from the time the systems were introduced.

The bug is due to code in the operating system that counts milliseconds rather than days. When this counter reaches 232 milliseconds, it crashes the system. It is perhaps the longest-living and most far-reaching software bug in history.[*]

---

[*] Wayner, Peter. *Free For All*. HarperBusiness. New York, NY. 2000.

Land of the Free Server

Each time you visit a website such as Amazon, Google (see Figure 3-1), or Orbitz, you touch a server running Linux. If you work in an enterprise that has an IT department, the chances are good that the IT people use Linux on some of their machines, perhaps for the servers that support your internal intranet or for the servers that run your enterprise websites.

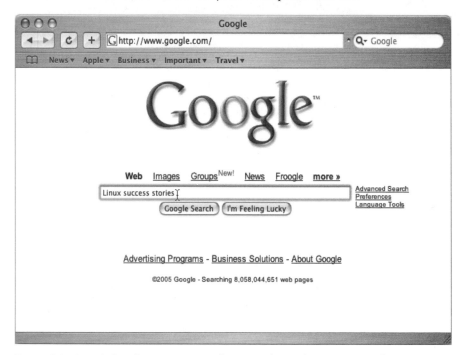

Figure 3-1: Google handles some 200 million searches a day using more than 100,000 Linux computers spread across multiple data centers.

If you use Federal Express to send or receive packages, your shipments are controlled by servers and computers, many of which run Linux. The U.S. Postal Service uses Linux servers to read the addresses on your envelopes. Yellow Cab uses Linux servers to connect you with a local taxi to pick you up for your ride to the airport, where you might get on a Boeing airplane designed and manufactured with the aid of Linux. Even your flight's operational support (including flight plans, network communications, runway analysis, and weather information) is provided by Linux servers.

Sales of servers using Linux are growing faster than sales of other operating systems with servers, according to the research firm IDC.[*] Linux is a relatively new competitor in the market for server operating systems—the most popular server system has historically been Unix and versions of Unix such as Sun Microsystems' Solaris. Microsoft is gaining some ground in this

---

[*] Hochmuth, Phil. "Linux server sales march on." Network World, June 8, 2005. See www.networkworld.com/newsletters/linux/2005/0606linux2.html?fsrc=rss-linux.

market with Windows, but the top four server hardware sellers—IBM, Hewlett-Packard, Sun Microsystems, and Dell—all support Linux, though Sun steers customers to Solaris.

One of Linux's many virtues is that it can run on just about any computing platform. Linux runs on about half of all *blade servers* in use today—not convenient holders for Zorro's swords but thin systems that plug into a chassis with a shared networking and power infrastructure. Linux is often deployed on dual-processor servers running critically important tasks. Linux can also be run as a partition on powerful machines such as IBM mainframes and Power processor-based servers and on Hewlett-Packard's Superdome servers.

During the decade that the Linux market remained fragmented, Microsoft paid little attention. As the market share of servers running Linux increased and companies such as Red Hat and Novell drew press attention, Microsoft responded by promoting fear, uncertainty, and doubt (a.k.a. FUD). Microsoft promoted the fear that as a Linux user—in particular, as a large company using Linux for your servers—you might be targeted by lawsuits over source code copyrights. Microsoft promoted uncertainty about the reliability of Linux itself. And Microsoft consistently pointed out how doubtful it was that customers would spend less with Linux than with Microsoft systems, given the need for costly support and services.

SUN MICROSYSTEMS: BEAM US UP, MR. SCOTT

Scott McNealy, CEO of Sun Microsystems, is an outspoken critic of Microsoft, open source Java servers, NHL hockey, the U.S. Government, venture capitalists, and the Wintel monopoly (Windows running on Intel processors). He even criticizes his own company, which markets an open system called Solaris, based on Unix, to support its bread-and-butter server and workstation businesses. When asked why Sun Microsystems never sold Wintel hardware, he responded, "You can't be a PC reseller and a computer creator company in the same company. . . . Every company that went onto Wintel ultimately hollowed themselves out; it was a self-imposed lobotomy."[*]

Scott McNealy was one of the first prophets of doom for the PC industry. In 2001, *PC Magazine* editor-in-chief Michael Miller took him to task for saying that the Windows PC, celebrating its 20th anniversary, was dead. "Clearly, people aren't about to throw their PCs out the window," said Scott, "though I'm sure they often feel like it. On the other hand, a lot of people and organizations are starting to realize that maybe they don't need that kind of technological hairball on their desks; there are much simpler information appliances available for the home, the office, and the classroom. Plus, people will increasingly access web services through mobile devices—wireless phones, pagers, and PDAs—more than they will through PCs."[†]

(continued)

[*] Orlowski, Andrew. "Scott McNealy on: Sun's secret weapon and its biggest mistake (not you, Apple)." *The Register*. December 6, 2002. See www.theregister.co.uk/2002/12/06/scott_mcnealy_on_suns_secret.

[†] Miller, Michael J. "Interview with Scott McNealy." *PC Magazine*. September 9, 2001. See www.pcmag.com/article2/0,1759,35769,00.asp.

In the same interview, Scott explained Sun's position as an open source software developer for its hardware business. "Sun is the most open technology company I can think of. We've always published our programming interfaces so that anyone can make a compatible product. We've also taken that openness a step further in recent years by making the source code for Solaris and our other software freely available. . . . We are a big supporter and a big contributor to the open source movement."

Scott believes that the funding for research and development (R&D) that commercial companies can bring to the party makes a big difference with open source software, such as Sun's Solaris operating system and StarOffice, Sun's Microsoft Office replacement. "I had a very interesting meeting with some Swiss company a year and half ago. . . ." remarked Scott to Andrew Orlowski in the online tech publication The Register.[*] "They decided not to deploy StarOffice because it's free. They said: it scares us, there's no contract, no agreement. So we put a price tag on it, and all of a sudden people are paying for it. You've seen more activity since we charged for it than you have the whole time it was free. It's a better product. And all of a sudden StarOffice is funding the R&D."

Scott tells it as he sees it with regard to Microsoft, such as his criticism of Microsoft's .NET strategy in response to Sun's Java, quoted by Peter Burrows in BusinessWeek. "They come up with a name for something we've been talking about for years, and then they act like they invented it. I guess if you've got a $200 million marketing budget, you can rewrite history. But name one thing they've ever invented on their own? Seriously, name one! . . . R&D and M&A (mergers and acquisitions) are the same thing over there."[†]

For a long time Sun was considered the only company left to stand up to Microsoft, but Scott acknowledges the open source movement as an important part of the opposition. "It's not just us," he told BusinessWeek. "If it was just us, we'd be toast. They've got $30 billion in cash. They could buy us for chump change. But we and a lot of other companies support open interfaces. It really is mankind against Microsoft. And mankind needs a bit of a break right now. That's why I think—no, I know!—that we're the ones wearing the white hat."

---

[*] The Register. December 6, 2002.

[†] "Q&A with Scott McNealy." BusinessWeek. November 19, 2001.
See www.businessweek.com/magazine/content/01_47/b3758010.htm.

Home of the Brave Desktop

The revolution will not be televised (as Gil Scott-Heron rapped in 1974), but it just might be brought to you by a small company like Xandros or a medium-sized company like Red Hat or a even a large company like Novell or IBM. In any case, you have to do some work to make the brave new Linux world happen on your desktop.

Linux gained popularity with server customers first, and server customers are an educated lot. Enterprises employ information technology (IT) people who can eat Linux installations for breakfast. While you can bravely do it all yourself, it is a daunting task to install Linux for a specific hardware configuration of graphics card, mouse, printer, and so on—it requires a bit of searching for documentation and actually reading it.

MICROSOFT-FUNDED LAWYERS FAIL TO KILL LINUX

There once was a fun-loving group of programmers in Santa Cruz, California, that called themselves the Santa Cruz Operation (SCO). These merry elves went about the business of providing support and software for Unix, the operating system of choice for minicomputer users of the 1970s and workstations of the 1980s. Based near the beach in a resort town, the original SCO epitomized the image of a company run by long-haired, bearded hackers rooted in counterculture values—and more inclined to use Elmer Fudd as a marketing tool than FUD (fear, uncertainty, and doubt).

Alas, by 1995, the market for Unix had dwindled, and Novell, which had bought the Unix source code from AT&T, sold its Unix business to SCO. As the original SCO programmers faded back into the labyrinth of nearby Silicon Valley or moved to other companies, SCO was taken over by lawyers who had probably never seen the beach at Santa Cruz. The mission of what is now called The SCO Group is as remote from Santa Cruz culture as you could imagine. The company exists to sue anyone who uses Linux or develops products or solutions using Linux. The method, not unlike the Spanish Inquisition, is to sow the seeds of FUD—fear, uncertainty, and doubt.

SCO has argued that it doesn't own just the Unix source code originally written by AT&T; the company also claims to own all additions to Unix that were ever made by companies that licensed Unix source code—including IBM, Hewlett-Packard, Sun Microsystems, and even Microsoft. According to SCO, any code IBM added to its version of Unix now belongs to SCO. And since IBM later donated that code to Linux, it's in Linux without SCO's permission. As a result of such donations, according to SCO, there are millions of lines of vendor-contributed, SCO-owned code in Linux.

Of course, IBM disagrees with this interpretation. Even so, of the million lines of Linux code that SCO claims IBM hijacked from Unix, SCO hasn't identified a single line that came from the original Unix source code. Yet SCO threatened lawsuits against large corporate users and even pursued one against DaimlerChrysler.

Microsoft knows a good disruptive effect when it sees one, so they jumped on this bandwagon big time. The company couldn't kill Linux, but Microsoft had no qualms about litigating Linux to death. Microsoft helped ensure that SCO could mount this fight by providing major financial help. In early 2003, Microsoft started paying SCO what eventually grew to $16.6 million for a Unix license, according to regulatory filings. Microsoft provided a second, though indirect, boost later in 2003 when it referred SCO to BayStar Capital, a fund that arranged a $50 million investment.

Microsoft might be paying the license fees because it simply believes SCO's Unix ownership claims have merit, even though the rest of the software industry does not. But arranging the BayStar Capital investment reveals Microsoft's ulterior motive—after all, why would Microsoft want to help prop up a company that is demanding millions in royalty fees from it? "Microsoft obviously has an interest in this," said Larry Goldfarb, managing partner of BayStar Capital, told CNET,[*] "and their interest is obviously in keeping their operating system on top." The licensing agreement is also unusual for Microsoft; years earlier, the company had fought hard against the same type of licensing claims from SCO's predecessor.

While SCO's plan to raise revenue from licensing has largely failed, the company succeeded in spreading clouds of doubt over Linux. As of this writing, a Michigan judge threw out all of SCO's claims against DaimlerChrysler, and SCO's lawsuit against Novell was dismissed. But large customers such as General Motors started demanding indemnification from any lawsuits concerning the origins of Linux. As a result, companies that distribute Linux, including industry leader Red Hat, now routinely indemnify their customers. As a user, you don't have to think about it.

---

[*] CNET News.com. November 15, 2004.

The companies that package Linux in a *distribution*—either on CD-ROM or for downloading—often include automatic installation programs or wizards that help you through the process of configuring the system for different hardware configurations. Distributions such as Xandros, Sun's Java Desktop System, and Lindows' Linspire offer easy Linux installations or PCs preloaded with Linux, and all the software you need for the desktop. You can even get inexpensive preloaded Linux PCs for under $300 from Wal-Mart. While Linux itself is free, companies make a profit selling packaged versions of the system on CD-ROM that include device drivers, utilities, and applications. Some of these companies, like Red Hat and Novell, offer services on the Internet for downloading software updates and obtaining support.

Linux is a great way to squeeze a few extra years out of an aging PC that is still chugging along with the crash-prone and highly insecure Windows 98. To migrate from Windows 95 to Windows XP, you most likely need more memory or even a new PC. But you can install Linux, a web browser, email, and other applications on an older PC for about $50. Computers starved for RAM (under 32 MB) can't really use it, but computers with 64 to 128 MB of RAM can run Linux with all its bells and whistles. By comparison, Microsoft Windows XP needs 128 MB or more.

Don't take my word for it. Just ask around at colleges and universities and other academic and scientific institutions. Robert Duncan III, a technologist at Bacone College, is using Linux to extend the life span of 15 of the college's older desktop systems. Using a combination of Linux, a memory upgrade, and new CD-ROMs on 133 MHz Pentium systems, his team has turned what would otherwise be obsolete hardware into serviceable Internet kiosks for the college's students. "Those machines are ancient in the Windows world and would wind up in some landfill if it weren't for Linux," Duncan said to *ComputerWorld*.[*]

How do you get Linux for your PC? The open source world is like a bazaar populated with merchants large and small. The best merchants attract the most business. In most cases, the software is free, and good service is available for a price. The software industry business model is changing to a model that charges for support and services and gives away the software—like a free cell phone with a monthly service. You no longer have to pay for shrink-wrapped boxes of software products that you have to integrate with your system on your own.

This model favors software companies—the merchants of this bazaar—that know how to integrate software from different sources and hinders companies that force their own products on the public without proper integration with other products. It also reflects the nature of software distribution on the Internet: Customers can download software and upgrades and keep their systems synchronized and up-to-date automatically, for a small monthly fee.

It can be challenging to shop around in the Linux bazaar, with hundreds of different distributions. It may seem overwhelming and confusing, but much groundwork has been done—the files and applications available with one distribution can usually be moved to another distribution. Aside from the

---

[*] McMillan, Robert. "Analysis: The business case for desktop Linux." *ComputerWorld*. IDG News Service. December 24, 2004. See www.computerworld.com.au/index.php/id;1048043952;fp ;16;fpid;0.

desktop environment, there are few differences between one Linux distribution and another, and the application offerings are pretty much the same.

Many people find installing Linux easier than installing Windows, because most Linux distributions install the applications, utilities, and tools along with the operating system. Depending on the distribution, it is possible to have a fully operating system in anywhere from 10 minutes to 2 hours. It is true that some Linux distributions are crude and ask too many cryptic questions about your graphics card, sound card, Ethernet hardware, etc. But others, such as SimplyMEPIS (www.mepis.org), can recognize your PC components automatically and install the proper software drivers.

SimplyMEPIS and Knoppix are good examples of Linux distributions that offer the goods. Both are distributed on a single CD with everything you need, and you can even run the system off the CD without installing it on your hard disk. Mozilla is typically provided as the default browser (see Chapter 9), and in some cases (such as SimplyMEPIS), Macromedia Flash, Real Player, Mplayer, and Java are all set up to work automatically. These distributions also install OpenOffice.org, the open source alternative to Microsoft Office (described in Chapter 4).

The *desktop environment* is the most important point of contact with the computer. You use it to copy files and folders, hunt for the icons or names of applications to launch them, open and save files, and send documents to the printer. SimplyMEPIS and Knoppix both offer the KDE desktop environment (shown in Figure 3-2), but you can change the window manager to something that looks more like Windows XP, such as IceWM (www.icewm.org).

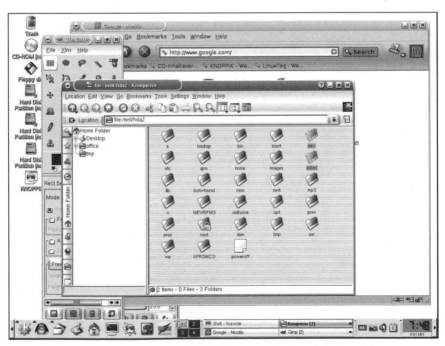

Figure 3-2: The Kool Desktop Environment (KDE) makes Linux (in this case, the Knoppix distribution) look and act somewhat like Windows XP. Also shown in this figure are the tools window for The GIMP (for image retouching), the file manager, and the Mozilla browser.

YOUR CHOICE OF DESKTOP ENVIRONMENTS

Linux desktop environments such as the KDE and GNOME look and act somewhat like the Windows XP environment. KDE, originally designed to run on Unix, provides a consistent look and feel for applications designed to run in the environment, along with Windows-like menus and toolbars. It includes a web browser, file manager, window manager, help system, tools and utilities, and an ever-increasing number of applications. More than 800 developers contributed to the project.

GNOME (GNU Network Object Model Environment) is one of the most popular desktop environments for Linux and Unix platforms and is included in most major distributions of Linux. (And yes, GNU is a recursive acronym for GNU's Not Unix; it refers to the GNU project to create a completely free operating system that looks and smells like Unix.) As you can see in Figure 3-3, GNOME offers a Macintosh-like interface and an extensive development platform for building applications that integrate into the desktop environment.

These two desktop environments dominate the Linux world. Both GNOME and KDE are in a continual state of flux, with their development teams trying to find the right mix of intuitive interface, bundled applications, and bells and whistles. Both are more than adequate as desktop environments when you compare them to Windows XP or the Macintosh; the differences are, for the most part, important only to application developers. KDE provides a robust environment that makes it easier for developers to create applications with menus that look very similar and work the same way. GNOME provides more capabilities for micromanaging menus and toolbars with custom code.

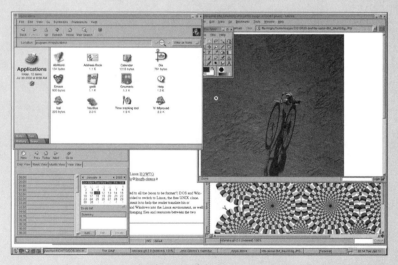

Figure 3-3: The GNU Network Object Model Environment (GNOME) makes Linux look and act somewhat like a Macintosh. Also shown are the windows for The GIMP (for image retouching), the file manager, a calendar program, and the Mozilla browser.

NOTE *You can change the background, color scheme, sound, window decorations, icons, and entire themes for KDE or GNOME and download themes that change your environment automatically. Visit the kde-look.org site for KDE themes or the art.gnome.org site for GNOME themes.*

Nothing sleeps in the world of open source software. Desktop environments for Linux are evolving quickly, because there is no standard environment dictated by someone like Bill Gates. Competition is driving innovation, even though the software is given away. For example, Sun Microsystems had developed Project Looking Glass (see Figure 3-4 and Figure 3-5), soon to be available to the open source community as a collaborative project, that offers a 3D desktop environment with window transparency, rotation, zoom, multiple desktop workspaces, and miniaturization.

Figure 3-4: In Project Looking Glass, your CD or movie database becomes a 3D jukebox, where titles are joined with images to make finding what you want easier than ever, and CDs spin in 3D space to bring to the front the title you want to see.

Figure 3-5: This view of Project Looking Glass shows word processing, video, and web browser windows in 3D. You can interact with existing 2D applications while learning how to use new 3D applications.

Linux in Your Pocket

Why *not* Linux in your pocket? You don't need Microsoft software. Pocket devices—handheld computers, personal digital assistants (PDAs), Internet-enabled cell phones, digital music players, digital video players, and anything else you can slip in your pocket—are essentially new territories for applications and systems.

Even if you are married to Microsoft Office, Outlook, and Internet Explorer, you won't be using the same versions of these applications in pocket form—these applications have to be re-engineered to work with different types of pocket devices. You have more application choices with pocket devices because open source alternatives are available that can synchronize with Microsoft software on desktops. These alternatives might just be better than the re-engineered stuff.

"Where Linux takes root is in new applications, like web servers and handheld devices," predicted Harvard Business School associate professor Clayton Christensen, the management guru/author of *Innovator's Dilemma*, at the Future Forward conference in October 2004. "As those get better, applications will get sucked off the desktop onto the Internet, and that's what will undo Microsoft."[*]

WHAT DOES BILL GATES THINK OF OPEN SOURCE?

Bill Gates, as you know, wasn't born yesterday. Many think of him as a programming wizard, when in fact he is an unabashed businessman. He does have an opinion of open source software, which he expressed to the Australian media at a briefing in June 2004.[*] "You know what my toughest competitor is?" Gates asked reporters at the media briefing. "It's pirated software. . . . If you really look around, you'll find way more pirated Windows than you'll find open source software. Way more." When pressed for his opinion of open source software, Gates said Microsoft's software represented a "dramatically higher, better choice than anything you'll get in the open source realm. It's true the press has taken a few design wins and said, 'Hey, look at that.' And you know, that's great; it's *almost helpful to us* to have a few of those." (Italics added.)

What does he mean by that? Design wins, a.k.a. innovations, are "almost helpful to us" but not quite. Too bad for Microsoft customers—those innovations are lost on the boys from Redmond.

---

[*] Ferguson, Iain. "'Windows' toughest competitor is pirates' —Gates." ZDNet Australia. June 28, 2004. See http://news.zdnet.co.uk/software/windows/0,39020396,39158862,00.htm.

Linux already runs well on a variety of processors from Intel, Motorola, IBM, and others and behaves similarly on all of them. Linux could soon be in even more pockets following the release of the first specification and reference implementation from the CE Linux Forum (Celf), a consortium of manufacturers that aims to optimize the operating system for information appliances

---

[*] LaMonica, Martin. "Microsoft advised to learn to love Linux." CNET News.com, October 18, 2004. See http://news.zdnet.co.uk/software/windows/0,39020396,39170562,00.htm.

and other devices. Celf includes consumer electronics heavyweights Panasonic, Sony, Hitachi, NEC, Philips, Samsung, Sharp, and Toshiba.

Wicked Cool Linux Applications

They're everywhere. You can find open source applications that mimic commercial applications or serve as alternatives to get the job done. Open-Office.org, for example, is a free alternative to the Microsoft Office suite and is discussed in Chapter 4. Commercial applications are available for Linux as well. Lawyers and legal professionals will be happy to know that WordPerfect runs on Linux.

Those who bring Linux home for family computing are in for a surprise: there are many free and commercial applications for playing with media. Got MP3s? Nearly all Linux distributions support the playback of MP3 sound; for example, KDE Player plays MP3 files as well as Windows Media files.

Many multimedia playback programs for Linux use the same free shared library known as xine (available from http://xinehq.de), which enables these programs (a.k.a. *front ends*) to play back CDs, DVDs, and video CDs (VCDs). The xine shared library and player also decodes multimedia files like AVI, MOV, WMV, and MP3 and displays multimedia streamed over the Internet. It uses the Windows video codecs instead of trying to reverse engineer each video format. Xanim (available from http://xanim.polter.net) is an excellent free video player that plays a wide variety of animation, audio, and video formats.

Got photos? Manage your digital photos with Lphoto, which includes a simple plug-and-play feature that interfaces with digital cameras, allows album-to-CD and album-to-DVD copying, and gives you tools to create MP3 soundtracks on custom DVD slideshows. Lphoto is an open source project financed, sponsored, and maintained by Linspire. It supports the Debian, Linspire, MandrakeSoft, Knoppix, SuSE, and Xandros Linux distributions. Digital cameras supported by Lphoto include models from Sony, HP, Canon, Nikon, Olympus, and other major brands.

Creative professionals are not left out. For an alternative to Photoshop on a Mac or PC, try The GNU Image Manipulation Program (The GIMP), a free open source program from www.gimp.org that offers similar functions for manipulating and retouching photos and composing images. The GIMP, as it is called (not just GIMP) also runs on Macintosh and Windows systems as well as Unix. Larry Ewing used an early version of The GIMP to create his now-famous Linux penguin logo (a.k.a. Tux). He explains how he did it on his website (www.isc.tamu.edu/~lewing/gimp).

NOTE *Scooby Doo, the computer-generated dog in the Warner Bros. film of the same name, was created using Linux and Film GIMP, the motion picture version of The GIMP. Developed by Caroline Dahllöf, a programmer at Rhythm & Hues Studios, Film GIMP makes it easy to retouch film frames to remove dust or wire rigs. Rhythm & Hues produced character animation and visual effects for films such as* Babe *and* The Flintstones in Viva Rock Vegas, *as well as the polar bear commercials for Coca-Cola.*

WINDOWS APPS IN WINE COUNTRY

You are better off using alternatives to Windows-based applications with your new Linux system. But if you stubbornly want to run Windows-based applications like Quicken or Adobe Photoshop, or even Microsoft applications, *you can.* Even better, you can even get free open source software to mimic Windows so that these applications feel at home. With WINE, Windows-based applications actually improve with age—you can run the programs designed for older versions of Windows as well the programs that run with the current version.

WINE (WINE stands for WINE Is Not an Emulator, yet another attempt at finding humor in recursiveness) is an ongoing project by open source developers to circumvent one of the major pillars of the Microsoft monopoly: Windows itself. The problem is that software written for Windows only works if you use a version of Windows from Microsoft. Products such as the Connectix emulator for the Mac come with a version of Microsoft Windows, because even if you emulate a PC on a Mac, you still need the Windows system to run Windows software. Specifically, you need the Windows application programming interface (API), which provides the hooks for application developers to provide system-level functions, such as menus and buttons, without having to write them from scratch. Most applications are written to work with the Win32 API for Windows.

The WINE project (www.winehq.com) is attempting to duplicate the Win32 API, so that software written for the Win32 API can run in WINE without any Microsoft code. *Wine does not require Microsoft Windows,* as it is a completely alternative implementation consisting of 100 percent Microsoft-free code. Even better, WINE can use the dynamic link libraries (DLLs) that are often supplied with Windows to control devices and memory. If your graphics card or similar hardware supplier provides software drivers as Windows-compatible DLLs, you can presumably use them with WINE instead of Windows.

WINE does not emulate the Intel x86 processor and is therefore not as slow as a PC hardware emulator. Windows-based applications that behave themselves— that is, they don't make system calls—will run just as fast as on Windows, according to the folks at the WINE project. For example, WINE works now with Microsoft Word and Excel—you can run these applications on a Linux system without Windows. Corel used WINE to migrate the Windows version of WordPerfect to Linux.

Commercial applications such as CodeWeaver's CrossOver Office for Linux (www.codeweavers.com) are built on WINE and provide support for popular Windows-based applications and Microsoft applications. CodeWeaver made the process of installing applications much easier than if you use WINE by itself. CrossOver Office offers direct support for Visio, Internet Explorer 6.1, Microsoft Office 97/2000/XP, Quicken, Photoshop 7.0, DreamWeaver, and Media Player 6.4. The new version can run Apple's iTunes application with iPod updating and music downloads from the Apple online music store.

For anyone who already owns Windows 98 and Microsoft Office, CrossOver Office is a painless way to continue to use these applications on Linux. According to *ComputerWorld,*[*] digital animation studios Pixar, DreamWorks SKG, and Disney have moved a combined total of 2,400 of their technical workstations to Linux, using CrossOver Office to run software such as Adobe Photoshop.

---

[*] McMillan, Robert. "Analysis: The business case for desktop Linux." *ComputerWorld.* IDG News Service. December 24, 2004. See www.computerworld.com.au/index.php/ id;1048043952;fp;16;fpid;0.

Got newsletters? Scribus (www.scribus.org.uk) is a dedicated desktop publishing program similar to Adobe PageMaker. It offers professional-quality page layout suitable for newsletters, magazines, and flyers. Scribus is also a complete Portable Document Format (PDF) editor. You can even create PDF forms that can be verified as authentic using digital signatures.

For a convenient searchable list of Linux applications, check out the Linux nonprofit organization site (www.linux.org/apps).

WHERE DOES BILL GATES GET HIS IDEAS?

Garbage cans brimming with other people's thrown-out code. That's what Bill said in an interview with the editor of *Programmers at Work*, a book by Microsoft Press:[*]

Interviewer: "Is studying computer science the best way to prepare to be a programmer?"

Gates: "No, the best way to prepare is to write programs and to study great programs that other people have written. In my case, I went to the garbage cans at the Computer Science Center, and I fished out listings of their operating system."

---

[*] Lammers, Susan. *Programmers At Work: Interviews With 19 Programmers Who Shaped the Computer Industry*. Microsoft Press. April 1, 1986. Interview with Bill Gates. See pages 76, 77, 80, and 83.

Revolution? We'd All Love to See the Plan

You say you want a revolution? Open source software represents a true revolution in the way software is tested, debugged, distributed, and sold. It is a revolution in the way that new, innovative software can be built on top of the best existing software. It is a revolution in the way that inventors are rewarded for their work. It is a revolution in the way that customers can solve their information technology problems by using free software and "subscribing" to paid support. It is a revolution in the way that software developers can share code across physical, corporate, and national boundaries. It is a revolution in the way that it fosters innovation anywhere in the world and contributes everywhere to the global economy. It is a revolution in the way that it defeats the Microsoft monopoly.

Most importantly, the open source movement is a revolution in the way that bugs are fixed. In the late 1970s, I worked in the engineering department of a computer company as a technical writer, producing the manuals. The writer's job was to translate programming jargon into readable English and, along the way, explain how the software worked. Occasionally, the writers would need to put a little spin on the writing and make the reader think the software worked fine, when in fact it didn't. One of our pet phrases back then was, "That's not a bug, that's a feature."

With commercial software, quality suffers because companies spend more time adding new features than fixing bugs. Microsoft Word is an excellent example of a piece of software bloated with features that many people never use, yet still buggy after all these years. By comparison, the free-for-all bazaar of the open software market produces code that is hammered on by thousands of developers eager to find flaws or add new features and improvements. When a bug pops up, thousands of programmers jump on it, and the best fix wins.

But what makes the open source movement a *movement* rather than a chaotic exercise in futility is the fact that improvements *must be shared*. The fixes and improvements might never make it out to the public if it weren't for the licensing restrictions placed on open source software—designed not to limit its free distribution, but to establish a feedback loop that works to everyone's advantage.

THE COPYLEFT LICENSE

Always leave a copy wherever you go. That's the mantra of the open source movement. The pioneers of this movement invented a new kind of license, now referred to as the *General Public License (GPL)*. While the GPL gives organizations the right to run, modify, and distribute the software, it also includes a "copyleft" clause. Basically, any new work that contains, in whole or part, software licensed under the GPL, must also be licensed under the GPL. For example, Linux is governed by GPL, so if a development group adds even a small chunk of Linux code to its software, the source code of the new software must now be shared with everyone else.

The pioneers of open source used the word *free* to mean the freedom to use the software, to study its source code and adapt it to your needs, to redistribute copies to your friends and neighbors, and to redistribute your own improvements to the software—provided that you also contribute those improvements back to the original software developers to include in the next freely distributed version. Like free beer, free software costs nothing; like free speech, it can inject new ideas and spur innovation, but only if there is an audience to hear it. In short, developers can improve and fix bugs to create a new version, but they can't sell the improved version without donating the improvements back into the free version.

The GPL guarantees that no one can build and sell commercial software based on open source software without contributing back to the movement. You may well wonder how anyone could make money in this scenario, but companies are doing just that by providing support—making the software easier to install or configure, customizing the software for a particular environment or simply packaging an excellent collection of free software and selling the package. When these companies improve a piece of free software that is governed by GPL, they donate their contributions back to the owner/manager of the software for redistribution.

Some open source authors decide to give away their creations without any restrictions, but this act of generosity can backfire. John Gilmore, a founder of Cygnus Solutions (an open source software support company acquired by Red Hat) and a developer of free encryption software, once released a program called PDTar, used to bundle together groups of files into one easily managed file known as a *tarball* (more Linux jargon). He put no restrictions whatsoever on it. The code was eventually ported to DOS by someone else, and for years, Gilmore received emails from people who wanted to get the DOS version to work properly. But Gilmore didn't have the source code for the DOS version and couldn't help them. Gilmore decided to use the GPL for his next offering.

(continued)

The forced sharing required by GPL is troubling to companies that have spent millions of dollars enhancing open source code to create their own proprietary applications. While most of these companies want open source software to succeed, they also want to add proprietary value to these software offerings and charge for them. To address this need, the open source community has created a variety of licensing agreements based on the original GPL that help companies protect their proprietary creations based on open source code. These licenses arose from the desire to ensure continued involvement of commercial organizations in open source projects, potentially increasing positive contributions. One model is the Netscape Public License, which governs the use of the Netscape browser source code— anyone can make changes and modify the software, but Netscape is under no obligation to share improvements made by others.

Questions about licensing pop up because some commercial products are based on open source code. Large portions of Apple's Mac OS X came from Mach and BSD, both of which were released with licenses that offer more freedom than GPL. Apple has returned the favor by sharing the source code to these parts of the system, but the company is still able to keep much of its offering proprietary. The parts that Apple shares are improved by the wider community of open source developers. So while the copyright issues for a given software product may seem murky at best to those who contributed to it, the software is improved by the open source method anyway, and everyone benefits.

The open source movement is rooted in the same ideas that fueled the American Revolution in 1776, as echoed by Peter Wayner in *Free For All.* "The free software movement certifies that we are all created equal, with the same rights to life, liberty, and the pursuit of bug-free code."[*] It's about the freedom to choose better software without getting locked in. The open source movement tolerates all newcomers, as long as they share their source code. It tolerates not only the fine, upstanding corporations trying to build legitimate businesses supporting open source software, but also the con artists and carpetbaggers trying to make a fast buck.

What the open source movement does *not* tolerate is a tyranny of the few. It does *not* tolerate Microsoft's proprietary, monopolistic hold on the software industry.

There is no surer road to a Microsoft-free computing life than open source software. The debate is not so much about whether Windows or Linux is better or less costly today; it's about which system will take you into the future without costing you a fortune. Microsoft lost ground to open source software in servers and Internet software, and may lose more ground in the next wave of information appliances and pocket devices. The next generation of programmers now attending high school have no previous allegiances or need to run Windows applications, especially when they can't afford them. The best and brightest kids are already the biggest fans of free software. The Linux brand is not as strong as the Microsoft brand, but the code is better. Which foundation do you want to build on today?

---

[*] Wayner, Peter. *Free For All.* HarperBusiness. New York. NY. 2000.

PART II

REHAB FOR YOUR MICROSOFT ADDICTION

4

SLAY THE WORD
AND YOU'LL BE FREE

You hold in your hands something you don't see every day: a book written on a computer without Microsoft Word.

You probably think Word is the stumbling block—the first, last, and final reason why you can't escape Microsoft software. But alternatives exist, and this chapter is all about them. You can use commercial products like WordPerfect, or free software such as OpenOffice.org Writer or AbiWord, or text editors such as TextEdit, which comes with the Mac.

In fact, it was possible to skip Word years ago to produce books that use graphical layouts. Children's books, for example, are typically composed and finished using a page layout program such as Adobe PageMaker or QuarkXPress. Large coffee table books with high-quality photographs are nearly always composed in page layout programs, because only those programs can do justice to reproducing the photographs in a proper graphical layout. Text, formatted or otherwise, has always been the easiest type of data to process. So it stands to reason that it must be possible to *use an alternative to Word*.

And yet, so many people continue to use Word because they need to work with Word documents. Some swear by it, and others swear at it. The application has been around far too long; people should have other choices by now. "Monopolies become their own worst enemies—particularly in businesses that live or die by technological innovation," wrote James Gleick in *The New York Times Magazine*. "They get soft. They make poor research choices. They bleed both profit and invention. They poison the marketplace that created them."[*]

Microsoft Word Is Not the Final Word

I'm a veteran Word addict, now reformed. Since the late 1980s I relied on Word for all writing and editing. So why do I bite the Word that fed me?

All that time I paid a tithe to the gods in Redmond so that I could eat, paying for upgrades and even migrating to more powerful computers just to run new versions. When the software continued to behave erratically, upgrade after upgrade, I began to feel misused and abused. I had heard rumors that Word harbored viruses, that Word reported back to Microsoft the details of your hardware configuration every time you launched it, and that Word was a manifestation of the devil. I had creepy feelings that somehow Microsoft could read what I was writing.

Of course it's all Microsoft's fault. Word's creepiness is directly related to the random suggestions it throws at you when you least expect them and the way it corrects your grammar before you can finish the sentence. Word reinforces bad rumors and ugly feelings by acting so stubbornly and annoyingly the same as it has since 1995. Yes, if you spend some time, you can eventually figure out how to turn off or adjust some of the most annoying features (see Figure 4-1). But this is *your time* I'm talking about. You already paid for the program; why should you also have to spend more time teaching it to behave?

Let's not even go into all the bad things Word does, for fear of inducing headaches or even nightmares . . . Like how Word applies the same idiotic default settings to any image you place or table you create, regardless of what came before. Or how, after two decades, I can still make it crash by using the DELETE key to delete characters past the beginning of a paragraph into previous lines of text.

Word is bloated beyond belief. Who actually uses the Data Merge Manager to create form letters? Who customizes Word menus so thoroughly that they can no longer find the spell-checker? How often do you want to choke that paper clip character that pops up with inappropriate suggestions (see Figure 4-2)? How many Word docs have you been unable to open for some reason or another, and when was the last time you got a flawless result by saving in an older Word doc file format?

Nearly 20 years ago, I used Word style definitions to define my book chapters so that they could easily be sucked up into Adobe PageMaker for FrameMaker, only to find that publishers used QuarkXPress, which either ignored or mangled my style definitions, rendering them irrelevant. I cranked up that Microsoft monster just to compose emails, only to find that it converted some of my text into some alien alphabet that others couldn't decipher.

---

[*] Gleick, James. "Making Microsoft Safe for Capitalism." *The New York Times Magazine.* November 5, 1995.

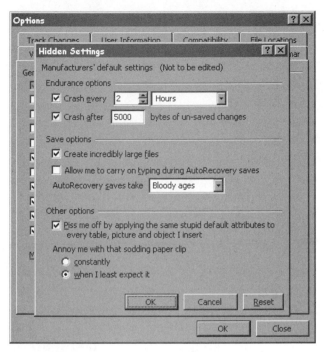

Figure 4-1: Don't you wish you could find these hidden settings in Word? (Thanks to Dr. Norman Clark in the Dept. of Communication at Appalachian State University, Boone, North Carolina.)

Figure 4-2: Don't you wish this little guy would just go away? Word can be so annoying with these suggestions. (Thanks to Dr. Norman Clark in the Dept. of Communication at Appalachian State University, Boone, North Carolina.)

I tried early alternatives that fell short. I even tried using PageMaker and exporting styled text into Word document files. Ultimately, I had no choice but to continue to use Word. My clients sent me Word documents that I could not open unless I used Word too. I sent Word documents back to them because that's what they wanted. Who knows what evil may have lurked in those Word documents?

What Up, Word Doc? A Format for Disaster

The *Word document format* is the addiction. Not Word itself or some special feature of the program, but the Word doc file format. For a long time, the only way to open a Word doc file was to use Word; without alternatives, businesses migrated to Word and the rest of the Office package and got stuck there. As Word doc files proliferated (and as Microsoft wiped out the competition in word processing programs), they hooked everyone they touched.

Just what is in those files? More than you realize. Word files can violate your privacy. The program is most often configured by default to automatically track and record changes you make to a document. A record of all changes is silently embedded in the doc file every time you save it. It's easy as pie for someone to recover this record and see all the revisions. Most Word document files contain a revision log that is a listing of the last 10 edits of a document, showing the names of the people who worked with the document and the names of the files used for storing versions of the document.

A WEAPON OF MASS DELUSION

Word documents are notorious for containing tracked changes and revisions that could be embarrassing if discovered, and they are easy to discover. The British government of Tony Blair learned this lesson the hard way. In February 2003, 10 Downing Street published an important dossier on Iraq's security and intelligence organizations—the same dossier cited by Secretary of State Colin Powell in his address to the United Nations later that month. It was published as a Word document. A quick examination of hidden revision logs in the Word document revealed that much of the material in the dossier was actually plagiarized from an American Ph.D. student.[*]

Dr. Glen Rangwala, a lecturer in politics at Cambridge University, discovered that the bulk of the 19-page document was directly copied without acknowledgment from an article in *The Middle East Review of International Affairs* titled "Iraq's Security and Intelligence Network: A Guide and Analysis" (September 2002), written by the student. As a result, during the week of June 23, 2003, the British Parliament held embarrassing hearings on the Blair dossier and other PR efforts by the UK Government leading up to the Iraq war.

[*] Smith, Richard M. ComputerBytesMan.com. June 30, 2003. See www.computerbytesman.com/privacy/blair.htm. See also Rangwala, Glen. "Intelligence? The British dossier on Iraq's security infrastructure." *The Campaign Against Sanctions on Iraq.* See www.casi.org.uk/discuss/2003/msg00457.html.

And why is the Word doc file format such a moving target? Try to collaborate on a document with a random group of Word users using different versions (Word 97, Word 2000, Word XP, Word 2003, and a couple of Mac versions), and you'll see what a mess you can make with Word doc files. As longtime high-tech pundit John Dvorak pointed out in his *PC Magazine* column,[*] "It's clear the program is in decline, with too many patches and teams of coders passing in the night. It's about time that it's junked and we get something new. This code can no longer be fixed."

SERVES THEM RIGHT

Ambulance chasers from The SCO Group suing DaimlerChrysler for using Linux forgot to remove tracked changes from a Word doc that identified their previous defendant, Bank of America, and demonstrated the litigation possibilities of Word templates. The press loved it; the SCO Group's credibility was ruined.[*]

----

[*] CNET News.com. March 6, 2004.

The Titanic of Text Editing

You don't want to trust your most important documents to the Word doc file format. One reason is that files are extremely large—it seems like Microsoft stores the design specs and blueprints for the Titanic along with your text. These files are often many orders of magnitude larger than ordinary text files. You can spend a lot of time sending or receiving these files over a network, and they eat up more disk space than they should.

Moreover, Word files are not secure—they can contain code that can destroy your computer. Word lets people create custom programs called *macros* for modifying their Word documents. Excel offers the same feature. But since Word and Excel let you save the macros along with the documents, and since it is possible to hide a virus in the macro code, these documents could easily be turned into Trojan horses carrying viruses. The code can be set to execute as the document opens. In fact, Word documents are now the most common carrier for viruses.

TIP *Don't use Word as your "helper" application for .doc files in Windows. As soon as Word opens a document, your computer could catch a virus—whether you use Word's File menu, click a Word document on the desktop or in a file list, or click an email attachment that happens to be a Word doc file. Open your browser's preferences, and set the helper application for .doc files to something other than Word. You might want to register WordPad as the helper application for a Windows system. Otherwise, choose an alternative to Word such as WordPerfect or OpenOffice.org Writer, both described in this chapter.*

----

[*] Dvorak, John C. "Kill Microsoft Word." *PC Magazine.* September 7, 2004. See www.pcmag.com/article2/0,1759,1631430,00.asp.

THIEVES USE WORD TO STEAL FILES

Details about one of the largest security holes in Microsoft Word were first published on August 26, 2002 to the popular Bugtraq security list, a service hosted by SecurityFocus, a subsidiary of Symantec.* The security hole has still not been corrected. Essentially, an information thief can steal files from the computer of a person using Word 97.

If you use Word 97 and an unknown person sends you a document to modify, be aware that when you return it, the Word document may contain a hidden copy of files from your computer. The Word document will not be flagged by anti-virus programs. It will also not appear to Word 97 to contain any macros.

The copied files aren't visible in Word, but they are clearly visible using Notepad or Wordpad. The copied files could be documents, Excel spreadsheets, or anything else; they could be located anywhere, even on a secure server. If you have permission to read a file, and you use Word 97 to edit a document from someone who is secretly an information thief, that person could grab the file using "spy" code that can scan for hundreds of files and the INCLUDETEXT field, one of many hidden fields embedded in Word docs. The only way to prevent a file from being stolen is to manually check the fields, which you can find in the document's Properties panel.

If you use Word 97, you shouldn't open and modify a document from someone you don't trust, unless that person will never get the document back. The scheme works best with Word 97, but Word 2000 and 2002 could also be conscripted into service if the attacker can persuade a victim to print the document first.

The security hole is outrageous, yet Microsoft has declined to fix older versions of Word, angering IT professionals. "The only suggestion Microsoft has come up with—examine field codes in your document manually—is so lame I don't know if I should laugh or cry . . . or scream," wrote Woody Leonhard, Certified Office Victim and publisher of the newsletter *Woody's Office Watch*.† "Can *you* look at a field code and know if it will automatically suck in a sensitive file? How can hundreds of millions of Office users be expected to tell the difference between a safe field code and a spy?"

Microsoft has also angered the community of bug fixers by complaining that the details of this security hole should not have been disclosed without Microsoft's first performing tests. It was only after Woody Leonhard published details in his newsletter that the mainstream press got a hold of the story. Microsoft was forced to make a statement about the problem since the Associated Press was about to release the story to newspapers all over the world. But you have to admire Microsoft's PR machine—the company managed to convince the press that it had disclosed the problem voluntarily.

---

* Gantman, Alex. "Security side-effects of Word fields." Bugtraq Archive. See www.securityfocus .com/archive/1/289268/2002-09-09/2002-09-15/2. See also Lemos, Robert. "Microsoft warns of thieving Word docs." CNET News.com. September 12, 2002. See http://news.com .com/2100-1001-957786.html?tag=fd_top.

† Leonhard,. Woody. *Woody's Office Watch*. September 18, 2002. See www.woodyswatch .com/office/archtemplate.asp?v7-n44.

Stuck Inside of Pages with Those Unprintable Blues Again

How typical is this scenario: You receive a 20-page Word document from a client, and you need to print it. The document contains graphics—in particular, slides copied from PowerPoint right into the Word doc. But nothing comes out of the printer. Turn the printer off, restart, and wait for the system and printer to rethink everything . . . but still the pages don't come out. Hell freezes over, but the document won't print. Word docs are notoriously buggy when it comes to printing graphics, especially "objects" from other programs like PowerPoint, and even more especially when those objects include text.

TIP FOR WORD ADDICTS

You are nearly always better off copying the slide from PowerPoint and using Paste Special in Word to paste it as a "picture" rather than an object. What's so special about Paste Special? It gives you choices besides the lame choice offered by Word, which is to paste it as an object. You can use Paste Special to paste the slide as a bitmap image, which may get through the printer; otherwise, your printer may hang indefinitely as it tries to decipher the PowerPoint object. You would think that after two decades inhabiting the same labs in Redmond, the PowerPoint and Word development teams should be able to work together to get graphics and text to print together.

Word is supposed to be a text editor that offers WYSIWYG (What You See Is What You Get).[*] It means, roughly, that what you see on your computer monitor is the same as what you get on the printer and vice versa. The first true WYSIWYG editor was a word processing program called Bravo. Invented by Charles Simonyi at the Xerox Palo Alto Research Center in the 1970s, it became the basis for Simonyi's work at Microsoft, including Word.

Somehow, something went awry, because now it's "You Don't Always Get What You Want"[†]—everything changes from computer to computer depending on which fonts are installed. A document produced with Word on one computer may end up with radically different formatting and pagination on another computer, even using the same version of Word.

The reason for these and other printing and formatting anomalies is this: Word silently reformats a document based on the computer's printer settings and fonts. This is bad news for certain kinds of documents, such as forms, that rely on elements precisely positioned on a page. In other words, Word documents are not guaranteed to look and print the same way on every computer and printer. The document's fonts may not be available on another computer, and the substitute fonts force the reformatting and cause pages to break in strange places. You can thank, among other things, the competing technologies for rendering fonts, which have befuddled the desktop publishing industry for two decades.

Maybe you could care less about fonts, as long as you get the document printed. But some of us want the printed document to look vaguely the same from one printer to the next. Thanks to the many differences in fonts and character spacing from one computer to the next, and from one printer driver to the next, you can't trust Word documents to look the same.

---

[*] Pronounced "whiz-ee-wig." Thanks to The Dramatics for "What You See Is What You Get," released in 1971, and also to Tina Turner for "What You Get Is What You See," released in 1986; as for Britney Spears, "What U See (Is What U Get)" appears to be a rip-off.

[†] Thanks to the Rolling Stones, or rolling fonts in this case.

TANGLED UP IN THE FONT WAR

Printing problems can be traced back to the legendary Font War of the late 1980s, in which Microsoft and Apple faced off against the father of desktop publishing, Adobe Systems. As everyone knows, a digital font is a mini-program that enables a system to display and print text with a typeface (such as Palatino) set to a particular size (such as Palatino 12). While Adobe didn't exactly invent this concept, the company *did* invent PostScript and a font format that works with PostScript (the Type 1 format). The combination enabled computers to print with high-quality typefaces on different laser printers and with better quality using the same font on high-resolution imagesetters. This combination revolutionized high-quality printing in the late 1980s, and most of today's printers use PostScript.

Adobe's font format dominated desktop publishing until Microsoft and Apple—strange bedfellows at that time—developed the TrueType format to challenge Adobe's dominance. They did it to try to force Adobe into opening its proprietary Type 1 format. However, typographers weren't crazy about TrueType's quality. But even typographers have to eat, so these two formats now dominate computing with an uneasy truce. Both formats work with Windows, Macintosh, Linux, and Unix systems.

The industry giants involved in the Font War were so embarrassed by their greed that they joined together eventually to impose yet a new format, called OpenType, that slapped TrueType and Type 1 together. "That was 1996," wrote Clark Kim in *Magazine World* in 2002. "OpenType today is as popular as the U.S. Olympic hockey team in Canada."[*] OpenType is supposed to work with everything. It is also supposed to provide richer linguistic support and advanced typographic control. While Microsoft and Adobe support it, the gaggle of small type foundries around the world are not yet on board. The transition to OpenType hasn't been easy. It is technically challenging to do OpenType fonts, and they've already got their hands full with Type 1 and TrueType.

Word uses the fonts installed in your Windows or Mac system. When you first install Windows, only a limited number of fonts are available, but as you install other software, other fonts are added to Windows like new genes to the gene pool, and those fonts automatically become available to Word. As we all merrily computed our way into the 21st century, our systems sprouted different fonts from all these different installations. When you create a document on one system, using its fonts, and then transfer that document to a different system, different fonts are substituted, with unpredictable results.

Conversion programs exist, and fonts in both formats are ubiquitous. When they show up in your system bearing the same name (for example, Palatino in either Type 1 or TrueType formats), your system and printer can get as bewildered as you must be at this point.

---

[*] Kim, Clark. "For Font's Sake." *Magazine World.* 2002. (See http://magazines.humberc .on.ca/magworld2002/talkingtech/font.html.

Adobe created the PDF (Portable Document Format) standard to enable the exchange of documents without printing problems, but Microsoft has never put much effort into making its PDF export function work well—possibly because Microsoft would rather people use the Word doc format rather than a portable format.

> **TIP FOR WORD ADDICTS**
>
> So you want to muck about in Word's preferences and try to alleviate the refor-
> matting problem so that Word docs look more similar from computer to computer
> and printer to printer? It's not that easy. Word gets font metrics information from
> your output device; every time you change the print driver (even switching from one
> PostScript driver to another PostScript driver, or using the same driver for a different
> printer), text may be reformatted, pages may reflow, and line breaks may be different.
> Printer margins (i.e., unprintable areas defined by the output device) also influence
> the reformatting. Word offers an option to cut down on this reformatting: the Use
> Printer Metrics To Lay Out Documents switch in the Tools ▶ Options ▶ Compatibility
> window should be turned off. However, it doesn't eliminate the reformatting. Simply
> moving a document from the Windows 95/98 system to Windows NT or Windows
> XP can cause reformatting. Good luck with that.

Get Angry about Word Docs

There is only one way out of Word madness: stop sending Word docs to
people. Only Word can open these files, so by sending Word docs, you force
other people to use Word. The specification for Microsoft Word documents
is a closely guarded secret, and since Microsoft chooses not to create versions
for other operating systems (such as Linux), people who use those systems
are left out in the cold. Keep in mind that Word doc files produced with one
version of Word might not even be readable by other versions of Word—
forcing others to upgrade their versions. The Word doc format is not a true
standard. Microsoft changes it from time to time, most likely to force users of
older versions to buy the latest version.

Richard Stallman, the founder of the Free Software Foundation, believes
the use of the Word doc format hurts us as consumers and hurts the industry
in general. "The worst impact of sending Word format is on people who might
switch to free systems: they hesitate because they feel they must have Word
available to read the Word files they receive. The practice of using the secret
Word format for interchange impedes the growth of our community and the
spread of freedom."[*]

Whether you move off Word or continue to be addicted to it, you should
know how to save your documents in a file format that others can use and
that can be attached to an email without worry. Standards for document files
exist, and even Word supports them to some extent.

Rich Text Format (RTF)

RTF files are readable and useful across systems and applications. RTF files
preserve some font information (such as italics, bold, font sizes, and so on),
and people can import the files into their word processors (including Word)
to edit them. You can be sure that the RTF file doesn't harbor any viruses,
because it doesn't contain any macros.

---

[*] Stallman, Richard. "We Can Put an End to Word Attachments." GNU project. See www.gnu.org/
philosophy/no-word-attachments.html.

The RTF files produced by Word *can* get crazy if they include complex formatting, tables, graphics, or objects embedded from other Microsoft applications, so you may want to simplify your document first. On the other hand, whatever application you use to open the RTF file might simplify things for you—the text will appear (more or less) the same, with page breaks, italics, tables, and possibly even footnotes, but most of the other Word-related junk not recognized by your application will be ignored.

NOTE   *RTF uses the American National Standards Institute (ANSI), PC-8, Macintosh, or IBM PC character set to control the representation and formatting of a document, both on the screen and in print. See the Rich Text Format specification at http://latex2rtf .sourceforge.net/rtfspec.html.*

TIP FOR WORD ADDICTS

As a general rule, you can lose the revision logs and other Word weirdness by saving the Word document as an RTF file that people can edit easily or as a PDF file that looks great but can't be edited easily. Choose **File ▸ Save As** and pick the RTF file format from the Format drop-down menu. Creating a PDF file is more complicated, thanks to Microsoft—see the section "PDF Was Made for This" later in this chapter.

Portable Document Format (PDF)

PDF files preserve the look, the feel, the fonts, the graphics, the pagination, headers, footers, footnotes . . . everything. Everything is exactly as it should look.

PDF is ideal for distributing finished documents, including PowerPoint presentations and Excel spreadsheets. It's especially useful for forms that must print the same way on every printer and look the same on every computer. Even the fonts are taken care of—you can automatically embed into the PDF file the font characters the document needs. The main drawback is that people can't easily edit the text unless they buy Adobe Acrobat. Unfortunately, PDF files are very large, and PDF files from untrusted sources might also carry viruses. But the risks of catching a virus by viewing and printing a PDF file are slim. See the section "PDF Was Made for This" later in this chapter.

Plain ASCII Text

Plain ASCII (American Standard Code for Information Interchange, pronounced "ask-ee") text files contain only the text of your document with no formatting whatsoever (no fonts, no spacing, and tables are turned into text spaced with tabs). Plain ASCII files can't harbor viruses (except perhaps as source code that can't execute by itself), which makes them safe. All text editing programs can edit ASCII text files, which date back to the Model-T era of the computer industry. Any decent spreadsheet program can read an ASCII file's tab-delimited characters saved from a table and convert the mess back into a table.

NOTE   *Programmers use ASCII text files to write programs, but the text files have to be interpreted or compiled into code for the programs to work.*

ASCII is a standard developed by ANSI to define how computers write and read characters. It was designed at first for teletypes and extended for displays and modern printers. If you've received ASCII text files, then you know that the text might all be in a single line, 10,000 words long, or have weird characters and control codes scattered about. It might appear stunted with only 35 characters per line, and you spend half a day positioning the cursor just so and deleting backward to remove these line breaks (an operation likely to crash Word).

NOTE   *The ASCII set of 128 characters includes letters, numbers, punctuation, and control codes (such as a character that marks the end of a line). Each letter or other character is represented by a number: an uppercase A, for example, is the number 65, and a lowercase z is the number 122. (Software engineer Jim Price has a nice ASCII chart at www.jimprice.com/jim-asc.htm.)*

Hypertext Markup Language (HTML)

HTML files contain the codes for formatting web pages (and email). HTML is essentially ASCII text with formatting *tags* neatly separated by angle brackets from the rest of the text. Today, HTML files can contain code such as Java-Script, which hackers can use to link to other websites and embed viruses, spyware, adware, and other bad things, but plain HTML (without code) is safe. Unfortunately, Word doesn't create a plain HTML file—it adds a lot of stuff you probably won't want or need (see Figure 4-3).

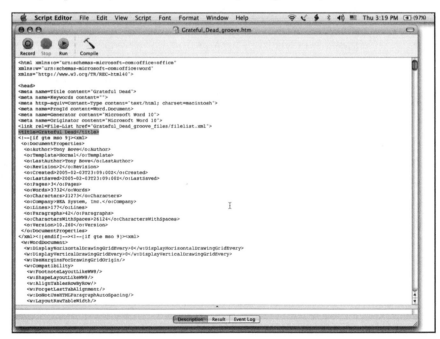

Figure 4-3: Word puts all this junk at the top of every HTML file it creates, guaranteeing that you won't know what the heck is going on inside. You can get rid of most of it and use the standard HTML codes for defining a header and title.

Aliens Kidnapped My Characters!

If you've ever created an ASCII text file from a Word doc, or opened one in Word or some other program, you probably ran into problems with Word's special characters. What's so special about em dashes, single and double quotes with curls, and the sequence known as ellipses (three periods in a row)? They've been around for long time, included on typewriter keyboards since at least 1914.[*]

Proper style calls for using these special characters to enhance readability. But Word on the PC seems to sabotage the documents so that they can't be used with the Mac version of Word without considerable reformatting. You get these funny characters (see Figure 4-4) that look like they're part of an alien alphabet from a distant planet. You also get them when you convert Word docs to plain ASCII text.

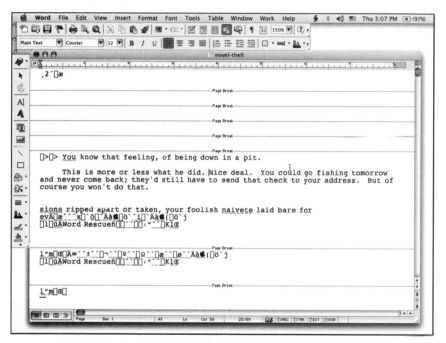

Figure 4-4: Word's special characters look like an alien alphabet when converted to ASCII text, or when converted from the PC to the Mac version of Word (or vice versa).

If you continue to use Word, you might want to consider at least converting these special characters to something else before sending ASCII or HTML versions of your document. You don't have to convert anything for PDF versions, because the special characters look fine. Even if you just use Copy and Paste to put Word text into an email message, you may find these characters lurking about in your message. Here are quick steps to change these special characters *before* converting to ASCII or HTML:

1. Choose **AutoCorrect** from Word's Tools menu. This opens Word's AutoCorrect dialog box.

2. Select the **Auto Format As You Type** tab, and uncheck the option 'Straight quotes' with 'smart quotes', as shown in Figure 4-5. (Click to remove the check mark, turning it off.)

---

[*] See the Virtual Typewriter Museum at www.typewritermuseum.org.

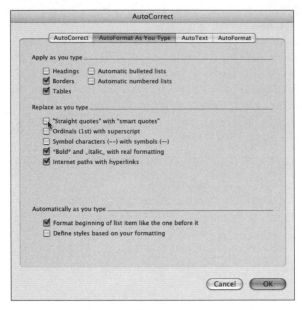

Figure 4-5: Don't let Word's smart quotes get in the way when converting Word docs to the ASCII or HTML formats or pasting copied Word text into an email.

But don't stop there! You still have to use the Replace command, replacing all instances of a single quote (curled) with a single quote (straight):

3. Choose **Edit ▸ Replace** and type a single quote for the Find box and the same single quote for the Replace box (yes, that's right—the same character). Click **Replace All** to perform the replace operation for the entire file (or selected text). Word automatically changes each curly quote to a straight quote that can pass the ASCII test.

    You can replace the characters in only a portion of the document by first selecting the portion and *then* clicking **Replace All**. The replacements occur only in the selected text.

4. Repeat step 3 with double quotes. Word automatically changes the curly quotes to straight quotes that can pass the ASCII test on all computer systems.

5. Repeat step 2, unchecking the option to the replace symbol characters (–) with symbols (—). Then repeat step 3 with em dashes (replace with a double dash, as in "--"), en dashes (replace with a single dash), and ellipses (replace with three periods in a row).

Use Alternatives to Word

When you're a hammer, every problem looks like a nail. (And when you're a nail, you wish there were no hammers around.) And when you're a Word user, every problem looks like it needs something from Word's menus or toolbars to solve.

The industry needs an alternative, if only to keep Word honest. Word is expensive (more than $200 for the stand-alone retail version, as this is written), tends to be a memory hog, and the built-in macro features are inherently insecure, providing an excellent breeding ground for viruses. Documents generated by Word also have the bad habit of hiding extra information (such as deleted text and personally identifiable details about the file author) in their headers. And files created in Word usually aren't readable by other word processing software, because Microsoft keeps Word's document format proprietary.

If you use Word on a PC, OpenOffice.org Writer offers the easiest transition to an alternative. WordPerfect also offers a look and feel that comes close to matching the Word's menus and toolbars, but OpenOffice.org Writer (hereafter known as OOo Writer) matches Word on the PC function for function and even looks just like it. If you use Word on a Mac, you can also use OOo Writer, but it looks like the PC version, which is somewhat of a downer. But the OpenOffice.org volunteers have scheduled a native Mac OS X version to come out real soon now. I used OOo Writer on the Mac in its current form to write this book.

You can fool people into thinking you are using Word by using one of these alternatives and then saving your documents in the Word doc format—just for them. For everyone else, you can save RTF documents that others can open and edit in any word processing program, or save PDF files that can be opened by anyone using Adobe Reader or similar PDF viewer. These alternatives also have their own native file formats, which are not as ubiquitous as the Word doc format and therefore not as prone to carry viruses.

WordPerfect: The Legal Remedy

For a commercial alternative that costs about the same or less than Word, consider WordPerfect. Lawyers and legal assistants swear by WordPerfect for legal contracts and briefs, possibly because it has been around long enough to be entrenched in that professional industry. It was the first word processor to offer automatic paragraph numbering and automatic footnote numbering and placement on pages. WordPerfect used almost every possible combination of function keys with the CTRL, ALT, and SHIFT keys, making it easier to use than the word processor of the day (WordStar, my first love).

Originally written for Data General minicomputers, WordPerfect migrated to the IBM PC in 1982. The program's popularity took off with version 4.2 in 1986, and in 1989, WordPerfect 5.1 for DOS became the word processing market leader. Then Microsoft moved in for the kill.

Microsoft started with WordPerfect's function keys, pre-empting them by creating incompatible keyboard shortcuts for Windows 3.0 that conflicted with them (e.g., ALT-F4 became Exit Program instead of WordPerfect's Block Text). The DOS version's impressive arsenal of finely tuned printer drivers was also rendered obsolete by Windows' use of its own printer device drivers.

"Microsoft knows that the technologically perfect product is rarely the same as the winning product," wrote James Gleick in *The New York Times Magazine.* "Time and again its strategy has been to enter a market fast with an inferior product to establish a foothold, create a standard, and grab market share."[*]

One problem was that WordPerfect's function-key–centered user interface did not adapt well to the Windows paradigm of mice and pull-down menus. Another problem was that WordPerfect took too long to migrate to Windows 3.0, which became the most popular operating system ever. But the main problem was that Microsoft engineers had advance information about Windows.

Novell, the company that bought and later sold WordPerfect in the mid-1990s, eventually sued Microsoft for restraint of trade, charging that Microsoft withheld "critical technical information" about Windows. Novell also charged that Microsoft deliberately excluded WordPerfect from the marketplace by using monopoly power to prevent hardware manufacturers from offering WordPerfect to customers.[†]

Microsoft defended itself by pointing out that its application development group (responsible for Word) and its system group (responsible for Windows) were simply able to "fly in formation," as CEO Steve Ballmer liked to put it. Only this formation was more like a bomber run.

WordPerfect eventually landed at Corel as a much better, cleaner, and faster product with some excellent features that Word lacks. For example, it shows a preview, right in your document, when you are considering changing the font, size, or alignment of the text, allowing you to change your mind before committing to alterations. It offers a "reveal codes" feature (see Figure 4-6) that lets you "open the hood" on any section of text and make changes to formatting by changing the codes directly. As a result, WordPerfect is less likely than Word to surprise you with automated reformatting. It also uses its own settings for print options rather than forcing you to set them each time in the Windows print driver.

WordPerfect 12 Office Suite includes Quattro Pro for spreadsheets and Presentations for presentations. It can import and save various Word and Office doc formats and RTF files with almost perfect back-and-forth compatibility. It can also save documents in the PDF format, with hyperlinks if you use them. WordPerfect's "compatibility toolbars" let you save documents in Microsoft's formats with a single click—you can even substitute icons and menus that approximate Microsoft's user interface instead of WordPerfect's. A Legal toolbar provides easy, one-click access to specialty tools for the legal community, including the Pleading Wizard, the Clipbook, the Concordance tool, and support for EDGAR electronic document filing. WordPerfect 12 Office is not just for lawyers; it's a solid product for all kinds of word processing, and Corel (www.corel.com) provides adequate support that is as good as if not better than Microsoft's.

---

[*] Gleick, James. "Making Microsoft Safe for Capitalism." *The New York Times Magazine.* November 5, 1995.

[†] LaMonica, Martin. "Novell sues Microsoft for sinking WordPerfect." CNET News.com, November 12, 2004.

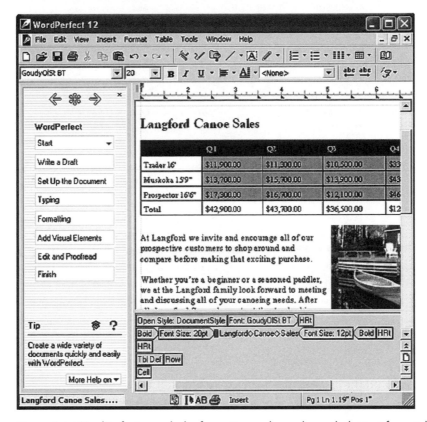

Figure 4-6: WordPerfect reveals the formatting codes underneath the text for quick adjustments.

OpenOffice.org Writer: A Free Alternative to Word

OpenOffice.org (OOo) Writer is part of the open source OpenOffice.org package, which started its life as StarOffice, a competitor to Microsoft Office for IBM OS/2 and Unix systems. Sun Microsystems bought it and converted it to an open source project called OpenOffice.org. It includes Writer for word processing, Calc for spreadsheets, Impress for presentations, Draw for drawing graphics, and conversion utilities for various file formats, including all Microsoft formats.

NOTE *OOo is not some hobbyist's dream from the days of teletypes. In the first month after OpenOffice.org was released (May 2002), the project reported nearly a million downloads. Nobody knows exactly how many people use it, but most estimates put it at more than 10 million.*

OOo is free—you can download versions for Linux, Unix, Solaris, Windows, or Macintosh (OS X) from the OpenOffice.org site (www.openoffice.org). You can also get it on CD or as part of a book-CD package, such as *OpenOffice.org Writer* by Jean Hollis Weber (O'Reilly Community Press). And here's something you can't do with Word or the rest of the Office package, but you can do with OOo: you can legally install it on as many computers as you want. You can even give it to your friends.

NOTE   *If you or your company prefers a traditional relationship with a software vendor, you can purchase StarOffice from Sun Microsystems for $75.95 for a single copy or $50 per copy for 150. StarOffice is an enhanced version of OpenOffice.org, with additional translation filters, fonts and clip art, a manual, and a database (see www.sun.com/ software/staroffice/6.0/index.html).*

A frequent criticism of open source software is that you have to pay for support, but you can get free support for OOo if you subscribe to its free mailing lists. This support is as detailed and as accurate as any you can get from most paid technical support services.

If you know Word, you can be comfortable with OOo Writer in just minutes (see Figure 4-7). OOo Writer matches Word feature for feature and even beats Word in some areas. For example, the Stylist floating palette for setting formatting styles is more convenient than Word's style catalog and extends to more than just paragraphs and characters. OOo Writer also offers text frames and lets you use styles with them, making it far easier than Word to set up multiple columns or a newsletter layout.

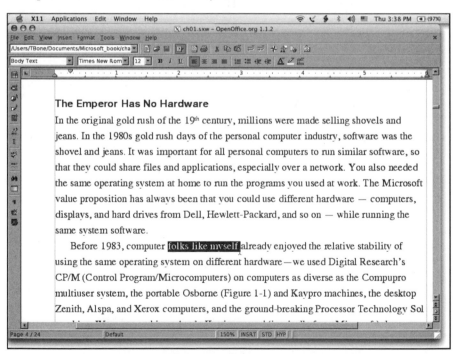

Figure 4-7: OpenOffice.org Writer looks just like Word and matches it feature for feature.

I've spent many frustrating hours with Word trying to make different headers and footers work properly in a long document. But you can control headers and footers far more easily in OOo Writer, because these elements are text frames attached to page styles that you control from page to page. And if you've spent a night wrestling with why Word's autonumbered lists are so screwed up, you'll be happy to know that OOo Writer's autonumbering works perfectly every time.

OOo Writer's menus look just like Word's, even to the point of offering the confusing choice of Configure or Options in the Tools menu. Autoformat and Autocorrect? They're in there, and you can customize them and turn them on or off. Envelopes and labels, fields, outlining, track changes, versioning? They're in there—maybe by different names and in different menus, but they're in there. The developers of OOo were determined to provide everything Word offers, and since there haven't been many real innovations added to Word since about 1995, it's an easy target.

In all this good news, there must be some bad. Indeed, OOo Writer has trouble importing Word docs that use some of Word's more esoteric features, such as the STYLEREF field (which OOo Writer converts to ordinary text). I've also discovered anomalies importing Word docs that use cross-references— although you can use OOo Writer to create cross-references without a problem. Forms don't translate well, and macros are either ignored or preserved for future use with Word (if you intend to save your document in the Word doc format).

TIP   *OOo Writer imports Word files without translating or executing macros. The program does not support Visual Basic or any form of internal macro, so even if the document's macros contained a virus, it most likely would not harm your computer. The program does give you the option of preserving macros in Word documents, so that they can be used when someone opens the document in Word again. In other words, you can import the Word doc into OpenOffice.org Writer, bypassing any virus, save the document back in Word format, and pass that virus along to someone else who still uses Word. But it wouldn't be very nice to do that.*

OOo Writer can save documents in various Word doc formats—including Word 6.0, 95, and 97/2000/XP formats, as shown in Figure 4-8. Assuming the Word user has the same fonts you used, the document should look the same, except that the bullets in a bulleted list may use an unexpected character rather than a bullet symbol. (You can avoid that problem by setting the bullet character in OOo Writer's Options tab for the list style.) Without the same fonts, the document might have differences in pagination, paragraph length, and paragraph alignment. You can also import or save HTML or RTF files and save a PDF file that looks exactly like the document in OOo Writer, fonts and everything, no matter what computer you use to view and print it.

Considering the difficulties of writing translation filters for importing, exporting, and saving files in different formats, what is unusual is not that OpenOffice.org's filters have problems, but that they have so few. Still, you should be prepared to do a bit of manual cleanup when importing Word docs into OOo Writer (or into any other program for that matter).

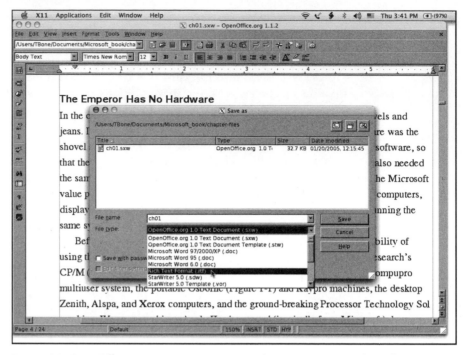

Figure 4-8: OpenOffice.org Writer can import and save various Word doc formats as well as RTF.

AbiWord: A Simpler Free Alternative to Word

AbiWord is part of a larger project known as AbiSource (www.abisource.com) started by the SourceGear Corporation, which later released the source code to a developer community that quickly formed around the project. The project's goal was to come up with a free office suite that would run on any operating system out there, and the community has largely succeeded, with more than 2.5 million downloads. AbiWord runs on Windows, Linux, Mac OS X, FreeBSD, and Solaris. It supports right-to-left, left-to-right, and mixed-mode text for European, Hebrew, and Arabic languages, and offers dictionaries for more than 30 languages.

AbiWord looks just like Word (no surprise there), except its icons are larger (see Figure 4-9), it loads faster, and it has less of a memory footprint, using only about 6 MB of RAM compared to Word's 30 MB or more. It doesn't try to match Word feature for feature, but it offers most of the features you'd expect from a word processor. You can employ tables, bullets, lists, images, footnotes, endnotes, and styles, just like Word. It even offers mail-merging for creating form letters and replacing fields with text from databases or spreadsheets.

If you are familiar with Word, you can be very comfortable with AbiWord; if you have no experience with Word, you won't miss all the obscure features that make Word a bloated memory hog. You may prefer AbiWord over Open-Office.org Writer for the same reason—simplicity. AbiWord's code is written to be tight and fit in small memory spaces; to do this well, it separates some of the extraneous functions into plug-ins. AbiWord lets you install plug-ins such as a dictionary, a thesaurus, a Google searcher, and translators from Babelfish and FreeTranslation. Also available are AbiPaint for painting simple images and graphics, and AbiGimp for photo and image manipulation. The Google plug-in lets you search Google with your selected text.

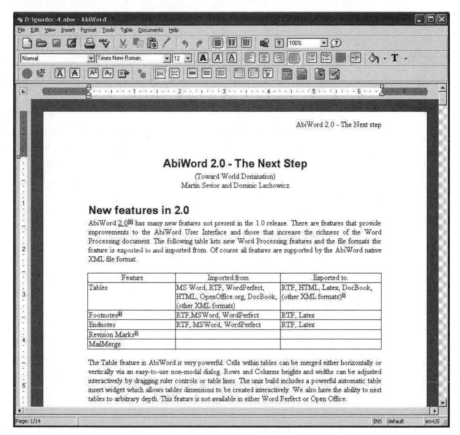

Figure 4-9: AbiWord, a free open source application, looks just like Word but uses less memory and runs on just about every type of computer system.

AbiWord can import Word docs, and import and export OpenOffice.org and WordPerfect docs, as well as RTF, HTML, and even XHTML files. It even offers a command line for executing some of its functions, to make it easier to run operations on a server, such as generating form letters, printing documents, or converting documents to another file format. Like OpenOffice.org, AbiWord saves a document in a compressed ASCII text file with XML (eXtensible Markup Language) markups, which makes the document file easy to open and read using any text editor and easy to process with XML tools. While OpenOffice.org Writer gets more publicity as an open source alternative to Word, AbiWord is a lean, fast, and cross-platform open source alternative that looks more like Word, especially on a Mac.

How to Collaborate on Documents without Word

Let's get down to brass tacks: How do you collaborate with all those other people out there who are stuck using Word?

Here's what I do: These days I use a Mac PowerBook running OS X, but I could be using a PC laptop just as easily, running Linux. Either way, I can use a free text editor, such as TextEdit on the Mac, to write all my text—book chapters, white papers for high-tech companies, web pages, and email messages I want to compose at my leisure before sending.

I then copy the text into OOo Writer, and I apply styles for book chapters and whatnot, controlling the page layout. I can send the finished draft in RTF or Word doc format. The recipient can't tell that I used OOo Writer.

Collaboration is a tougher nut. Most people assume that means allowing other people to make changes directly to your document. This is the Word model—send out a Word draft with Track Changes turned on, so that people can make changes and see other folks' changes. People can also add comments that others can see. I can use OOo Writer to import a Word doc with tracked changes, add my own changes, and save them back to another Word doc, but I don't like doing it.

The problem is that you have to trust everyone. People could turn Track Changes off, make changes, and then turn it back on, and no one would be the wiser (unless they laboriously compared the text from the one version to the next). Even if you trust everyone, if you forget to turn Track Changes on for reviewers, they might make changes that aren't tracked without realizing how much of a problem they may be causing. Heck, in Word, you can't even track some of the changes made to tables (fortunately, it warns you). There is no secure way to collaborate using the Word doc model.

To collaborate securely—by this I mean make drafts available for review comments and incorporate them back into the draft—I export a PDF version from OOo Writer and invite comments. When I receive commented PDFs back from reviewers, I make the changes myself, in OOo Writer, based on the comments. This is a far more secure method of collaboration. It doesn't require retyping—you can copy text from a PDF comment and paste it right into a document without any trouble. (The next section provides more details about using PDF.)

There's another way to collaborate that lets others make changes directly—it's just not as secure, and you have to trust the reviewers. I submit my book chapters this way. I send the first draft in the OOo Writer format to my editors, who make changes and add comments (OOo Writer offers tracked changes and commenting just like Word) and send them back to me. You can even use OOo Writer to import Word docs with tracked changes and comments and save a document back in the Word doc format with the same tracked changes and comments (and your own ones added in).

Collaboration with documents can quickly get out of hand when others don't have the same fonts you have. Character sizes and spacing can change everything from the way lines break to the pagination and placement of footnotes. You might be referring to page 10 while someone else opening the document on a different system with different fonts would need to look at, say, page 9 or 11. And you can forget about trying to collaborate on complicated page layouts using Word, OOo Writer, WordPerfect, or any other doc file format. PDF was made for this.

PDF Was Made for This

I was there when John Warnock, co-founder of Adobe Systems, first unveiled PDF to analysts in 1991. With a gleam in his eye and a silent nod to the analysts who had written extensively about the Font War that had nearly been his undoing, Warnock introduced PDF as if it were already a standard and read a statement that has since become the PDF manifesto: "Imagine being able to send full text and graphics documents—this means newspapers, magazine articles, technical manuals, and so on—over electronic mail distribution networks. These documents could be viewed on any machine, and any selected document could be printed locally. This capability would truly change the way information is managed."[*]

Okay, I thought, sounds wonderful so far. PDF would solve many of the print problems plaguing the desktop publishing industry. It would do so by encapsulating the font, graphics, and page layout information in a standard format everyone could use. Indeed, by 1996, PDF had become a standard in the high-quality pre-press and color printing industry. But why not provide a format that people could *edit*? I asked Warnock this question back in 1991, and he pointed out that the leading page layout programs, namely Aldus PageMaker and QuarkXPress, used proprietary formats, and these companies would never agree to cooperate at the editable document level. If they had agreed back in 1991, the Word doc format would not be so ubiquitous. By 1992, I was using PageMaker to compose a newsletter, sending it to the printer as PDF and exporting it to the Word doc format whenever I needed to spin off an article for a magazine that required Word doc submissions for additional editing.

The Adobe PDF file has since become the de facto standard for distributing documents in a secure, reliable way. The lack of an editing capability is, in this scenario, a blessing, because you can distribute a PDF and know that the text can't be altered or copied without your knowledge—you can even digitally sign the PDF so that readers can verify its authenticity. With a track record of more than a decade, PDF has been adopted by governments and enterprises around the world to reduce reliance on paper. You already use it today to file your U.S. income taxes. It's the standard format for the electronic submission of drug approvals to the U.S. Food and Drug Administration (FDA) and for electronic case filing in U.S. federal courts. It is also the standard format used for advertisements in newspapers and magazines.

Why is PDF so good for distribution? It preserves the fonts, images, graphics, and layout of any source document, regardless of the application used to create it and regardless of what fonts you have in your system. PDF

---

[*] Warnock, John. "John Warnock's 'Camelot' signalled birth of PDF." Planet PDF. January 18, 2002. See www.planetpdf.com/enterprise/article.asp?ContentID=6519.

files can be shared, viewed, or printed by anyone using the freely distributed Adobe Reader software (which you can grab from www.adobe.com; more than 500 million copies have already been downloaded). PDFs include embedded fonts and color profile information for more accurate color rendering across different systems. You can expect the PDFs you create to look the same way on another computer as it does on your computer.

All the word processors described in this chapter can export PDF files, even Word. In some systems, all you need to do is pretend to print the document and choose a PostScript printer driver to save the output as a PostScript file. Adobe offers the rather expensive Adobe Distiller product to convert PostScript to PDF, but there are also free applications, such as Free PDF Converter (www.primopdf.com) and Pdf995 (www.pdf995.com), and inexpensive commercial products, such as CutePDF (www.cutepdf.com). Adobe also offers server products for creating PDFs in an enterprise, eliminating the need for PDF creation applications on desktops.

Adobe never pursued the ability to edit PDFs except with its own applications. Adobe offers Acrobat for creating, combining, and exchanging PDF files, which lets you collect documents, emails, graphics, spreadsheets, and other attachments into a PDF file that preserves the integrity of the layout, whether the pages are oriented horizontally, vertically, or mixed. Acrobat also allows you to password-protect PDF files to prevent unauthorized viewing and altering, while also enabling authorized reviewers to use commenting and editing tools.

Adobe Acrobat provides excellent commenting and markup tools. You can draw attention to something with lines and arrows, draw boxes and free-form shapes around portions of text, add comments in separate windows, and even add voice comments and attachments, as shown in Figure 4-10. When you receive a PDF file with comments appended to it, you decide which comments to incorporate—and it's easy to copy and paste comments from the Adobe Reader or Acrobat window into your document. You can even use Acrobat to export the text in PDF files—including comments—into RTF files or Word docs. And you can search PDF files for words appearing in the text and in annotations, bookmarks, and data fields.

NOTE *Adobe offers an online service for creating PDFs from your documents. It not only accepts Word and WordPerfect documents, but also Adobe Illustrator, InDesign, FrameMaker, PageMaker, and Photoshop files. Visit https://createpdf.adobe.com to learn more.*

PDF is the easiest way out of the conundrum of using flaky Word docs and other Office docs to collaborate on documents or publish them to the Web. It is also the most useful format for sending documents to printers. The free Adobe Reader application can open, display, and print PDF files on all versions of Windows and Macintosh systems and Linux. The same PDF file will print on a cheap inkjet printer as well as on an expensive imagesetter. PDF files can contain multimedia elements like movies or sound as well as hypertext elements like bookmarks, links to email addresses or web pages, and thumbnail views of pages.

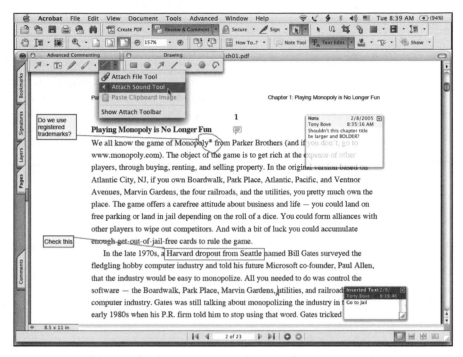

Figure 4-10: Adobe Acrobat lets reviewers mark up text for corrections, draw attention to details, add comments, and even voice opinions as well as attach files (such as background material). None of this stuff changes your original document, so you retain control.

TIP FOR WORD ADDICTS

PDF Writer is a printer driver that installs automatically into the Microsoft Office environment on Windows as a virtual printer, but don't use it. PDF Writer is just not as good as Adobe Distiller for creating PDFs with bookmarks for easy viewing or for pre-press systems and high-quality color printing. Always print to a PostScript file and then use Distiller or a similar tool to create a PDF. If you install Acrobat on a system containing Office, it adds macros to Word, Excel, and PowerPoint that automate the creation of PDF files. Whenever you select the **Export to PDF** option, the application will create a PostScript file and launch Distiller to automatically convert that code to a PDF.

Mac OS X uses PDF technology within the operating system itself. Apple calls this technology Quartz, and it runs as a layer on top of the kernel of the system, rendering all two-dimensional objects. As a result, PDF is now the standard document format for the Mac, and native Mac applications can create and import PDFs without the need for outside programs. PDF is not exactly open source, but it *is* an open file format specification, and Adobe makes information available to anyone who wants to develop tools to create, view, or manipulate PDF documents (which is how Apple developed Quartz).

With so much knowledge about PDF available in the developer communities, one wonders why Microsoft's support for PDF is so minimal. "Microsoft is fighting to keep Office as the standard archival format for documents," said Rob Helm, an analyst with Directions on Microsoft.[*] "If companies were to standardize on PDF, Office would become just one PDF authoring tool among many. It's a very long-term potential threat, but Microsoft can afford to look several steps ahead."

And so should you. For a look into the future, see how easy it is to display and print documents with Macs and Linux systems. They use PDF.

---

[*] Becker, David. "What's behind Microsoft's Office moves?" CNET News.com. December 1, 2003. See http://news.zdnet.com/2100-3513_22-5111644.html.

5

DE-MICROSOFT YOUR OFFICE

Like word processing, presentations and spreadsheets—
the first tools of the personal computer revolution—
have fallen under the authority of the Microsoft monopoly. As a result, presentations are less effective at the art
of persuasion than ever before, and spreadsheets are
less accurate than ever before. This is progress?

It would be an understatement to say that Microsoft Office, which combines and integrates Word, Excel, and PowerPoint, dominates the corporate
world. It's as if there were only one type of pencil in the world and one pencil
company, and the sharpeners it sold were bulky, clumsy to use, and constantly
in need of upgrading. Microsoft accomplished this domination by making
the license terms for Office attractive for businesses. The license was based
on concurrent usage. Companies could install a copy on a server and pay
only for the maximum number of copies in use simultaneously. When Microsoft ended this practice, Office was already entrenched. Today's license is
much tighter, and the cost of using Office in a corporate environment has
gone way up.

A lot of businesses got caught by the short hairs when Microsoft dis-
continued the Small Business Edition of Office in 2001. Upgrading from the

Small Business Edition to Office XP Professional Edition by the deadline of July 31, 2002 cost small businesses about $200 per copy; after the deadline, the same upgrade cost about $330 per copy. Microsoft also revised its two-year contract licensing policies at the same time. The net effect was to force companies to either pay for upgrades by the deadline, or risk losing contracts that guaranteed the same licensing fees for two years. Such strong-arm tactics are part of the reason the corporate world is starting to look for alternatives to Microsoft Office.

What a great time for another hairball release from Microsoft. Most places have no budget for training or anything else, yet we are all supposed to stop and wonder in amazement at another worthless Office release. —A reader of The Inquirer, commenting on the announcement of Office System 2003[1]

The other reason is the perception that productivity is going down as software complexity goes up. Microsoft claimed "dramatic cost reductions and high returns" were possible with Office 2003, according to research the company sponsored that evaluated a small sample of 14 companies, all of which likely received excellent technical support from Microsoft during the study. But anyone who's been on the receiving end of Microsoft tech support knows that a true return on investment (ROI) study would include the costs of training, professional support, and integration with other Microsoft products, notably Windows Server 2003, Office Infopath 2003, and Office Sharepoint Portal Server 2003. Office comes alive in conjunction with these products, possibly increasing productivity, but at what cost? Where's the payoff for individuals who use Office on its own? The Microsoft-sponsored studies don't mention ROI. "I wonder if [it's] because they are wary of the results they would get," mused AMR Research analyst Jim Murphy to *eWeek.*[*]

There once was a time when spreadsheets made you more productive, and when presentations created on a computer were far more compelling than they are today. The complexities of Office are even more bewildering today than they were 15 years ago, when it took over the spreadsheet market with Microsoft Excel. And Office has stifled the art of persuasion by crowding out all other presentation alternatives with PowerPoint, the king of sleazy slideshows. How did this happen, and what can you do about it?

Calculating with Incense and Spreadsheets

It should come as no surprise to learn that the inventors of the spreadsheet and the first companies to market spreadsheet software were refugees from the Sixties counterculture. How often have you looked at a spreadsheet and thought, what were they smoking?

Before computers, paper ledgers were trusted because they weren't so complicated that you couldn't recalculate them by hand. But spreadsheets are far more complex, especially ones created in Excel that use multiple work-sheets. The truth is a formula you can plug into a spreadsheet cell and never see again, nor question. Rows and columns of numbers seem accurate—but who really knows? You have to trust the spreadsheet maker and the program that made it, including its automatic formulas. But as spreadsheets proliferate through a company without any means of updating their information, they become multiple versions of the truth.

---

* Dignan, Larry. "Suite Returns: MS Office Survey Lacks ROI." *eWeek.* November 4, 2003. See www.eweek.com/article2/0,1759,1371771,00.asp.

You want truth in a formula? Consider the spreadsheet in Figure 5-1. The formula in cell A5 uses the addition operator. The sum of these three cells is 2. The conclusion: Excel treats TRUE as 1 and treats FALSE as 0. Except that it doesn't: the formula in cell A6 uses Excel's SUM function. In this case, the sum of these three cells is 0.[*]

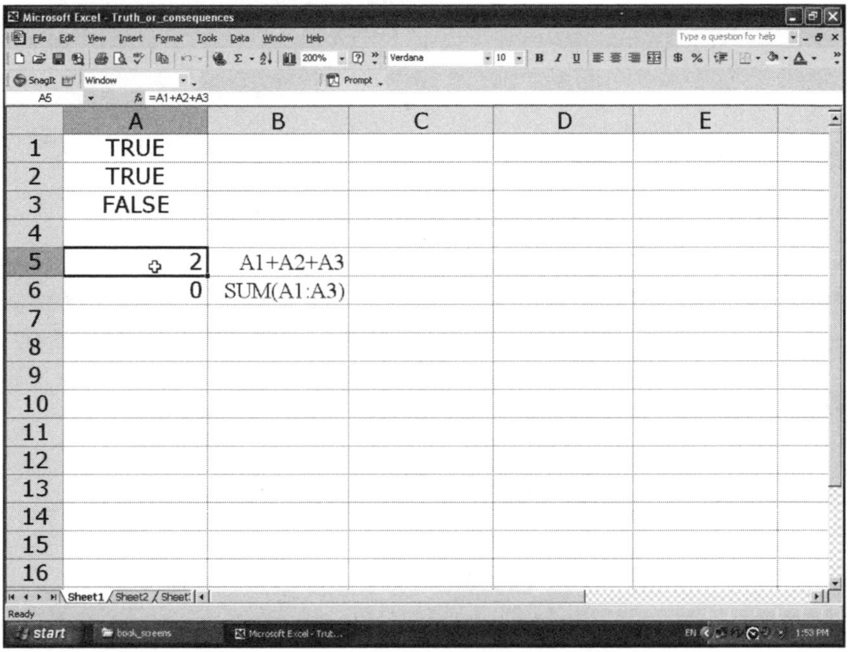

Figure 5-1: Truth depends on what formula you use. The cell range A1:A3 contains Boolean values (TRUE or FALSE). Add them up one way you get 2; add them up with the SUM function and you get 0.

People who use Excel generally fall into these categories:

Rows and columns

You need your information presented as a table, perhaps with a pie chart and some graphs. Maybe you also need a few formulas such as subtotals, totals, and financial calculations—enough to present a home budget, a simple income statement, or a loan interest calculation. For this category, using Excel is like driving a Mack truck through a toll booth for a trip to the local grocery store. You won't use one-tenth of its features, but you'll pay a steep price and need days of training just to drive the bulky thing. There are plenty of simpler alternatives, and some of them are absolutely free.

Invoices, statements, and formal business reports

Excel is designed to handle these projects and offers a multitude of features and options—but so do all the Excel alternatives. The key to making these spreadsheets work is the ability to integrate them with databases and core applications as part of automatic processes. That is what the

---

[*] Note that OpenOffice.org Calc, an alternative, provides the correct answer—2.

standard eXtensible Markup Language (XML) is designed for, and open source alternatives do XML much better.

Databases and custom applications

Excel can manage information so that it can be imported into databases and used with custom applications. Developers that work with Excel use it because it's there; more often than not, they develop custom applications that take apart the Excel file and move the information through filters and process automation software. Much of this "middleware" between Excel and the database is open source software that works with XML. You can use any Excel alternative that uses XML.

BRIEF HISTORY OF THE KILLER APP

The personal computer revolution is generally thought to have started with the spreadsheet, known back then as the *killer app* ("app" for application) for PCs. Driving this change was the need for personal productivity and access to information locked up in the corporate mainframes managed by IT fiefdoms. The first killer app was VisiCalc, which, by itself, made the Apple II—the first mass-marketed personal computer—useful in business.

Before anyone knew about that, in 1980 I gave a roomful of people at the Menlo Park public library a demonstration of an early version of VisiCalc. I used an Apple II equipped with an 80-column display card and TV monitor. At first, I showed them simple, blank rows and columns and talked about how you could dream up an entire business, or at least a household budget, with these rows and columns. Reams of market research and analysis have since been published about the efficacy of spreadsheets for business and personal productivity, but at that time, no one knew what the heck I was talking about. So I whipped out a standard IRS Form 1040 and displayed an equivalent version of the form in VisiCalc. If the spreadsheet could free their taxes by eliminating the accountants, I thought they would believe in the personal computer.

I wish I could say that the true personal computer revolution started right there in that room—that people took control of their financial lives, putting accounting firms out of business and throwing lawyers out into the streets.

Nothing so dramatic ever happened, but people did seize on the spreadsheet as the primary reason for getting a personal computer. VisiCalc eventually lost momentum to Lotus 1-2-3, the killer app for the IBM PC. Lotus 1-2-3 is still around but has largely been dethroned by Excel. It all happened in the late 1980s, and not much has happened since. While Excel spreadsheets are prettier, and some businesses find specialized ways to use the application and its set of formulas, there is not much more you can do with Excel that you couldn't just as easily, perhaps more easily, do with the original verison of VisiCalc from the early 1980s.

Going by the *Computer Desktop Encyclopedia* definition that a killer app is "an application that is exceptionally useful or exciting," I think we can all agree that Excel is no longer a killer app. Small business advocate Jim Blasingame offers a more precise view:[*] "Killer apps create new markets and destroy old ones; launch new corporate ships and sink old corporate vessels; create hysteria while concurrently wreaking havoc; build wealth while simultaneously destroying fortunes." That sounds more like Excel: It helped build the market for Office while destroying the spreadsheet market of the 1980s; it helped launch the Microsoft monopoly while sinking companies like VisiCorp (makers of VisiCalc); and it made Bill Gates very rich.

[*] Blasingame, Jim. "Small Business and the Killer App." Small Business Network. 2001. See www.smallbusinessadvocate.com/cgi-bin/articlesbybtsub.cgi?art=211.

Excel offers so many options that the program can be confusing to users—the Options dialog (see Figure 5-2), for one, is a candidate for worst user interface ever. Typically, it takes two or three tab clicks to locate the desired option, and there are 13 tabs, each chock full of options! But the main problem is inconsistency—some of the options affect only the active sheet, and others affect Excel as a whole. These options are scattered all over the place, and some are sprinkled into the Customize dialog. Even worse, the Options dialog offers a number of buttons that, when clicked, display other dialogs that contain even more options.

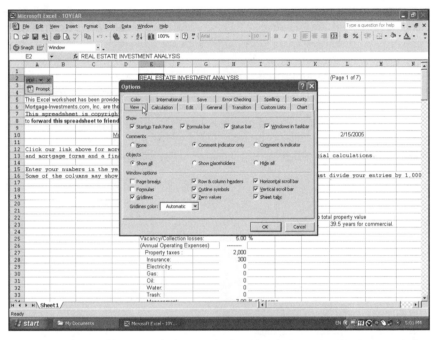

Figure 5-2: The world's worst dialog can be found right here: Excel's Options dialog. Can you find the Advanced Encryption option? How about the Web options?

Reviewers of the newest versions of Excel for Windows and Mac platforms have largely been, well, *disappointed.* "The real innovation is the Page view, showing you how your printed spreadsheet will look while you work with live data; beyond that, though, it's a little disappointing," said one.[*] "We'd even argue that many of the features, such as formula error-checking, should have been provided as a service update." Another wrote,[†] "This latest release of Excel can be summed up in one word: DISAPPOINTING." Even earlier upgrades were not up to snuff. "Microsoft's Excel 2002 facelift may leave a lot of spreadsheet jockeys disappointed," reported *PC World.*[‡]

[*] Microsoft Excel 2004 for the Mac review. *MacUser.* May 2004. See http://macuser.pcpro.co.uk/macuser/reviews/58395/microsoft-excel-2004.html.

[†] Walkenbach, John. "Excel 2003 Review." The Spreadsheet Page. See www.j-walk.com/ss/excel/xl2003.htm.

[‡] Walkenbach, John. "First Look: Excel 2002." *PC World.* May 31, 2001. See www.pcworld.com/reviews/article/0,aid,49607,00.asp.

Get the message? Excel is a dog. But don't be ashamed of yourself for wallowing in the misery it causes. Alternatives exist, but they don't get much publicity—perhaps because, given a choice, technology journalists would rather write about iPods than spreadsheets. What they haven't written yet is that Microsoft Excel is the last T. Rex of the spreadsheet world, because free alternatives are emerging to steal its eggs.

Excellent Alternatives

You may already have an Excel alternative in your system that's easier to use than Lotus 1-2-3. If you switched to a Word alternative as described in Chapter 4, an Excel killer may be part of the package—OpenOffice.org and WordPerfect Office are two examples.

OpenOffice.org Calc (see Figure 5-3), part of the free OpenOffice.org suite, offers the same set of analysis and graphic tools as Excel. OOo Calc runs on Windows, Linux, Sun Solaris, and Mac OS X, and can open and save spreadsheets in all Microsoft Office formats as well as the standard XML format. The StarOffice version of this software includes some additional features and corporate support at a fairly low price.

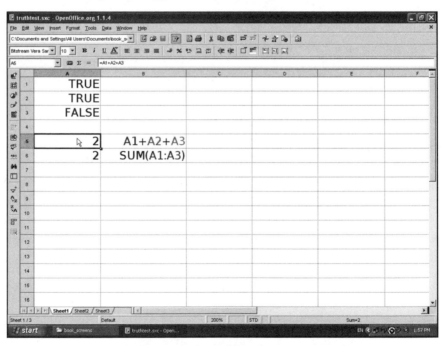

Figure 5-3: OpenOffice.org Calc offers all of the same features as Excel, and also gets the logic correct. (See Figure 5-1 for Excel's logic.)

OOo Calc is impressive. Version 1.1.2 can correctly import and export a complicated Excel spreadsheet that contains numerous sheets, formulas, and embedded charts. Calc supports a complete range of financial functions, including MIRR (modified internal rate of return) and ISPMT (interest of a credit or investment with constant redemption rates—defined as "returns the straight-loan payment interest" in Excel). It also offers an Excel-like wizard to help you through the process of creating graphs.

Support for the XML format, an open standard, makes it possible for Office alternatives such as OpenOffice.org to provide greater portability of files from platform to platform and a high degree of interoperability with any other software that supports XML. Since many browsers support XML, you can automatically view OpenOffice.org documents using a web browser locally or over the Internet. While many alternatives to Lotus 1-2-3, OOo Calc, and Quattro Pro can open or import workbook files, you may still need to use Excel, but you can save a spreadsheet from Excel, without using the Excel workbook format, in three essential ways:

1. Save it as a worksheet or entire workbook you can use again, with all its formulas and formatting intact, in another spreadsheet application. Let's say you have a complex spreadsheet that models the dietary habits of elephants in Kenya or calculates the positions of the stars for your next astrology reading. You don't want to save the data alone—you want the formulas as well, so that you can move the worksheet or entire workbook to another program, such as Lotus 1-2-3 or OOo Calc, ready to make calculations.

2. Save the information as tabular data you can use in another program, such as a word processor, database, or another spreadsheet application. You can, for example, save a budget spreadsheet as a table to use in a budgeting plan created with a word processor. You get the results of all calculations, but you lose the formulas for them.

3. Save (or export) the information as a published document or web page with formatting intact (but not formulas). Use this approach to distribute spreadsheets to people who need only to view or print the information.

It all depends on how you plan to use the information. To migrate all of your Excel workbooks with formulas and formatting intact to another spreadsheet application such as Lotus 1-2-3 or OpenOffice.org Calc, you can use the other application to open the Excel workbooks directly. You can also save all the workbooks from Excel into another format.

Saving Formulas as Well as Data

Microsoft grudgingly accepts the fact that there are alternatives to Excel and lets you save worksheets and entire workbooks into some of the more popular formats with the formulas and calculations, sometimes even the formatting. Of course, every time you do this, Excel warns you that you may lose something in the process—a subtle piece of FUD that shouldn't worry you. Here are the other formats you can use when saving spreadsheets:

WK4, WK3, and FM3 formats for Lotus 1-2-3
These formats save all worksheets and charts in the workbook.

WKS, WK1, and FMT formats for Lotus 1-2-3, and WQ1 for Quattro Pro (DOS version)

These formats save only the active worksheet, i.e., the one you have displayed in front, so you have to save each worksheet in a workbook separately to transfer them.

Microsoft XML

With some versions of Excel, you can save the entire workbook in this format, but you lose any charts and graphs, macro sheets, custom views, drawn object layers, outlines, scenarios, shared workbook information, Visual Basic projects, and user-defined function categories. You also can't save password-protected worksheets. Read more about Microsoft's version of XML in the section "XML's Like Team Spreadsheet" later in this chapter.

Saving Only the Data

You may want to liberate a spreadsheet's data to use in another program—for example, to format as a table using a word processor or to use in a database program, such as an address book. You have a lot more choices for saving data formats than you have for full spreadsheet formats. With the exception of XML, these formats save only the active worksheet; you have to switch worksheets and save each one separately:

Microsoft XML

Although Microsoft's version of XML includes proprietary extensions, you can use XML, if your version of Excel supports it, to transfer information to applications that accept XML (and there are lots of them out there). All worksheets in the Excel file are saved.

CSV (comma-separated value)

The CSV file format is often used to exchange data between disparate applications. Actually, there is no real standard for the CSV format—there is only the 800-pound gorilla known as Microsoft's CSV format. As is the case with most exchange formats since XML, CSV files have become somewhat of a legacy format; most new applications use XML. CSV files use commas and double-quote characters to separate cells of data. If you open a CSV file in a text editor, you see lots of commas and quotes. Even blank cells are saved, separated from other cells by commas. Fortunately, you don't have to parse this stuff yourself, because all spreadsheet applications and most database applications can import the files. CSV includes different formats for Mac and Windows (actually DOS). Choose the appropriate system to ensure that the text file uses the correct combination of tab characters, line breaks, carriage returns, and other characters.

Tab-delimited or space-delimited text file

This format is a straightforward text file with data elements separated by tabs or spaces. It is similar in most respects to the CSV format, except that tabs or spaces are used rather than commas, and you might even be able to read the data.

DBF 4 for dBASE IV, DBF 3 for dBASE III, and DBF 2 for dBASE II

These formats are designed to feed data into various versions of the ancient (but still used) dBASE application. Much newer database applications prefer XML or even SYLK.

SYLK

A spreadsheet SYmbolic LinK file is a sparse and cryptic ASCII text file containing information that a spreadsheet application can recognize and use to create the rows and columns correctly (and, in some cases, formulas and calculations as well). It was originally designed to work with Multiplan, another ancient spreadsheet program, but it is also supported by lots of other programs, including address books in PDAs. Excel *seems* to save a "dumb" SYLK file that contains only data when opened or imported by other programs. However, Excel actually *can* open the SYLK file it created and leave everything intact. What's going on? Calculations and formulas are supported only if you use Excel to open the SYLK file; otherwise, you get just the data.

DIF (Data Interchange Format)

DIF, like SYLK, is a program-independent method of storing data as ASCII text files so that the information can be reconstituted as rows and columns in a spreadsheet. The format is compatible with just about all database applications, languages, and operating systems.

Saving a Document You Can Publish

You may want to save a spreadsheet as a published report to post on the Web or distribute by email, or in a format you can use with a word processing or page layout program. If so, try the following options:

Tab-delimited text file

This format saves a single worksheet in a normal ASCII text file with data elements separated by tabs and each row ending with a hard return as if it were a paragraph of text. This format makes it easy to convert the data, which is already in tabular form, into a table. All you need to do in a word processor is select the information and set the tabs to the desired spacing to make the table look right. Most word processors offer tabs with left, right, or center justification settings to line up text or the decimal points of numbers.

Web page (HTML)

This format saves the data from multiple worksheets but adds way too much HTML code that you don't need. (You may want to strip out this code using a text editing or web page authoring program.) Nevertheless, it presents the information in tabular form suitable for a web page.

PDF

This format preserves the fonts, graphics, and tabular layout of the entire workbook. You can expect the PDFs you create to look the same way on another computer as it does on your computer—exactly the same as if it had been printed. PDF files can be shared, viewed, or printed by anyone using the freely distributed Adobe Reader software (see the section "PDF Was Made for This" in Chapter 4).

XML's Like Team Spreadsheet

Microsoft is evolving Office into a tool that is deeply tied into a company's core applications, further entrenching Microsoft systems and software into all levels of business computing. Part of this effort entails subverting the XML standard format and driving open source software back into the underground.

For many businesses, Office already serves as the maddeningly familiar interface for databases that hold critical business information. People use Word, Excel, and Outlook to fill out and submit electronic forms to core applications and to prepare up-to-date reports from business information scoured from company databases. If all this activity could be better accomplished with XML and secure web portals, Microsoft's hold on businesses with Office might loosen. So Microsoft is moving quickly to embrace XML and incorporate the standard into its vision of Office-dominated computing.

Microsoft XML is not the native file format for Office, but it lets companies move data in and out of Excel, Word, and PowerPoint—with some conditions. Gary Edwards, OpenOffice.org's representative on the OASIS Open Office XML Format Technical Committee, points out, in an interview with internetnews.com, that the use of XML "is only available to the most premium customers who purchase licenses to a whole rash of Microsoft application and server products."[*] Microsoft's strategy is, once again, to lock large swaths of the business market into using its products.

Open source advocates see this move as treachery of the highest order, and they envision the destruction of XML itself, or at least its marginalization, as Microsoft adds extensions to the standard that work only with Office. A similar move by Microsoft years ago nearly capsized Java and sparked a lawsuit from Sun Microsystems.

XML was designed to *increase* the portability of documents, not to decrease it. The markup language does not affect content—you can use or strip out XML's embedded markup tags to reproduce the document's content. But Microsoft has extended XML to include a wide range of active functions that *do* affect content.

A Microsoft XML document can, for example, activate ActiveX components to perform functions with other applications, interact with a dynamic link library (DLL), or pass tagged content to a Visual Basic script. Developers can use Microsoft XML tools to make documents that automatically update themselves or documents that can't be emailed to people who are not on a predefined list. It can even be used to make documents that delete their own contents if called up after some pre-specified date. This goes way beyond standard XML usage into dangerous territory, and the reason Microsoft did it was to turn Office documents into clients for server-based processes.

---

[*] Joyce, Erin. "Microsoft, Open Source Claim XML Success." internetnews.com. November 26, 2003. See www.internetnews.com/ent-news/article.php/3114271.

With these capabilities available, fraud detection is far more difficult, if not impossible. You can receive a secured document on CD that can still be subverted by a bad guy able to spoof the remote server. Even more likely, your documents might become unreadable due to a glitch or server upgrade. Documents might refuse to display themselves on PCs that fail to meet hardware identification or software licensing checks. Truth, once again, could be compromised, as the same document could show different content to different people or at different times.

Microsoft XML documents represent the ultimate in viral marketing. People who get them from clients or suppliers have no other option than to license the same Microsoft products. In many ways, Microsoft XML documents are designed to be open source killers, since it is likely that a Microsoft XML document opened using OpenOffice.org Writer or Calc *won't* function properly as an interface to data stored on a remote Microsoft Server. Microsoft will once again crow that open source software can't keep up with innovation.

Nevertheless, Microsoft needs developers to buy into its vision and create applications that build on Office and Microsoft's extended XML. The company is even offering peeks under its kimono at *some* of the proprietary source code for the latest version of Office. But at every turn Microsoft is bumping up against open source software that uses XML as a standard. And guess what? Developers *like* open source software, so Microsoft faces an uphill battle.

For example, the Apache Cocoon project and its various spinoffs and competitors offer a better way to meet the needs addressed by Microsoft's promised document management capabilities.* Cocoon makes it possible to use a building-block approach in building web solutions and applications, hooking together components without requiring programming.

The Security Assertion Markup Language (SAML) and other XML work spun out of the Liberty Alliance offer a complete, functional framework for document authentication, user identification, and access authorization.† Liberty Alliance provides the technology, knowledge, and certifications to build identity into the foundation of mobile and web-based communications and transactions.

These solutions work now—there's no need to wait for Microsoft's next version of Windows or to lock your company into Microsoft products. What Microsoft has realized, and what many developers have known all along, is that standard tools such as Java and standard formats for data such as XML are the Trojan horses for freedom and independence from Microsoft.

Speaking Truth to PowerPoint

You call them *decks*, *presos*, *PPTs*, or just *powerpoints*, and you know how pervasive—and unpersuasive—they are. PowerPoint presentations have been inducing catalepsy in boardrooms and conference halls for nearly two decades.

---

* See http://xml.apache.org/cocoon.

† See www.projectliberty.org.

The corrupting power of PowerPoint is so strong that otherwise normally articulate speakers turn into zombies mumbling the bullet points that appear on the slides behind them. PowerPoint's entrenchment in business and education as part of the Office suite discourages the use of any other tool for presenting information, especially graphical information, thus locking out any possible innovation. You either spend an inordinate amount of time fiddling with fonts and tweaking graphics, or you opt for the preprogrammed instant slideshows in which you simply add text. Its lockstep linear model forces all presenters to organize their shows as if they were slides from summer vacations or transparencies from a police academy freshman training class. For sales, marketing, and PR executives, analysts, government bureaucrats, and educators, PowerPoint is a forced addiction.

"Imagine a widely used and expensive prescription drug," Edward Tufte wrote in *Wired Magazine*,[*] "that promised to make us beautiful but didn't. Instead the drug had frequent and serious side effects: It induced stupidity, turned everyone into bores, wasted time, and degraded the quality and credibility of communication. These side effects would rightly lead to a worldwide product recall."

PowerPoint represents the last of its kind—the linear slide presentation tool—a dinosaur stalking the new world of interactive media that simply won't give up. PowerPoint tends to confine the speaker to a single pre-set path, limiting the creator's options, discouraging spontaneity, and diminishing flexibility. Limited to a linear presentation of one slide after another, each containing fewer than 40 words (about eight seconds of reading), PowerPoint makes it difficult for an audience to understand context and evaluate relationships between sets of data without considerable voiceover accompaniment. Contrary to popular belief among PowerPoint graphic artists, the more intense the detail of a visual presentation, the greater the clarity and understanding. This is especially so for statistical data, where the fundamental analytical act is to make comparisons.

According to Microsoft estimates, at least 30 million PowerPoint presentations are made every day. Today's business speeches seem naked without them. Thanks to the ubiquitousness of PowerPoint, people expect speakers to use slides and are often more comfortable staring at the slides instead of the speaker.

Slides can be useful as signposts that promote the subject matter and the speaker's version of the truth. But more often than not, presentations exaggerate the truth and cloak the presenter in a mantle of false respectability and professionalism, thanks to PowerPoint's instant presentation templates. As Ian Parker pointed out in his brilliant essay on PowerPoint in *The New Yorker*,[†] "PowerPoint is strangely adept at disguising the fragile foundations of a proposal, the emptiness of a business plan; usually, the audience is respectfully still (only venture capitalists dare to dictate the pace of someone else's

---

[*] Tufte, Edward. "PowerPoint is evil." *Wired Magazine.* Issue 11.09, September 2003. See www.wired.com/wired/archive/11.09/ppt2.html.

[†] Parker, Ian. "Absolute Powerpoint: Can a software package edit our thoughts?" *The New Yorker.* May 28, 2001.

slideshow), and, with the visual distraction of a dancing pie chart, a speaker can quickly move past the laughable flaw in his argument. If anyone notices, it's too late—the narrative presses on."

A TALE OF TWO DISASTERS

The Columbia space shuttle crash of February 1, 2003 was caused, according to NASA, by faulty foam insulation. However, the Columbia Accident Investigation Board at NASA also criticized the use of PowerPoint to present life-threatening information. According to the board's report,* when NASA engineers assessed possible wing damage during the mission, they presented the findings to senior managers in a confusing PowerPoint slide—so crammed with nested bullet points and irregular short forms that it was nearly impossible to untangle.

The 2003 war in Iraq was sold to the world using PowerPoint. Colin Powell used it to make the U.S. case to the United Nations that Iraq possessed weapons of mass destruction. The weapons were never found, but the PowerPoint slides were convincing as a weapon of mass delusion. "Perhaps PowerPoint is uniquely suited to our modern age of obfuscation," wrote Clive Thompson in *The New York Times Magazine*, "where manipulating facts is as important as presenting them clearly. If you have nothing to say, maybe you need just the right tool to help you not say it."

---

* Thompson, Clive. "PowerPoint Makes You Dumb." *The New York Times Magazine.* December 14, 2003.

The history of PowerPoint is not pretty. It all started in bowling alleys and police precincts in the 1940s—where overhead projectors were first used.

Slide presentations danced behind the podiums in conference halls for decades before ordinary folks learned how to create them. An army of graphic designers, photographers, and audio-visual specialists were employed to produce them. Then along came the personal computer and low-cost projection equipment.

Ironically, the original PowerPoint was inspired by one of the first hackers ever to be despised by the U.S. Government enforcement agencies: Whitfield Diffie, a long-haired mathematician, former peacenik, and co-developer of public key cryptography. Diffie created a small graphics program in 1981 at Bell-Northern Research labs to help storyboard slides for a speech. Bob Gaskins, who was the head of computer science research at Bell-Northern at the time, built on the idea and collaborated with Dennis Austin to develop Presenter (eventually renamed PowerPoint), the first graphics program for creating slide presentations.

The first version appeared in 1987 and ran only on the Mac. Shortly thereafter, Microsoft swooped down from Redmond and gobbled up Gaskins' fledgling company for $14 million in cash. By 1990, Microsoft had made considerable changes to PowerPoint and added a complex set of new features to make its integration into Microsoft Office more tantalizing. The popularity of Office solidified PowerPoint's hold on the market, and Aldus Persuasion, its only competitor—and a much better program for creating more flexible, non-linear presentations—was left in the dust.

DHARMA AND DOGMA

The idea that businesses around the world use PowerPoint to push their agendas is not so dangerous. What *is* dangerous is that Microsoft supplies PowerPoint and other applications to schools at a substantial discount.

Although the software originally was intended for the business market, by 1998, teachers found it useful for presenting lessons and helping students hone their proficiency with computers. That means kids are learning to think in terms of sound bites and bulleted lists. Sherry Turkel, noted author[*] and director of the Massachusetts Institute of Technology's Initiative on Technology and Self, pointed out in an interview in *The Chicago Tribune*[†] that PowerPoint is "an exemplar of a technology we should be quite skeptical about as a pedagogical tool. . . . PowerPoint doesn't teach children to make an argument. It teaches them to make a point, which is quite a different thing. It encourages presentation, not conversation. Students grow accustomed to not being challenged. A strong presentation is designed to close down debate, rather than open it up."

Rather than learning to write a report using sentences, children are being taught how to formulate client pitches and infomercials, thanks to Microsoft and PowerPoint.

---

[*] *The Second Self: Computers and the Human Spirit* (1984) and *Life on the Screen: Identity in the Age of the Internet.*

[†] Keller, Julia. "Is PowerPoint the Devil?" *The Chicago Tribune.* January 22, 2003. See www.siliconvalley.com/mld/siliconvalley/5004120.htm.

PowerPoint was intended to free the ordinary business person from being beholden to graphic designers, audio-visual production companies, and other intermediaries to produce slide presentations for them. Alas, Microsoft shackled the business world to PowerPoint's parade of boring templates and clip art. Today, businesses employ people at high salaries—presumably experts in their fields—who spend way too much time choosing type fonts and experimenting with amateurish clip art.

As it is human nature to be intimidated by technology, business people are not comfortable with a blank PowerPoint screen and feel compelled to fill it with instant content. In an effort to make presentations easy to create, Microsoft supplies templates with the AutoContent Wizard, but these actually limit your ability to express yourself and choke the very life out of creativity. The templates are both generic and specific, with titles like "Managing Organizational Change," and folks who've never had an original thought in their heads can simply add logos and speaker's notes. Even those who think they're too clever to use templates tend to fall back on the default settings. So, it's no surprise that all of these boring presentations use the same colors, the same fonts, and the same arrangement of bulleted lists, with variations only in backgrounds, logos, and gratuitous graphics.

Efforts to get people to use multimedia were stymied in the mid-1990s by the lack of a standard format for presentation delivery. Applications that could combine animation, a soundtrack, digital video, and special effects flourished in niche markets but never caught on with the mainstream. Once again, the Microsoft-backed file format—in this case, the dreaded PPT file from PowerPoint—hooked everyone on the bland, excruciating style of presentations we still suffer to this day. With more than 300 million users worldwide and a share of the presentation software market that is said to top 95 percent, the word "powerpoint" is now synonymous with any computer presentation that consists of one interminable slide after another.

In 1997, Sun Microsystems' chairman and CEO Scott McNealy, "banned" PowerPoint. "Why did we ban it?" he replied to Ian Parker in *The New Yorker*,[*] "Let me put it this way: If I want to tell my forty thousand employees to attack, the word 'attack' in ASCII is 48 bits. As a Microsoft Word document, it's 90,112 bits. Put that same word in a PowerPoint slide, and it becomes 458,048 bits. That's a pig through the python when you try to send it over the Net."

McNealy's concern is shared by the American military, according to Parker. "Enormously elaborate PowerPoint files (generated by presentation obsessives—so-called PowerPoint Rangers) were said to be clogging up the military's bandwidth. Last year, to the delight of many under his command, General Henry H. Shelton, the chairman of the Joint Chiefs of Staff, issued an order to U.S. bases around the world insisting on simpler presentations."

I once had the honor of creating the keynote presentation that former Apple CEO John Sculley gave at Tokyo COMDEX. He insisted on throwing out the graphical slides with bullet points produced by his marketing group. Instead, he opted for slides with a single word or phrase in bright yellow on an all-black background, such as "Trends," "Markets," "Revolution," etc. It was a very effective speech. Yet even with just words on blank slides, the PowerPoint file was too large to copy from computer to computer by email. For translation into Japanese, it made more sense to send the words in an email message rather than send the PowerPoint file.

Speaking Alternatives to PowerPoint

As hypertext pioneer and author Ted Nelson once said, we live in media as fish live in water. He popularized the idea that you could link text and pages to other works and allow readers to follow the links, presaging the Web's Hypertext Markup Language (HTML). A hallmark of the Web and HTML is the ability to dip into the information sea, travel in any direction, and change directions at will, interactively . . . A web browser (yes, even Microsoft's Internet Explorer) can display HTML information on the screen just like PowerPoint can display slides, but you can also click text items as links to navigate different routes into the information.

The most inexpensive approach to replacing PowerPoint in your life is to use a free web browser and web page (HTML) creation tool. (Chapter 9 provides more details on this topic.) Web browsers such as Netscape, Mozilla, Firefox, Safari, and Internet Explorer are already equipped to do most of what PowerPoint does—display text in various sizes and colors, show images (including animation), and play video and sound (with standard plug-ins). Most

---

[*] Parker, Ian. "Absolute Powerpoint: Can a software package edit our thoughts?" *The New Yorker*. May 28, 2001.

computers in lecture rooms and conference halls have one or more web browsers preloaded on them. Your web page presentation can be stored on CD-ROM or on a portable hard disk or simply be posted on the Web.

Consider these advantages of web pages over PowerPoint slides:

- You can open multiple windows simultaneously, activating "slides" as you speak by clicking them. You can use different size windows to show big points, little points, demos, etc.

- You can keep windows open to show relationships between data points on different slides. You can even keep a table of contents window open and jump to any slide at any time.

- Each window can have multiple links to other windows. Your examples or demos can be web pages from other sites, which launch quickly because you are already in a browser. You can also effortlessly put your presentation on your own website for the audience to review later.

- No special reader or client is required to view the presentation, whether it is posted on the Web or run off a hard disk or CD-ROM. All you need is a standard browser and a free plug-in for multimedia (which is likely the same or a similar plug-in required for PowerPoint to do multimedia).

One of the problems with PowerPoint is the difficulty of layering information properly, so that a presenter can clearly show the connection between individual pieces of information. PowerPoint's slide-by-slide sequencing fragments related pieces of information. But with a web page approach, a bullet point can open up to reveal a deeper explanation, which can then transition into a movie or 3D animation, which can have any number of documents, in any format, attached to it as well—all viewed through a normal web browser.

The drawback to using a web browser to play a presentation is that you don't have snazzy transitions or bullet points that build from a single slide, although you can create these using a plug-in such as Macromedia Flash. This is not much of a drawback, however, considering that we've all seen these so-called "special" effects for two decades, and we're mostly sick of them.

TIP *To use a web page as a slide, use a large type size for text, keep your text brief, and use contrasting colors. Most web-authoring applications (such as Macromedia Dreamweaver) let you control these aspects easily. Add photos or images in the JPEG or GIF formats—you can even use animation in the GIF format without a plug-in. The most common formats for video and audio are QuickTime and Windows Media Player, both of which work on Macs or PCs. Flash is also becoming a standard format for web animations, graphics, and video.*

If you still want to do conventional slide presentations with snazzy special effects, you don't need PowerPoint. Besides, linear presentations may still be appropriate in some circumstances. For example, you might not want to jump into a new presentation style right before that big road show for investors, technology analysts, government bureaucrats, or bank managers. *They* expect to see a slide presentation, and you don't want to disappoint them. There are several alternatives to using PowerPoint for typical slide presentations.

Mac users can get a decent alternative. Keynote 2, supplied with the iWorks package from Apple, offers an unmatched combination of ease-of-use features and advanced support for multimedia, including scalable graphics, loads of smoothed fonts, dual displays, etc. It imports and exports all of the file formats you're likely to need, including the dreaded PPT (PowerPoint) format. You can use Keynote's built-in iLife media browser to add your own photos, movies, and songs, or you can import data and media from other applications. Some of Keynote's ease-of-use features can't be found in PowerPoint, such as the ability to resize and rotate an image or object. To do so, you simply drag one of the selection points of a Keynote object, and a little yellow rectangle shows you the degree of rotation or the current size of the image. You can't do this in PowerPoint without going through its menus. Keynote also allows you to import Adobe Photoshop files directly.

The OpenOffice.org suite, described earlier in this chapter as a free replacement for Excel (and in Chapter 4 as a replacement for Word), includes a PowerPoint alternative called Impress. For all its mimicry of Microsoft Office, OpenOffice.org Impress manages to improve on Microsoft's dismal user interface in some small, helpful ways, such as adding a vertical tool bar for common shortcuts and a floating window for paragraph styles (see Figure 5-4). Fonts in the Font menu are shown in their native typefaces, making it much easier to choose.

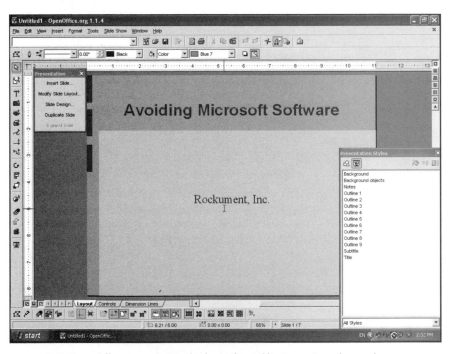

Figure 5-4: OpenOffice.org Impress looks and acts like PowerPoint but makes composing slides easier with shortcuts and a floating Presentation Styles window.

OOo Impress is by far the best value for your money; you don't need money. It runs on Windows, Linux, Mac OS X, or Sun Solaris and stores its documents in XML for compatibility with other applications. The StarOffice version of OOo Impress from Sun Microsystems includes some extra features such as a database, special fonts, template, clip art, some file filters, and, most importantly, training and support from Sun.

Astound Presentation (www.astoundcorp.com), a powerful commercial alternative to PowerPoint, can add multimedia effects to imported PowerPoint files that PowerPoint itself can't produce. Astound lets you place multiple objects on a slide with timeline synchronization for precise frame-by-frame animation and synchronizing with sound. You can also export the presentation as a web page in HTML or Dynamic HTML with just one click.

Corel Presentations, included in the WordPerfect Office suite described in Chapter 4, has all the features of PowerPoint with additional support for animation and sound within slides. Not only can it import and export Power-Point files, it can also produce Flash files for publishing on the Web.

Another free application for making presentations is Kpresenter, included in the free KOffice suite (www.koffice.org) for Linux, Unix, and other systems running the KDE desktop. It offers a simple feature set and can import PowerPoint files and export web pages.

Do yourself a favor and wean yourself off PowerPoint presentations. If you must create slides, consider the one-word-per-slide approach that John Sculley took in Tokyo (which was certainly easy to translate into Japanese). Speak directly to your audience—don't use slides as anything more than a visual prop. If you must communicate bullet points, consider posting a more wordy version on the Web where people can find it, download it, and print it on their own time. Remember, friends don't let friends use PowerPoint.

6

MEDIA LIB: MICROSOFT-FREE
MUSIC AND VIDEO

A major battle is brewing in the digital media industry, and once again, you and I are the innocent victims. If you ever bought a Betamax VCR or a laser videodisc player, or even an eight-track music cartridge for your car, you know what I'm talking about. The format becomes obsolete or unplayable, and you have to buy the music or video again. What you may not realize is that CDs are not the final solution to this problem for music, nor are DVDs the solution for video. These discs can become unreliable after 15 years or so, even if you don't play them much. For example, I purchased CDs that were played only a few times during the last 15 years, and yet some tracks skip or don't play at all. The big music labels don't lose sleep over this, because they profit when you buy the same music more than once.

Not just the music labels but the entire entertainment industry is unhappy with the idea of people copying and sharing digital media. But the entertainment industry is not to be trusted. It has fought every new development that seemed to threaten current revenue streams by offering content through new channels it didn't completely control. It fought the player piano at the turn of the previous century in order to protect sheet music, until piano rolls opened up gigantic new music markets. It fought cassette tapes until record companies figured out how to sell prerecorded tapes at truck stops. It fought the VCR until corporations figured out how to make billions with a video after-market. Technology companies have always toppled entertainment industry opposition by opening up new opportunities to sell products and services, not by doing the entertainment industry's bidding.

NOTE *The player piano was a digital recording and playback system. Companies bought sheet music and copied the notes to make the holes (zeros and ones) in the piano rolls, which they sold by the millions without a penny's compensation to the music publishers. They were the first digital pirates.*

Alas, technology titans today are joining the entertainment industry in leading us down the garden path toward more restricted and expensive media. The fight over digital media pits our two favorite archenemies—Microsoft and Apple—against each other for dominance over copy-protected formats. Neither company is innocent; both are quite willing to court the entertainment industry's demands for stricter control over copying the music and video you've already purchased. In particular, music labels have enlisted technology companies to help fight a losing battle against music enthusiasts who distribute free MP3 songs, styling themselves as the Florence Nightingales of media, ministering to the cash-poor. Music consumers who simply want to maintain indestructible backups of their purchases are caught in the crossfire.

Microsoft, as a monopolist, has way too much power and shouldn't be allowed to enforce the entertainment industry's anti-copying agenda. But even if you could care less about Microsoft's dominance, you might care that Microsoft's technology for digital media favors the entertainment industry, not the consumer.

*The only thing wrong with Microsoft is that they have no taste, they have absolutely no taste. . . I have a problem with the fact that they just make really third-rate products.
—Steve Jobs, Apple CEO[1]*

Apple is criticized for offering a closed, proprietary platform—the iTunes online music store and the iPod, which is the only type of player that will play songs purchased from iTunes. Apple has captured nearly the entire market for portable music players and online music stores with products that are irresistible as well as fashionable. Despite its closed nature, the platform accommodates the standard MP3 format as well as its own protected format for purchased music. Apple also lets you burn CDs of purchased music, make unlimited backup copies, and copy the music to any number of iPods, but the service still ties playback to a specific set of computers that must be authorized to play the protected songs. And yet, this tradeoff is still a bit more liberal than the restrictions imposed on purchased music that uses Microsoft's protection technology. So far, no other company, and certainly not Microsoft, has been able to match the iTunes and iPod combination for convenience and popularity.

The media war is far from resolved, but given Apple's emergence as owner of the digital music space, there is at least *one* way to escape the not-so-jolly Green Giant of Redmond. Now, the heat is on for the open source community and Microsoft competitors to maintain that momentum.

Windows Media Player: Just a Pawn in Their Game

Windows Media Player is the flagship component of Microsoft's media technologies. It promises to make multimedia content "secure" through digital rights management (DRM)—Microsoft style.

Microsoft has worked hard to establish the Windows Media format for audio and video in the entertainment industry. The company established a broad alliance with Disney in 2004, under which Disney will license Microsoft's DRM tools and explore ways the companies can release content together. The newly minted competitors to the Apple iTunes online store, such as the new and improved Napster and Microsoft's MSN Music, sell music in the Windows Media Audio (WMA) format and link automatically to Windows Media Player. The format is now supported by dozens of would-be iPod killers and is even used on copy-protected audio CDs.

New iTunes competitors offer a different way of acquiring music: an all-you-can-hear service that charges a monthly subscription fee, somewhat like a premium cable TV channel. Microsoft and other companies envious of the iPod's success believe fans of alternative players will prefer to pay a low monthly fee for ongoing access to hundreds of thousands of songs, instead of buying songs or albums one at a time. As these services started up in late 2004, they were hampered by the absence of technology that would allow users to copy songs to portable devices in a protected format that would expire after a given period, since the songs were merely "rented" rather than purchased. So in early 2005, Microsoft introduced copy protection technology called Janus. Janus adds a timestamp to WMA files for use with portable music players, so that subscription services such as Napster can offer rented songs that expire after a given amount of time.

For example, Napster to Go makes available the company's catalog of one million songs with time-stamped tracks. Every time the music player is connected to the computer, the songs are checked against the user's subscription, and they won't play if the user hasn't kept up with the payments.

None of these competitors has dampened enthusiasm for the Apple iTunes online store, available to Mac and Windows users through iTunes, which still sells more music than any other online store. Apple's position in the computer industry doesn't allow it to dictate standards, so it supports the currently popular standard (MP3) as well as its own formats.

By comparison, Microsoft has the power to make its software the de facto entertainment industry standard for encoding and playing back *all* digital media, including music, web video, and DVDs. To get entertainment industry support, Microsoft wants to convince the music industry first and then the film/video industry that the PC is a *more secure* platform for copy protection than CDs or DVDs. Reading between the lines, you might draw the conclusion that, with Microsoft technology, your purchased music and video will be even harder to copy, even if the copying is legal (such as copying for personal use).

Microsoft has gone a step further, with its Secure Audio Path (SAP) technology built into Windows Media Player and the operating system, to force certification of device drivers in order to make protection schemes work, thereby limiting consumer choices to hardware that enforces the rules. In a sense, Microsoft is trying to lock people into its chosen hardware the way Apple did with its proprietary hardware. The difference is that Microsoft can use its clout in the PC industry to make or break other companies, whereas Apple goes its own way to profit from innovation.

Not content with a passive protection system (such as iTunes), Microsoft set up Windows Media Player to obtain information about the songs you rip from CDs and the DVDs you play, and report that information back to Microsoft. That means Microsoft can extend copy protection to the digital versions of songs you rip from your own CDs. By comparison, Apple's iTunes gets song information from the independent Gracenote database (www.gracenote.com) and doesn't report any information back to Apple.

You can turn off the reporting options in Windows Media Player, but you rob yourself of legitimate features, such as capturing song information so that you don't have to retype it. You can also limit your use of the Internet so that it can't report back, but Microsoft makes it quite difficult to upgrade a computer to fix defects without Internet connectivity. If Microsoft chose to, it could use the information it receives from your computers to track down music and video pirates or even consumers who innocently make copies of their purchases for personal use.

It truly is time to say no to Microsoft's gambit to standardize media copy protection technology.

The Rights Stuff

Intellectual property rights are confusing to even the most experienced copyright lawyers. Imagine if the companies that made phonograph turntables in the early 1960s were able to decide whose records you could listen to and the labels sold records that couldn't be played in different countries. Media players that enforce digital rights management are just like those finicky phonographs—they make it harder for people to share the content they purchased or to play that content on different machines.

There is no copyright law here, or in any other country, that enables an author to control *where* you enjoy creative works once you've paid for them. And yet, today's DVD players won't play discs with region codes from different countries. When the legislators wrote the copyright statutes that granted authors the right to control the display, performance, duplication, derivative works, and so forth, they didn't leave out "geography" by accident. But the entertainment industry invented a business model and then invented a copyright law to prop it up.

"Copyright is a delicate balance," said Cory Doctorow from the Electronic Frontier Foundation, in a speech[*] to the Microsoft Research Group that tried

---

[*] From a talk by Cory Doctorow given to Microsoft's Research Group in Redmond on June 17, 2004. See http://craphound.com/msftdrm.txt.

to convince the company to abandon digital rights management. "It gives creators and their assignees some rights, but it also reserves some rights to the public. For example, an author has no right to prohibit anyone from transcoding his books into assistive formats for the blind. More importantly, though, a creator has a very limited say over what you can do once you lawfully acquire her works. If I buy your book, your painting, or your DVD, it belongs to me. It's my property. Not my 'intellectual property'—a whacky kind of pseudo-property that's Swiss-cheesed with exceptions, easements, and limitations—but real, no-fooling, actual tangible *property*—the kind of thing that courts have been managing through property law for centuries."

DRM, as Microsoft conceives it, won't deter the pirates who stamp out millions of high-quality counterfeit CDs and DVDs. Rather, it is designed as a "speed bump" that prevents the rest of us from copying the stuff we've already purchased. It won't stop college students from sharing music throughout a large dormitory's network, nor will it deter anyone who knows how to edit the Windows registry. It won't stop those who use Google to find protection-defeating software.

What DRM may do is turn ordinary, law-abiding citizens into small-time pirates, especially if the rights management system is inconvenient or too clumsy to use effectively. What Windows Media Player will do is report back to Microsoft any CD you rip into your digital music library, so that Microsoft can reach out and protect those songs from any further copying (by you or anyone else). Compare this kind of protection to Apple's iTunes, which lets you rip and burn your own CDs without any intervention or reporting.

CLUMSY RIGHTS MANAGEMENT TURNS CITIZENS INTO PIRATES

The simple digital rights management software implemented for the iTunes online music store doesn't stop you from burning CDs and copying to iPods as you wish, and you can authorize up to five computers to play the music you purchase, so there is little reason to circumvent the protection. It's not a clumsy system that might gobble your purchased songs in error and force you to buy them again. As long as you make backup copies of files, you can recover from any disaster.

However, the future is less certain, as the music industry experiments with copy-protected CDs that are similar to the inconvenient protection employed for DVDs. What if you want to make a copy of a DVD on tape for your kids in order to protect the disc from mishandling? As you may know, if you try to make a VHS tape copy of a DVD you purchase, it fails because a DRM system called Macrovision is embedded—by law—in every VHS player that messes with the vertical blanking interval in the signal and causes any tape made in this fashion to fail.

Macrovision can be defeated for about $10 with a gadget readily available on eBay—but you may be breaking the law if you use it. And the next time you want to get a DVD for your kids, rather than risking the money on a disc that could easily be destroyed with casual use, you might explore how to download it from the Internet for free and burn a custom disc for them. And so the technology and entertainment industries work hand in hand to turn ordinary law-abiding citizens into pirates. Arrrgh, mateys!

An innovation that disrupts copyright does so because it simplifies and cheapens creation, reproduction, and distribution. Businesses that exploit inefficiencies in the old production, reproduction, and distribution system are weakened by the new technology, but the new technology always gives us more art with a wider reach. DRM props up copyright laws that accommodate the business models and technologies of the previous generation. To abandon invention now robs tomorrow's artists of the new businesses, new reach, and new audiences that the Internet and the PC can give them.

Consumers have fought copy protection schemes before, and won. Sony, once the leader in portable music devices with the Walkman, offered a low-capacity digital player that used a brain-damaged DRM format that kept customers from freely moving their music back and forth between their devices. Customers stayed away in droves.

And yet Microsoft is shoving a more insidious form of DRM down our computer's throats. Purchased songs in the Windows Media format are tied to the hardware of your PC, so what happens when your PC fails and you have to reinstall Windows, or you need a new PC that uses a different display card or DVD drive?

The danger of ignoring Microsoft's move to bundle Windows Media Player with all PCs is that the software giant will control the media platform completely—directly through the operating system and the Windows Media Player client software, and indirectly by dealing out authentication signatures more quickly to hardware device vendors that maintain good relations with Microsoft. You would think there would be a legal challenge to this bundling, because it has far worse implications than the bundling of a browser with Windows that sparked the Justice Department's actions in the 1990s.

Beware the Encrypted Path in Windows Media Player

Let's take a look under the hood of Windows Media Player and see how DRM can screw up your digital music and video collections.

Microsoft's technology called Secure Audio Path (SAP), bundled into Windows ME and XP, requires video and audio cards to authenticate themselves to Windows before playing digital content. When the operating system accesses media files, noise is added so that if the audio is intercepted by a pirate attempting to copy it, the audio won't be listenable. Once the file makes it through the hardware device and passes it to Windows Media Player, the noise is removed and the file plays. The content remains encrypted throughout the process until the security system verifies that the path to the sound or video card and the card itself are valid and authenticated. No other application or plug-in can intercept the encrypted content, according to Microsoft. The solution provides protection for content owners but excludes other digital rights management systems, because it is shipped free with Windows.

So you can forget about using another program to apply equalization (such as boosting the treble or bass) or to produce visual effects synchronized with the music. The Microsoft SAP system does provide an audio signal for such programs, but it's such low quality, it's worse than useless.

Even worse, the SAP system limits your hardware choices and wreaks havoc with sound and video card driver updates. It gives Microsoft the power to determine what hardware it will allow to run Windows Media Player. Sound and video card vendors have to get their software drivers approved and signed off by Microsoft. Without a signed driver, DRM content won't play. So every time your sound card vendor releases an update, you have to wait until it is approved by Microsoft. If the vendor produced drivers for Linux or other competing systems, Microsoft might accidentally "forget" to sign off on the driver for several months. Eventually, the security system will most likely be expanded from sound and video cards to include CD readers, DVD readers, CD and DVD burners, scanners, printers, and even USB speakers.

By comparison, Apple's iTunes security is contained within iTunes itself, which behaves like any proper Windows application and functions with any PC sound card that works with Windows. Apple uses the AAC codec from MPEG-4 and its own digital rights management system called FairPlay. It lets you authorize up to five different computers to play the music on at any one time and to de-authorize any of them to make way for other computers. You can also burn purchased songs onto audio CDs, so you can rip the songs into any other format. FairPlay also allows unlimited copying to iPods. But the drawback is that FairPlay is not licensable to use with other portable music players.

You have to give Apple credit for striking a plausible balance between the desire of consumers to copy their music and the need to protect the copyright holder's interests. Besides, Apple is not a monopolist technology provider—you can use the Windows version without ever buying another piece of Apple hardware or software. You can use the MP3 format to copy songs easily to and from iTunes and any other music player or portable.

WAR ON THE EUROPEAN FRONT

Microsoft hasn't been able to extend its empire and conquer Europe without opposition. Indeed, our friends in Europe are trying to prevent Microsoft from controlling the platform for the delivery of and subsequent control over digital content.

What does the European Union recognize that our own U.S. Justice Department doesn't? That competition is important for innovation to occur. The European antitrust regulators took one look at Windows Media Player and concluded that Microsoft violated competition rules by "tying" the media player to Windows. The regulators hit Microsoft in March 2004 with a $617 million fine and ordered the company to offer PC makers a version of its Windows operating system with Windows Media Player stripped out.

Microsoft is also battling a civil antitrust suit involving its digital media business in the U.S., where rival RealNetworks is seeking up to $1 billion in damages. Otherwise, there are no antitrust actions against the company in the U.S. The prosecutors focused largely on the browser market in its actions in the 1990s, but they were so late to the party that the browser game was effectively over before they started. The Europeans are more up-to-date in their actions and may actually have some influence over the future course of digital media.

If Microsoft gets what it feels is sufficient market penetration for its DRM technology, the company could begin charging content companies every time they want to encode music or videos for play on Windows computers. Those music stars and composers who think that DRM is the only way to stop people from stealing music may be playing into Microsoft's hands—DRM, as developed by Microsoft, will most likely raise the cost of production and distribution and solidify the hold that large corporations have over media.

If Microsoft's record of dominating the PC platform is any indication, its dominance of the future media platform will guarantee a Windows-like experience, only extended to include all the world's TV sets. Consumers can look forward to more crashing software, bad human interface design, and viruses. Mercenary hackers have already discovered ways to subvert Microsoft's DRM technology in Windows Media Player to inflict spyware, adware, dialers, and computer viruses on unsuspecting PC users. When you try to play an infected media file, it tricks the system into searching the Internet for the appropriate license to play the media file. At that point, it redirects the unsuspecting person to a website that downloads the badware. How ironic it is that spyware and viruses could be activated by a so-called "anti-piracy" solution.

While there are plenty of alternative players, Windows Media Player's installation interferes with their operation. This is precisely why RealNetworks is suing Microsoft. If you're lucky enough to find a Windows PC that *doesn't* have Windows Media Player pre-installed, you can safely install other players; otherwise, you'll need to change the setup of Windows Media Player *in order to use them.*

> [Microsoft's business strategy is to] copy the product that others innovate, put them into Windows so they can't be unplugged, and then give it away for free.
> —Larry Ellison, Oracle Corp. Chairman[2]

How to Get Your Groove Back

When you double-click a music or video file or insert a music CD or a movie on DVD into a typical Windows PC, Windows Media Player starts up automatically, as if it were the only software on the machine allowed to play it. Microsoft set up Windows Media Player that way on purpose.

Most people simply use Windows Media Player without thinking about it. But why do all Windows-based PCs have to act this way out of the box? Where is the "differentiation" that manufacturers so desperately want to have in their products so that you might have reasons to choose from among them (besides price)? Why doesn't Windows offer a choice of other players, some of which are provided by the manufacturer and others that can be downloaded for free from the Internet?

More importantly, how can you keep Windows Media Player from starting automatically, so that you can try other players for your sound and video?

Windows Media Player version 10 (current as of this writing) *automatically* takes over all media on your PC, *installs Microsoft's rights management*, and spies on your music and video folders. It looks for new things to stuff into its library without your knowledge—*unless you intervene* by changing its options during the setup process or right after installing it. You are essentially about to put blinders on Windows Media Player to prevent it from performing certain tasks automatically.

> We welcome innovation and competition from Microsoft. But if Microsoft "breaks" competing products, and especially if it uses Windows leverage to do so, this harms customers and innovation.
> —Rob Glaser, RealNetworks CEO[3]

Whether pre-installed or upgraded, Windows Media Player is usually set up as the default for everything from CDs and DVDs to MP3 music files—shutting out all other players. It also tries to trick you into setting up Microsoft's MSN Music online music service as your active service by displaying a normal-looking license agreement (shown in Figure 6-1).

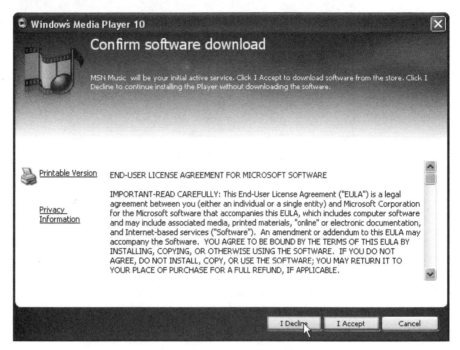

Figure 6-1: During Windows Media Player setup, don't accept the first wizard page as if it were just a simple license agreement. See the fine print at the top? Say no to Microsoft—decline the option to set MSN Music as your active online music service.

It is at this point that you would stop and think about iTunes, RealNetworks, and other players and services. The Internet is littered with free media players that are begging for your attention. So why would you use default setup options that shut out competing online stores and players or compromise your privacy?

You can get around the problem of shutting out other players by changing the file types associated with Windows Media Player. The Customize the Installation Options page in the setup wizard lets you change the file types, as shown in Figure 6-2. Click to remove the checkmark from each media or file type that you want to reserve for other players. I suggest you *only* check the box for Windows Media formats (as shown in Figure 6-2) and skip all other media types.

At the end of your Windows Media Player setup procedure, a dialog appears that lets you choose whether or not to search your hard disk and add files to its library, as shown in Figure 6-3. This is another important time to say no to Microsoft. Click the **No** button, so that Windows Media Player doesn't go off looking for media files to capture.

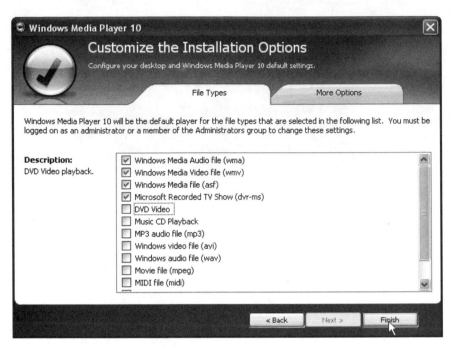

Figure 6-2: During Windows Media Player setup, be sure to uncheck the file and media types you may want to use with other players. Don't let Windows Media Player take over all these files and media types without a fight.

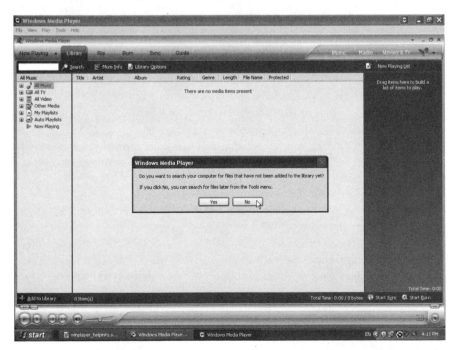

Figure 6-3: After Windows Media Player setup, be sure to say no again—this time to keep Windows Media Player from searching and storing in its library all the media files on your hard disk.

If Windows Media Player is already set up as the default player, you can still change the file types that automatically activate it. In Windows Media Player, select **Tools** ▶ **Options** and then click the **File Types** tab. Uncheck the file and media types that you may want to use with other players. Remember, you can *always* launch Windows Media Player and open any of these files or media types, but if you turn off this automatic feature, you will have more choices.

Liberating Media for Other Players

To disassociate media file types from Windows Media Player, thereby liberating them to be used with other players, select **Tools** ▶ **Options** and then click the **File Types** tab. Decide for each media type as follows:

Media Type	Recommendation
Windows Media file (asf)	Windows Media files with .asf, .asx, .wm, .wmx, .wmp, and .wpl extensions. While many other players can play these files, Windows Media Player will probably remain your choice for this type. Keep this box checked.
Windows Media Audio file (wma)	Windows Media files with .wma and .wax extensions. Windows Media Player is the best choice and the *only* choice for protected files, so keep this file type turned on.
Windows Media Video file (wmv)	Windows Media files with .wmv and .wvx extensions. While many other players can play these files, Windows Media Player will probably remain your choice here as well. Turn it on.
DVD Video	DVD Video files with .vob extensions. *Stop right there—* uncheck this if you want to try other DVD video players that run on Windows, such as RealPlayer or WinDVD.
Music CD Playback	Files with .cda extensions. Do you really want to use Windows Media Player for your audio CDs? How about iTunes or RealPlayer or a dozen other possibilities? Keep this unchecked.
Windows video file (avi)	Files with .avi extensions. Keep this unchecked, because there are many other players out there that support this type.
Windows audio file (wav)	Files with .wav extensions. iTunes offers more choices for converting .wav files into compressed formats. Definitely keep this unchecked so that you can try other players. Everything out there plays .wav files.
Movie file (mpeg)	Files with .mpeg, .mpg, .mpe, .m1v, .mp2, .mpv2, .mp2v*, and .mpa extensions. Windows Media Player on automatic for these files? Fuhgeddaboutit! Turn it off. Try RealPlayer, QuickTime, or an open source program such as MPlayer.
MIDI file (midi)	Files with .mid, .midi, and .rmi extensions. What MIDI composer do you use? There are lots of MIDI players out there—what does Microsoft really know about MIDI? Uncheck this as well. *(continued)*

Media Type	Recommendation
MP3 audio file (mp3)	Files with .mp3 and .m3u extensions. MPEG stands for Moving Picture Experts Group, a committee that recognizes compression standards for video and audio. Windows Media Player is the *absolute worst* choice for playing MP3 files. Definitely uncheck this baby. The noble MP3 format roams freely across the Internet and from application to application, and it should not have to put up with the disgrace of being played by proprietary Microsoft code. Check out WinAmp, RealPlayer, iTunes, whatever.
AIFF audio file (aiff)	Files with .aif, .aifc, and .aiff extensions. How insulting to Apple! Uncheck this type, which is the standard high-quality (uncompressed) format for Apple Mac users. Obviously, iTunes does AIFF better, and so do loads of other players.
AU audio file (au)	Files with .au and .snd extensions. Professional musicians and computer music nerds already have better tools for playing AU audio files. Uncheck this one too—try RealPlayer.

While you're changing options for Windows Media Player, consider turning off other automatic features that might haunt you later, such as the privacy options, so that Windows Media Player doesn't report your activities back to Microsoft.

To change options in Windows Media Player, select **Tools ▶ Options** and then click the appropriate tab to change its options:

Player tab

Turn off the Add music files to library when played option. Otherwise, Windows Media Player will stick its nose into your business. It makes no sense to fill up this library if you don't intend to use Windows Media Player much.

Player tab again

Turn off the Include files from removable media and network folders option to keep stuff you play on removable media—such as a CompactFlash card, data CD or data DVD, or on network-shared resources—from being automatically added to this library.

Rip Music tab

Make sure the Copy protect music option is turned off. This controls the music you rip from your own CDs. If you turn this on, the music you rip on your computer won't play on other computers, because Microsoft's DRM technology locks the music to play only on that particular computer.

Privacy tab

Be sure the Update music files by retrieving media info from the Internet option is turned *off* if you don't want Windows Media Player to report back to Redmond the identifier code and other information for every CD and DVD you play.

Library tab

Windows Media Player monitors folders for activity. If you add media files to the folders, it will automatically add them to the library. By default, Windows Media Player is set up insidiously to automatically monitor folders in the My Documents folder. You have to click the **Monitor Folders** button, as shown in Figure 6-4, and actually select each folder and remove it from the list, as shown in Figure 6-5, if you want to keep the program's hands off your media files.

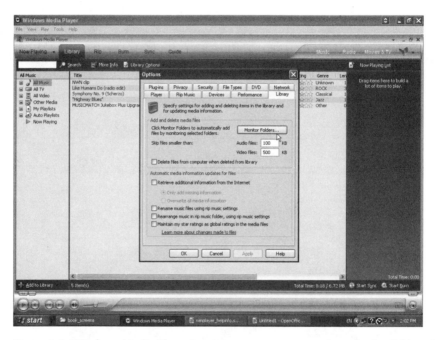

*Figure 6-4: Windows Media Player is set up to spy on your music and video folders, looking for new files to add to its library. To stop this arrogant takeover of your media files, click the **Monitor Folders** button in the Library tab of the Options window.*

Now that you've disabled Windows Media Player's automatic monitoring and startup options, you can install and use other players without interference from Windows Media Player.

When installing other players, pay attention to how they are set up for playing media and file types. For example, RealOne Player lets you set up the player to launch automatically when you open certain media and file types, but it also shows you which file and media types are assigned to other players, as you can see in Figure 6-6. This conciliatory approach is far better for managing an "ecosystem" of media players.

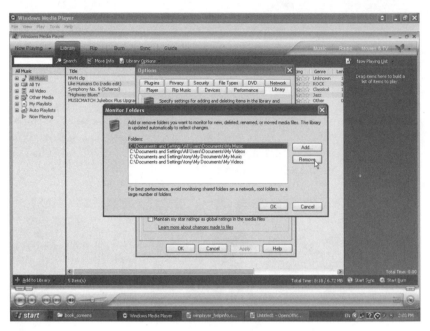

Figure 6-5: After clicking the **Monitor Folders** button in the Library tab of the Options window, as shown in Figure 6-4, you have to select and click **Remove** for each folder that you don't want Windows Media Player to monitor.

Figure 6-6: RealOne Player from RealNetworks plays nicely with other players and tells you which media and file types are assigned to which players. And see the `Periodically check my system . . .` option? This makes sure that your assignments are restored if any other application (such as Windows Media Player) changes them without your knowledge. Very cool.

Getting iTunes and Going Mobile

While there are several online music services competing with MSN Music, one has captured the lion's share of the market. As of this writing, Apple's iTunes Music Store offers nearly a million songs, with most songs available for download at the price of $0.99 each. You can even download an entire album for less than the price of the CD. The store also offers audio books from Audible.com.

When Apple announced iTunes, Apple chairman Steve Jobs remarked that other services put forward by the music industry tended to treat consumers like criminals. He had a point. Many of these services add a level of copy protection that prevents consumers from burning more than one CD or from using music purchased on other computers or portable players. Record labels had been dragging their feet for years, experimenting with online sales and taking legal action against online sites, such as Napster, that allowed free downloads and music copying. Although the free music attracted millions of listeners, the free services were under legal attack in several countries, and the digital music found on these networks wasn't of the highest quality (not to mention the widespread and sometimes intentional misspellings in the song information and artist names). Consumers grew even warier of file-sharing when the Recording Industry Association of America (RIAA), a trade organization looking out for the interests of record companies, began legal proceedings against ordinarily law-abiding folks who'd downloaded music for copyright infringement.

By all accounts, Apple has succeeded in offering the easiest, fastest, and most cost-effective service for buying music online, even though the music won't play on any portable players except iPods. Of course, Apple would never have gotten as far as it has without bowing to pressure from the entertainment industry to offer a form of digital rights management. Apple uses FairPlay, which lets you create backups of your song files and make as many copies as you want with no loss of quality. You can play the songs on up to five different computers, burn your own CDs, and use them on players such as the iPod. You can authorize up to five computers at once (any mix of Macs and PCs), or you can authorize them on the fly by removing authorization from an old computer and then authorizing a new machine and migrating your music library to it without a hitch. iTunes also lets you share a library over a local area network (LAN) with other computers running iTunes. You can even share your music library over a wireless network by using AirTunes and AirPort Express.

By comparison, Microsoft has expended (or, it could be argued, wasted) years of effort and millions of dollars to ensure that you can share music from Windows Media Player with every conceivable device, but it has somehow managed to ignore the most obvious music sharing experience—PC-to-PC sharing. While there are ways to share music this way with Window Media Player, you have to have more than the average amount of network-tweaking experience to do so. As of this writing, iTunes is the only player that lets you easily open and use a music library on another computer over a LAN.

On the Mac, iTunes is practically the only jukebox in town. And yet, Apple hasn't abused its position by putting out a less-than-functional program. If your Mac is rather new, you probably already have iTunes installed; all Macs sold since 2003 (and many before that time) come with iTunes and Mac OS X (version 10.1.5 or newer) pre-installed.

On Windows, iTunes has plenty of competition but is still one of the top five audio players—download it for free from www.apple.com. It requires either Windows 2000 or Windows XP. If you need an iTunes-like program for older versions of Windows, check out MusicMatch Jukebox (www.musicmatch.com), which also offers an automatic iPod connection.

The iTunes Setup Assistant takes you through the process of setting up the Windows version of iTunes. After clicking **Next**, the Setup Assistant displays a pane that helps you find music files on your PC, as shown in Figure 6-7, with these options:

Add MP3 and AAC Files

Turn on this option if you already have music files in the iTunes (AAC) format on your hard disk and want to copy those files automatically into the iTunes library. You might want to turn this off, however, because iTunes could find MP3 files that you *don't* want to add to your library, such as music for games. You should also turn this off if you use other music players, such as WinAmp, to play MP3 files.

Add WMA Files

Turn this option on if you want to add unprotected Windows Media audio (WMA) files to your iTunes library. This option automatically converts the WMA files to the AAC format. The original WMA files are left untouched.

iTunes offers playlists for organizing songs and burning CDs, including "smart" playlists that you can set up to reflect your preferences and listening habits. You use playlists to burn CDs and to copy music to an iPod, as shown in Figure 6-8. Putting music on an iPod is simplicity itself: you can update the iPod with playlists or with all your music. (If it doesn't fit, iTunes makes a playlist for you.) You can even customize your library to make the music sound just the way you like. The equalizer in iTunes has preloaded settings for all kinds of music and listening environments and gives you the ability to customize and save your own personalized settings with each song.

The Mac and Windows versions of iTunes are virtually identical, but there are a few differences. The Windows version lets you import WMA songs, while the Mac version, like most Mac applications, can be controlled by AppleScripts. Nevertheless, as Apple continues to improve iTunes, the company releases upgrades to both versions at the same time, and they're free to download.

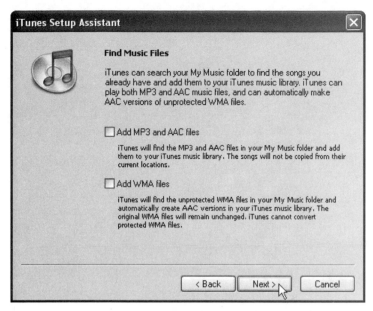

Figure 6-7: Apple iTunes for Windows gives you the option to search your hard disk for MP3 files as well as any songs in the iTunes AAC format. You can also automatically convert Windows Media (unprotected) files into the iTunes format.

Figure 6-8: iTunes lets you copy music from your library to an iPod in any number of ways, including by playlist.

Gonna Rip It Up: Importing CDs

You will want to decide which encoder and settings to use *before* ripping (importing) CDs into music files. Your choice depends on the type of music, the source of the recording, and other factors, such as whether you plan to copy the songs to an iPod or burn an audio or MP3 CD.

Power is also an issue with portable players like the iPod. Playing larger files takes more power, because the hard drive inside the iPod has to refresh its memory buffers more frequently to process information as the song plays. You might even hear hiccups in the sound.

The audio compression methods that are good at reducing space have to throw away information to do that. In technospeak, these methods are known as *lossy* (as opposed to *lossless*) compression algorithms. The AAC and MP3 encoding formats compress the sound using lossy methods, which means that they throw away information to make the file smaller, degrading the quality in the process. On the other hand, lossless encoders, such as the Apple Lossless encoder, compress the information slightly with no loss in quality or information, but the resulting files are still huge and skip may occur when playing them back on a portable device. The AIFF and WAV encoders, also lossless, do not compress the sound at all. These are the best choices for burning CDs, since it doesn't matter how huge the files are.

To get the best results when converting from one format to another, start with an uncompressed song in the AIFF or WAV format and then convert that song using an MP3, mp3PRO, or AAC encoder, or one of the open source encoders (such as LAME), all described later in this section.

The encoders provided with importing software such as iTunes offer general quality settings, but you can also customize the encoders and change those settings to your liking. With the MP3 or AAC encoders, the amount of compression depends on the bit rate that you choose and other options. The *bit rate* determines how many bits (of digital music information) can travel during playback in a given second. Measured in kilobits per second (Kbps), a higher bit rate, such as 320 KB, offers higher quality than a bit rate of 192 KB, because the sound is not compressed as much—which also means the resulting sound file is larger and takes up more space.

Besides the Windows Media format, which you should avoid like the plague, here are the most popular encoders for music, all of which are available in iTunes and most other music players that let you rip CDs:

AAC Encoder

All purchased music from the iTunes Music store comes in this format, but with FairPlay copy protection as well; the unprotected format is supported by other players, such as RealPlayer. Technically known as MPEG-4 Advanced Audio Coding, AAC is a higher quality format than MP3 at the same bit rate—meaning that an AAC file at 128 Kbps sounds better than an MP3 file at 128 Kbps. In my humble opinion, AAC offers the best tradeoff of space and quality for iPod users. It's suitable for burning to an audio CD, though not as good as AIFF or Apple Lossless encoder, and it's also excellent for playing on an iPod or from a hard drive. However, as of this writing, only Apple supports AAC.

Apple Lossless encoder

The Apple Lossless encoder, available only in iTunes, is a compromise between the lower-quality encoding of AAC or MP3, which results in smaller file sizes, and the large file sizes of uncompressed, high-quality AIFF or WAV audio. The Apple Lossless encoder provides CD-quality sound in a file size that's about 60 to 70 percent of the size of an AIFF or WAV encoded file. The virtue of this encoder is that you can use it for songs that you intend to burn onto audio CDs *and* for playing on iPods—the files are just small enough that they don't hiccup on playback, but they are still much larger than their MP3 or AAC counterparts.

AIFF Encoder

The Audio Interchange File Format (AIFF) is the standard digital format for uncompressed sound on a Mac, and it provides the highest quality digital representation of the sound. Like the WAV encoder for Windows, the AIFF encoder uses a Mac-specific version of the original Pulse Code Modulation (PCM) algorithm required for compliance with audio CDs. Use AIFF if you plan to burn songs onto an audio CD or to edit the songs with a digital sound-editing program. Mac-based sound-editing programs import and export AIFF files, and you can edit and save in AIFF format repeatedly with absolutely no loss in quality. The downside is that AIFF files take up enormous amounts of hard drive and iPod space because they're uncompressed. Don't use AIFF for songs that you want to play on an iPod or other portable digital music player, because they may hiccup on playback. Instead, use the Apple Lossless encoder with iTunes or convert the AIFF file to AAC or MP3. You can convert an uncompressed file to a compressed file without losing too much quality, but don't ever convert a compressed file to another compression format.

MP3 Encoder

The MPEG-1, Layer 3 format, also known as MP3, is supported by most computers and some CD players. The MP3 format offers quite a lot of different compression and quality settings, so you can fine-tune the format to get better quality, sacrificing hard drive space along the way. Use the MP3 format for a song that you intend to use with MP3 players, including the iPod, MP3 CDs, and applications that support MP3. Songs obtained from free online filesharing services are often MP3 files with bit rates as low as 128 Kbps. Converting them to an MP3 format with a higher bit rate doesn't improve the sound quality and only wastes space. You can't recover information lost in the first compression operation, and you can't "make it up" from scratch; whatever settings were used when the sound was first compressed are the final quality settings. Converting such files can only make them worse.

WAV Encoder

Waveform Audio File Format (WAV) is a digital audio standard that Windows PCs can understand and manipulate. Like AIFF, WAV is uncompressed and provides the highest quality digital representation of the sound. Like the AIFF encoder for the Mac, the WAV encoder uses a Windows-specific version of the original PCM algorithm required for compliance with audio CDs. Use WAV if you plan on burning the song to an audio CD or using the song with Windows-based digital sound-editing programs, which import and export WAV files. There is no difference between AIFF and WAV, except that AIFF works with Mac applications and WAV works with Windows applications. WAV files take up enormous amounts of hard drive and iPod space because they're uncompressed. Don't use WAV for songs that you want to play on an iPod. Instead, use the Apple Lossless encoder or convert the song to MP3 or AAC.

mp3PRO

The mp3PRO encoder supported by various programs (including Music-Match Jukebox and dbPowerAmp) creates smaller MP3 files that come close in quality to the larger MP3 files. The mp3PRO encoder can create files that are nearly 50 percent smaller, but its bit rate settings only go up to only 96 Kbps—suitable for mono records from before 1960 and voice recordings, but not much else. Use the MP3 encoder for higher bit rate settings.

LAME

LAME (a lame acronym for LAME Ain't an MP3 Encoder) is a highly evolved open source MP3 encoder, with quality and speed that rivals state-of-the-art commercial encoders. LAME started as a project to improve psycho-acoustics, noise shaping, and encoding speed, and is distributed freely as source code only. It requires the ability to use a C compiler, but many popular open source, shareware, and even commercial ripping and encoding programs include the LAME encoding engine (such as CDcopy for Windows, VideoLAN, dbPowerAmp, and Grip). LAME is also available for iTunes (from www.blacktree.com).

Burn It Again, Sam: Saving Music on CD-R

Until the online store formats sort themselves out, your best bet is to buy songs online and then burn them onto recordable audio CDs (CD-R format) so that you can rip the songs into whatever format you want.

What if you want to buy music in the protected Windows Media format from MSN Music and convert it to AAC to use on an iPod? Or vice versa?

Forget about converting a protected, compressed format such as Windows Media or AAC. After buying the songs, burn them onto an audio CD—*not* an MP3 CD, but a regular audio CD. You can then *rip* the new audio CD to create MP3 or AAC versions of the songs without losing much sound quality. There is no avoiding some quality loss by burning and re-ripping, but most ears won't notice the difference. The mantra is "Buy, then burn and rip."

Both iTunes and MSN Music let you burn the songs you buy onto multiple audio CDs, but that may change some day. Copy protection software can count how many audio discs you burn and keep you to a limited number.

The Real Thing and Other Alternatives

One company that has a history of kicking sand in the face of the bully is RealNetworks, founded by an ex–Microsoft marketing executive, Rob Glaser, who grew tired of Microsoft's monopolistic shenanigans. In U.S. courts and before regulators in the European Union, RealNetworks has argued that Microsoft's market abuses have made it difficult for companies to compete in the digital music business.

RealNetworks pioneered the use of audio on the Internet in 1995 by introducing a proprietary streaming audio format called RealAudio and the RealPlayer software. *Streaming* is the process of sending content (sound or video) in a protected set of bits to your computer over the Net. Your computer starts playing the content as soon as the first set of bits arrive, and more bits are transferred as you watch or listen, so that you experience the content as a continual stream.

The company now offers the Rhapsody online jukebox service and RealPlayer 10 (www.real.com). It recently joined with Comcast, the largest cable service provider in the U.S., to offer Rhapsody RadioPlus, a subscription-based Internet radio service that includes thousands of stations.

The company doesn't like monopolies and has repeatedly pressed Apple to open the iPod to rival music services. Eventually, RealNetworks introduced Harmony, a clone of the FairPlay copy protection used in Apple's iTunes store, without Apple's permission. Harmony lets you play Real content by wrapping the media in a FairPlay-like DRM layer. It doesn't interfere with iPod's FairPlay system or the iPod itself, but Apple did not appreciate this harmonic convergence and the latest upgrade to the iPod software, as of this writing, won't work with Harmony.

However, RealPlayer can handle just about every format you throw at it—all varieties of the Windows Media format and secure WMA files from Napster 2.0, and even the AAC format used in iTunes (not the protected music you buy, but the music you download or rip yourself). RealNetworks integrates its online store within the software and includes detailed descriptions of songs and artists culled from the Rhapsody subscription service. You can play purchased music on up to five computers and burn up to five CDs. RealPlayer also handles video formats and offers TiVo-like pausing and playback of live video and audio streams, with support for 5.1-channel sound when playing DVDs.

Another alternative is WinAmp (www.winamp.com), the most popular free media player for Windows PCs, offering a simple interface you can customize with "skins" and nice equalizer settings for fine-tuning the sound. WinAmp Pro (about $15) lets you rip CDs into MP3s and burn songs onto CDs as well as or better than any other rip-and-burn application. Both offer video playback as well as audio.

dbPowerAmp (www.dbpoweramp.com) for Windows is an excellent free alternative software player from the developer of the popular dbPowerAmp Music Converter program. The player has a small memory footprint and offers a familiar set of controls. One awesome feature is the ability to play WMA files and the ability to rate your songs. dbPowerAmp Music Converter is an ongoing development project that converts media files from one encoder to another. It gives you direct control over media file conversions using mp3PRO, AAC, VQF, and other encoders, and offers both Blade and LAME MP3 encoders, which are considered higher quality than your typical MP3 encoder.

Linux users have more choices for music players, most of which are free, although a recent patent crackdown on MP3 encoders has forced some developers to separate the MP3 ripping function into a pay-only plug-in. Nearly all Linux distributions support the playback of MP3 sound; for example, KDE Player plays MP3 files as well as Windows Media files.

Grip (www.nostatic.org) is a free, open source CD player and ripper for the Gnome desktop environment used with various flavors of Linux and Unix. It provides an automated interface, shown in Figure 6-9, for using MP3 (and other audio format) encoders, for ripping CDs into music files, and for retrieving track information from Internet databases. Grip works with DigitalDJ to provide an integrated music library with DJ playing features.

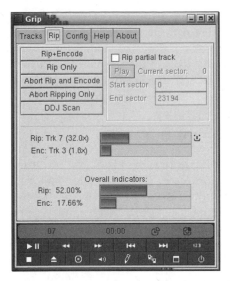

Figure 6-9: Grip is a free program for Linux for playing CDs and ripping tracks into MP3 files.

XMMS (www.xmms.org), a no-nonsense acronym for X MultiMedia System, is a free open source player for Unix and Linux systems that can play MP3 and WAV sound files. It looks a bit like WinAmp and offers similar features. You can download plug-ins to support other formats, including AAC, AVI, MPEG, and QuickTime.

Mp3blaster (www.stack.nl/~brama/mp3blaster) is an open source MP3 player for Unix, Linux, and Free/Net/OpenBSD systems. The program is set up for text commands, eliminating the need for a graphical environment such as X Window or Gnome, but that does not limit the way you can control the player. You still have the usual play, stop, pause, next track, and previous track buttons, as shown in Figure 6-10.

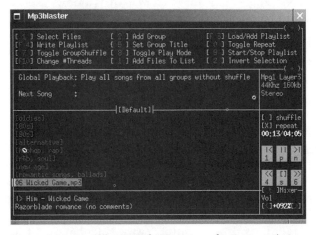

Figure 6-10: Mp3blaster, a free program for Linux and Unix systems, provides a complete set of functions for playing CDs and ripping tracks without the need for trendy graphical interfaces.

If you want to run a Windows-based media player in Linux, try Code-Weaver's CrossOver Office for Linux (www.codeweavers.com), which provides support for popular Windows-based applications. It duplicates the Win32 API, so that software written for the Win32 API can run in WINE without any Microsoft code. CrossOver Office offers direct support for the Windows version of iTunes, complete with iPod updating.

Internet Video: Running Down a Stream

The Internet is the newest frontier for video, and Microsoft dominates Internet video distribution through its Windows Media format, thanks to its monopolistic hold on the PC. Like sound, video can be streamed over the Internet to a computer from a server, so that it starts playing before the rest of it even arrives. While sound files can be small enough to download, it makes more sense to stream digital video because it takes up so much more storage space than audio. Full downloads take too long to satisfy the impulsive viewer.

The Godzilla, Moby Dick, and King Kong of digital video players are respectively Microsoft Windows Media Player, Real Player, and Apple QuickTime, and, by many industry accounts, King Kong from Cupertino is gaining on Godzilla from Redmond. Still, the Windows Media format is the format of choice for Internet video, because it affords the widest potential audience, given its free distribution with every Windows machine. That's too bad, because the format is not as good as QuickTime or Real for random access. If you're using the Windows Media Player to watch streaming video and you attempt to jump to another point in the video stream, the playback stops for a few seconds and then the audio starts playing—and it can be several more seconds before the video catches up. This makes Windows Media a bit annoying for viewers, except when playing a video from start to finish.

Video streams come from many sources; as a consumer, you can't predict their formats. This means that as a Mac or Windows user, you still need at least two players: one for Windows Media and Real formats, and QuickTime for QuickTime video. Real Player can handle both Real and Windows formats, as can some open source and commercial players. Fortunately, all of these players are free, and all can also handle the industry-standard MPEG formats for downloaded video.

Linux users, again, have more choices, most of which are free. Xanim (http://xanim.polter.net) is an excellent free video player that plays a wide variety of animation, audio, and video formats. MPlayer (www.mplayerhq.hu/homepage) is another great choice, with its laundry list of supported video formats: MPEG, VOB, AVI, Ogg/OGM, VIVO, ASF/WMA/WMV (that's Windows Media to you), QT/MOV/MP4 (that's QuickTime to you), FLI, Real, NuppelVideo, YUV4MPEG, FILM, RoQ, and PVA. You can use it to watch VideoCD, SVCD, DVD, 3ivx, and DivX movies.

The VideoLAN project (http://www.videolan.org) tries to support everything, including multimedia streaming of MPEG-1, MPEG-2, MPEG-4, and DivX files, DVDs, digital satellite channels, digital terrestrial television channels, and broadcasts on a high-bandwidth IPv4 or IPv6 network in unicast or multicast under many different operating systems. VideoLAN also features a cross-platform multimedia player, VLC, which runs on all GNU/Linux flavors, all BSD flavors, Windows, Mac OS X, Solaris, and even systems no one uses anymore, such as BeOS—just in case.

Give DVDs a Chance

Commercial DVDs, such as Hollywood movies, are typically encrypted with anti-piracy software called the Content Scramble System (CSS). Almost all Windows PCs and Macs with DVD players can play DVDs. The system software supports regional codes and is licensed to decrypt the CSS-protected content. Computers that offer a video output connector (such as S-video) must also support Macrovision technology in order to play copy-protected movies.

Most new computers equipped with DVD drives are set up to play a DVD automatically upon insertion. Some computer manufacturers, such as Dell, bundle DVD player software with a PC, but the bundled player is typically "overruled" by Windows Media Player, which installs itself as the primary DVD player software, unless you've changed the file type assignment for DVD Video (files with .vob extension) as described in the "Liberating Media for Other Players" section earlier in this chapter. If you've turned off this file assignment, Windows displays a dialog when you insert a DVD, giving you a choice of players on the system, as shown in Figure 6-11.

Figure 6-11: Windows can give you a choice of DVD player software if you first turn off the file type assignment for DVD Video in Windows Media Player.

Why not use Windows Media Player? It is, after all, free. Microsoft went to the trouble of providing these file type assignments, so why not leave them alone? Indeed, Windows Media Player is quite capable of playing DVDs and using sonic hardware that offers 5.1 surround sound. Real Player doesn't offer surround sound yet. But there are other players that offer this and more, such as InterVideo Inc.'s WinDVD, a simple DVD player that shipped with my Dell Dimension laptop, combining all the features you would expect to find in a standard consumer DVD player, in addition to some advanced functions such as the Dolby Surround Compatible option, which (depending on your hardware) gives you 2-channel plus Dolby Pro Logic surround sound. And it won't come as a surprise to learn that there are plenty of reasons *not* to use Microsoft's player.

Maybe you don't want to use Windows Media Player because you don't like its attitude, reporting what you play back to some database in Redmond. As with music CDs, when playing a DVD, Windows Media Player attempts to locate information associated with that DVD, such as the DVD name, title names, chapter names, director name, and release date. It sends a unique DVD identification number to WindowsMedia.com. According to Microsoft's privacy statement, Windows Media Player does not obtain and transmit back personally identifiable information, but I suppose it could in the future. Other Windows-based players that look up information for a CD or DVD can't put together all the information about your system the way Microsoft's software can. Besides, the Windows Media Player End User License Agreement gives Microsoft complete control over your computer to download security updates without your knowledge.

If you still want to use Windows Media Player but don't want it to report back to Redmond, select **Tools ▸ Options**, click the **Privacy** tab, and make sure the Update music files by retrieving media info from the Internet option is turned off.

Mac users already have DVD Player, which plays encrypted DVDs using licensed CSS decryption code in Apple's QuickTime application. The newest version offers closed captioning.

For Linux users, Xine (http://xinehq.de) is a very capable DVD player that can be easily extended with plug-ins available from Xine itself or from third parties. While Xine officially supports only the playback of unencrypted DVDs, you can get around that with xine_d4d_plugin, a third-party plug-in available on the Internet.[*] The legal status of this plug-in is debatable (see the "They Fought the Law and the Consumers Won" text box later in this chapter), but it's easy enough to find and install. Xine does not support DVD menus directly, but you can use a plug-in called dvdnav (prdownloads .sourceforge.net/dvd) that adds support for DVD menus to Xine. Xine also decodes media file types such as AVI, QuickTime, Windows Media, and MP3, and displays video streamed over the Internet in either Windows or Real formats.

---

[*] Try "Captain CSS's even newer xine page" (http://debianlinux.net/captain_css.html) or other links from the Xine website (http://xinehq.de).

The VideoLAN project (www.videolan.org), mentioned earlier in this chapter in the section "Internet Video: Running Down a Stream," includes a client that can play encrypted DVDs. Available for Windows, various flavors of Linux, and other Unix systems, VideoLAN can work with Linux desktop environments, including GNOME and KDE, and can use either X11, XVideo, SDL, or DirectX technologies for video output. To play encrypted DVDs, VideoLAN Client uses the library libdvdcss, which was written by the VideoLAN development team using the original DeCSS code as a reference. The only drawback to VideoLAN Client is that there is currently no support for DVD menus, so you can watch a movie but not access any of the "extras" that come with it.

MPlayer (www.mplayerhq.hu/homepage), also mentioned previously, can play most media files, as well as VideoCD, SVCD, DVD, 3ivx, and even DivX movies. MPlayer is complex and only recommended for programmers. It works with X11, Xv, DGA, OpenGL, SVGAlib, fbdev, and Aalib video technologies, and you can use SDL and some low-level card-specific video drivers (for Matrox, 3Dfx, and RADEON). Encrypted DVDs are supported using the libcss library and, optionally, libdvdread for chapter support (both of which you can find on the Internet separate from MPlayer), but you need to ensure that the libraries are installed before compiling, because MPlayer does not support plug-ins.

While the Mac has always maintained its lead as a superior alternative to Windows for playing entertainment content, including DVDs, Linux has lagged behind due to licensing issues with the Content Scramble System (CSS) for commercial DVDs. Thanks to the efforts of individual programmers who risked their livelihoods and jail time, several open source implementations of the CSS decryption algorithm have emerged for people to use with Linux and other open source systems.

The entertainment industry as a whole is moving quickly toward subscription services and rentals, which may not be the direction *you* want to go. According to the entertainment industry, even if you paid for a song six times over, you never bought the song, just the media it traveled in. This logic benefits the entertainment industry, not the consumers. People generally want a choice—buying or renting should be a decision you make because you like the content, not because you are forced into it by your playback equipment. Digital media should not be penalized with clumsy protection schemes that backfire by alienating the consumer without stopping the real pirates. And Microsoft should not be able to force clumsy copy protection schemes down the throats of PC users who think they have no other choice.

Media liberation starts with the liberation of music and video from Microsoft technology. If you don't want to pay a monthly subscription fee for the music you hear and the video you watch, you are better off using non-Microsoft players or switching to a Mac or Linux system.

THEY FOUGHT THE LAW AND THE CONSUMERS WON

Linux and open source software developers have had to resort to software of questionable legality to play encrypted DVDs. The licensing restrictions on the Content Scramble System for DVDs made it impossible to create an official CSS player and distribute the source code legally, and free distribution of source code is the very definition of open source. That put these developers between a rock and a hard place, with no legal way to offer open source software to play DVDs.

Open source developers came to the rescue with DeCSS in 1999, which let users copy a DVD and decrypt the video into a file that would then play on any computer. The Motion Picture Association of America (MPAA) took legal action and effectively made it forbidden to offer DeCSS for download or even link to it. One programmer in Norway was nearly jailed—after an appeal, he was acquitted of all charges in 2003.

The result was that the source code of DeCSS, leaked to the world by persons unknown, opened the CSS algorithm itself to public scrutiny. CSS was soon found to be susceptible to "brute force attacks"—methods of defeating a cryptographic scheme by trying a large number of possibilities (for example, exhaustively working through all possible keys in order to decrypt a message). As CSS is only a 40-bit encryption scheme and doesn't use all keys, a high-end home computer running optimized code would be able to brute-force it in about 24 hours.

The open source developers did the DVD industry a favor by pointing out the flaws of CSS. While CSS prevents most consumers from making convenient copies of their DVDs, it doesn't prevent pirates with the programming skills to break CSS and produce counterfeit DVDs.

Programmers around the world used the source code of DeCSS as a guide to create hundreds of equivalent programs, some merely to demonstrate the trivial ease with which CSS could be bypassed, and others to implement an open source DVD player for Linux and Unix systems.

Hackers also devised clever ways of distributing descriptions of the DeCSS algorithm, such as through steganography, through various Internet protocols, as a series of haiku poems, and even as a so-called illegal prime number. This is a prime number that, when interpreted a particular way, describes a computer program—its binary representation corresponds to a compressed version of the C source code. Because the program (the DeCSS algorithm) has been found illegal by American courts, this method of distribution has produced debate about whether the prime number itself could be considered illegal. Euclid never had to consider this question!

As of this writing, DeCSS (and several copycat programs that have not been specifically brought to court) can be readily obtained over the Internet, and the DeCSS algorithm is available as a plug-in or library that can be obtained separately. Some Linux distributions are able to install a DVD player incorporating a CSS implementation with a single command.

"The Net treats censorship as damage and routes around it," John Gilmore, developer of open source encryption software, told *Time* magazine[*] in 1993. The phrase has been widely quoted ever since. "The meaning of the phrase has grown through the years," wrote Gilmore on his website.[†] "Internet users have proven it time after time, by publicly replicating information that is threatened with destruction or censorship. If you now consider the Net to be not only the wires and machines, but the people and their social structures who use the machines, it is more true than ever."

---

[*] *Time*. December 1993. Reprinted many times since then, including *The New York Times* (January 15, 1996) and *Scientific American* (October 2000).

[†] See www.toad.com/gnu.

PART III

THE WHOLE NETWORK IS WATCHING

7

THE MESSAGE IS THE MEDIUM FOR INFECTIONS

Weinberg's Law (attributed to noted author and software consultant Jerry Weinberg) postulates that if builders built buildings the way programmers write programs, the first woodpecker that came along would destroy civilization.

Since the first personal computer virus was discovered in 1981, malicious hackers have tried to *be* that first woodpecker, sending out emails and messages containing hidden code that can cripple your machine. Over the last two and a half decades, the hackers' methods have spread to con artists, thieves, terrorists, and organized crime. Cyber-criminals can specifically target your business to commit fraud, steal intellectual property, and extort money by menace. Terrorists and spy organizations can disrupt communications and damage institutions and military systems. The Internet can be as lawless as Deadwood in the Black Hills of the Dakota Territory in 1876.

Microsoft is like the biggest saloon-keeper in Deadwood who takes advantage of the lawlessness to maintain its iron grip on the town. Rather than use its dominance to make Internet communications safer for everyone, the company designs its software products—in this case, Microsoft Outlook and Exchange—to lock people into using its other software products and to continue paying for updates and security packs, under the pretext of offering a safer computing environment. Microsoft will soon offer its own protection racket to keep you safe from its software. In May 2005, the company started testing an anti-virus subscription service called OneCare that may threaten the livelihoods of independent anti-virus software companies like McAfee and Symantec when it is finally released. Why would Microsoft do this? Because keeping your PC secure promises to be a profitable business, at your expense.

Standards do exist to help keep email safer, and many email programs adhere to these standards. The problem is, Microsoft "improved" and extended those standards and integrated Outlook with Office to entice its captive customer base into using other Microsoft applications—all at the expense of security.

NOTE *It is estimated that, as of October 2004, 20 percent of home computers were infected by a virus or worm, and that various forms of snooping programs such as spyware were on 80 percent of systems.*[*]

In classic Orwellian doublespeak, Bill Gates recently spun the lawlessness of the Internet into a positive view of Microsoft:[†] "The threats of cybercrime, viruses, and malware have sparked a new wave of innovation that's helping to make the computing ecosystem more secure."

Read that again. He's almost an echo of that Deadwood saloon-keeper, pointing to the violence in the street and beckoning for you to come into the relative safety of his saloon for a civilized drink—and to join his protection racket. It is to the credit of the Gates' public relations team that Microsoft has somehow escaped blame for this mess, because nearly all the security problems of recent years have been Windows-specific, as hackers take advantage of loopholes in Microsoft products.

Microsoft Windows is clearly more vulnerable to virus and worm attacks than any other system. "If you use a Windows personal computer to access the Internet, your personal files, your privacy, and your security are all in jeopardy," wrote Walt Mossberg in *The Wall Street Journal.*[‡] Microsoft has made PC attacks too easy, according to Mossberg, by carelessly opening numerous security holes in the operating system and its web browser. Outlook and Outlook Express work with Microsoft's browser to display HTML-formatted email, which is just one of the many departures from email standards that has helped to de-stabilize email security.

Microsoft's email programs, Outlook and Outlook Express, make your PC even more insecure than Windows by itself. If you have to use Windows, you can at least make your PC somewhat more secure by eschewing Microsoft's applications, including Office, Outlook, and Outlook Express.

---

[*] From a report by the National Cyber Security Alliance, a nonprofit commissioned by America Online to study home computer security. See www.post-gazette.com/pg/04300/401798.stm.

[†] Gates, Bill. "Viewpoint." *BusinessWeek.* March 22, 2005.

[‡] Mossberg, Walter S. "How to Protect Yourself From Vandals, Viruses If You Use Windows." Personal Technology column. *The Wall Street Journal.* September 16, 2004.

There are plenty of free email alternatives that are not as vulnerable to virulent vermin of the digital kind. You need diversity and innovation, not an eternally hazardous computing environment. "In biology, if the members of a herd are too genetically similar, a single disease can wipe them out," wrote Charles Arthur in *The Independent*.[*] "Ditto with computer systems: as Microsoft becomes increasingly dominant, the users of its programs are open to weaknesses that they may not know exist—until it is too late."

Please Mr. Postman (Is That a Virus in My Email?)

Email makes the world go round. Sometimes, it seems like a mystery how any work got done before email. Someone's job, and even someone's life, has probably been saved by a timely email. Someone's job was probably destroyed, too—by an email carrying a virus that damaged PCs. Email is a more potent form of communication than anything else, because it can carry software as well as messages.

You can thank the U.S. Department of Defense for developing email and the ARPANET, an embryonic version of the Internet. In 1971, computer engineer Ray Tomlinson experimented with a program that allowed users on the same machine—back when people time-shared a single mainframe—to send messages to each other. He made it work on ARPANET, and two years later, email comprised 75 percent of all traffic on the network.

NOTE   *In a redial of Alexander Graham Bell's famous experiment, the first email was sent between two computers that were sitting right next to each other, even though they were connected to the network. The first email message was "QWERTYUIOP."*

The first publicized *virus* to spread by email didn't appear until 1999. Before then, most email programs sent and received text-only messages that didn't include scripting code (although code could be attached as a separate file). The widespread adoption of email programs such as Microsoft Outlook, with its automatic address book features and HTML support, made it that much easier to spread a virus infection to others' computers by email. It's no surprise that the first widely disseminated email virus, dubbed "Melissa," was Outlook-specific and spread rapidly around the world.

If nothing else, the problems of macro viruses have shown the weakness inherent in Microsoft's dominance of both business software and home PCs.
—Charles Arthur, columnist, The Independent[1]

Outlook is more virus-prone than most other email software, even more than Outlook Express. This is due to support for ActiveX controls and VBScript that can enable the takeover of your machine without your knowledge. Outlook enables speedy distribution of infected Word documents automatically and en masse through its address book. (Fortunately, Outlook Express does *not* spread it through its address book.) While you can mitigate the spread of the Melissa virus and others like it by not using Outlook, you aren't entirely out of the woods. You could still be infected by the virus through a different email program or from some other method (such as copying a Word document).

---

[*] Arthur, Charles. "Microsoft's browser dominance at risk as experts warn of security holes." *The Independent.* July 5, 2004. See http://news.independent.co.uk/world/science_technology/story.jsp?story=537951.

HOW PCs GET INFECTED

A *computer virus* is a small program written to alter the way your computer operates without your knowledge or permission. A virus executes itself, often by placing its own code in another program's path of execution. A virus also replicates itself, by replacing other executable files with infected files. Some viruses are designed to damage programs, delete files, or reformat the hard disk. Others simply replicate themselves and make their presence known by presenting unwanted text, video, or audio messages, but even these seemingly less destructive viruses can take memory needed by legitimate programs and cause erratic behavior that can lead to system crashes.

Macro viruses use the macro programming languages of applications to replicate themselves automatically and infect data files. They are the most common viruses to spread by email, and they have cost corporations the most in repair time. When Visual Basic appeared in Microsoft Office 97, hackers used it to write viruses that could infect Word, Excel, PowerPoint, and Access files. Thousands of macro viruses roam in the wild; the known ones have names like "W97M.Melissa," "WM.NiceDay," and "W97M.Groov."

Trojan horses are like viruses, except that they don't replicate themselves. As the name suggests, Trojan horses pose as something benign, such as an ordinary text document. Unlike the wooden horse statue used by the Greeks to conquer Troy sometime around 1200 B.C., victims don't drag or in any way invite the Trojan horse into their PCs—it comes in as an unwanted email attachment and only executes if the victim is naïve enough to open it.

Worms are programs that replicate themselves from system to system all by themselves. Worms start out by inhabiting files such as Word or Excel documents and then they release documents to replicate themselves across networks. Viruses are often combined with worms to accelerate distribution.

You can't guard a Windows PC against attacks completely without installing and updating anti-virus software (from vendors such as Symantec/Norton or McAfee) and applying a bit of common sense. For example, don't open email attachments from unknown sources and don't use the preview panes of email programs (such as Outlook) that show the contents of a selected message automatically.

Melissa was the first Word macro virus and worm combination to use the Outlook address book to send itself to others via email. Its modus operandi was to send itself out to the first 50 or so names in the Outlook address book. It also infected the Normal.dot template file for Word to, thereby, infect all newly created Word documents that used this default template file.

The original Melissa virus did no major damage to PCs. Whenever the minute and day of the month were the same (as in 4:04 on the 4th of July), the virus inserted a phrase—a reference from the Simpsons cartoon series—into whatever document you were working on: "Twenty-two, plus triple-word-score, plus fifty points for using all my letters. Game's over. I'm outta here." But it flooded mail servers around the world with a deluge of messages, and many damaging viruses have followed Melissa's path. Variants called W97M.Melissa.U. and Melissa.U(Gen1) deleted system files. Some of these are still in circulation today.

HOW TO DIAGNOSE AN INFECTION

It's not easy to determine whether you've been infected by Melissa or any other Word macro virus. If you use Word, you can check the macros you have on your system for ones that you don't recognize, such as AAAZAO, AAAZFS, AutoOpen, FileSaveAs, or PayLoad. (Better yet, switch to a Word alternative that doesn't use macros, as described in Chapter 4) However, Melissa is one virus that changes Word settings before you have a chance to find out—it blocks access to the Tools ▸ Macro menu item in Word 97, or the Tools ▸ Macro ▸ Security settings in Word 2000, so that you can't check for extraneous macros or raise their security level.

Another way to detect an infection is to watch for unexplainable behavior on your system—except that much of the behavior of a Windows system is unexplainable to begin with! But one clear indication of virus infection is an unusual error message. Here are a few real-world examples:

```
This one's for you, Bosco.
ROBERTA TI AMO!
WindowError:010 Reserved for future mistakes
Just to prove another point.
And finally I would like to say: STOP ALL FRENCH NUCLEAR TESTING IN THE
PACIFIC!
```

The best way to detect a virus and defend yourself against viruses is to use anti-virus software such as the commercial offerings from Symantec (www.symantec.com) and McAfee (www.mcafee.com), which provide updates for new viruses. Figure 7-1 shows Symantec's Norton AntiVirus software at work on one of my PC laptops—it locates viruses, worms, Trojan horses, and adware (advertisements installed without your knowledge—see Chapter 9), and it lets you "quarantine" the infected files to examine them before deleting them. Free anti-virus programs are also available, such as avast! 4 Home Edition, a full-featured anti-virus package for Windows from Alwil Software (www.avast.com/eng/avast_4_home.html).

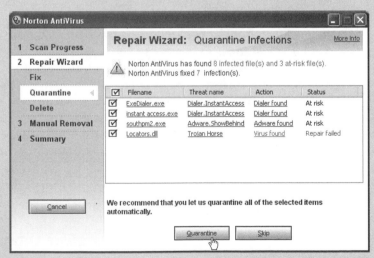

Figure 7-1: Norton AntiVirus finds malware on Windows PCs and gives you a chance to quarantine them before they do any further damage.

NOTE *Check out the latest information on virus attacks on the Symantec Security Response site (http://securityresponse.symantec.com) or independent sites such as F-Secure (www.europe.f-secure.com/virus-info), both of which offer new information daily about virus attacks. Check also Vmyths.com (www.vmyths.com) for the latest virus hoaxes.*

Outlook is an *email client,* and, like all email client software, it transfers messages, along with any attachments, to and from your hard disk. Another way to get email is to use a *web email* service, such as Yahoo! Mail, which lets you log into the service using any standard Internet browser. Rather than store messages locally on your disk, you can view them in your browser and delete them while they're still on your email provider's server. Web email is more secure than an email client, but it has its drawbacks. You are only protected while your messages remain on the server; once you save your messages and attachments on your machine, all bets are off.

TIP *Web email can't protect you from a virus embedded in the HTML formatting of the email message—only your browser can protect you from that, as explained in Chapter 9.*

NOTE *For excellent advice on how to keep your home computer secure from outside attacks, follow the 10 steps outlined by the National Cyber Security Alliance (NCSA), a nonprofit chartered to educate consumers and businesses about cybersecurity (www.staysafeonline.info/home-tips.html).*

Look Out for Outlook

Microsoft Outlook is insanely complicated to set up and use. It's hard to believe that an application designed for emailing, scheduling, and contact management would need a 1,000-page book,[*] with at least 50 pages devoted to setup and startup. Comparable programs on the Mac—Mail, Calendar, and Address Book—require little if any documentation; indeed, you could get by on just the help messages.

*Microsoft is now talking about the digital nervous system. I guess I would be nervous if my system was built on their technology, too.
—Scott McNealy, CEO, Sun Microsystems[2]*

Experts point to the vulnerability of Outlook as evidence of fundamental flaws in many Microsoft products.[†] Rather than bugs, the problem is a flawed approach to software design that's driven by an impulse to include as much functionality as possible at the expense of security. Microsoft brought its older scripting capabilities for automating its applications forward into the Internet age without making them as hacker-proof as Internet-based scripting languages. The company didn't move fast enough to adapt to security threats in the Internet age, putting more than 90 percent of the desktop PC market at risk.

---

[*] Boyce, Jim. *Microsoft Office Outlook 2003 Inside Out.* Microsoft Press. 2004. Pay particular attention to the 40 pages in Chapter 10, "Securing Your System, Messages, and Identity."
[†] Gomes, Lee. "Love Bug Prompts Security Experts to Poke at Microsoft's Weak Points." *The Wall Street Journal.* May 24, 2000.

With all the coffee brewing in the Seattle area, you'd think Gates would wake up and smell it. Microsoft brought this security dilemma on itself by basing its success on tying applications to each other and to Windows. Word and Excel were joined at the hip by a common scripting language and even common components, so that if you used one, you were compelled to use the other. Microsoft then went one step too far and bundled its all-purpose email and scheduling program, Outlook, with these applications and tied it to its browser, Internet Explorer. "Microsoft has built the ideal virus transmission mechanism into the operating system," said Gartner Group analyst John Pescatore in CNET.[*]

To be fair, Microsoft has tried to address some Outlook security problems by turning off certain features as default settings—such as ActiveX controls—and issuing patches for the system and application software. But Outlook is vulnerable by design. If you want all that power to trade data and code with other Microsoft programs like Excel and Word, security is the price you pay. If you want to share address books, email libraries, forms, and calendars with associates using Microsoft Exchange and Outlook, keep in mind that this information is the lifeblood of your business, and you shouldn't be trusting it to this patchwork of powerful but vulnerable applications. Even when conscientious users and administrators patch their software, this only closes the barn door after the horses have fled.

A prolific worm called Bagle, first discovered in January 2004, is still kicking around the Internet—an indication that Microsoft's method of distributing fixes as patches does not reach all the way out to the rank-and-file PC user who thinks a patch is something you wear to quit smoking. Bagle can spread through email without using email attachments. The HTML formatting codes in the message can harbor a Windows ActiveX control that takes advantage of a vulnerability announced and patched by Microsoft in August 2004.

Microsoft issues security updates and patches regularly, but mainstream PC users barely know about them. Do you even know if the IT manager for your business network keeps up with Microsoft's steady stream of server patches? Besides, it is highly likely that you would not get through a full installation of Windows XP on a machine connected to a public network without it being infected or saddled with spyware before you even have a chance to patch it.

NOTE   *Microsoft got tough with attachments in Outlook. It bans more than 70 different types of files as email attachments by default. You can see the list at the Microsoft Office Assistance Page (http://office.microsoft.com/en-us/assistance/HA011402971033.aspx).*

---

[*] Festa, Paul, and Joe Wilcox. "Microsoft criticized for lack of software security." CNET News.com. May 5, 2000.

Avoid Infections, Part 1: Don't Get Attached to Attachments

No matter what email client or method you use to get email, you can still be infected by an email attachment. In Outlook, you might be warned about an attachment, but the software only gives you the choice of saving it to your disk or opening it (see Figure 7-2). It would be more logical to offer a Delete button, but logic and convenience are not Outlook's strong suits.

If you set Outlook or any other email program for Windows to block attachments by file type or scan for attachments, make sure you know what type of file is actually attached. Some viruses targeting Windows use a double filename extension, such as .jpg.vbs (to disguise a VBS program as a JPEG image). If Windows is set to *not* show the extension for known file types, the recipient may see the attachment listed as a harmless JPEG file, not as a potentially dangerous VBS file. Choose **Tools** ▸ **Folder Options** or **View** ▸ **Options**, depending on your version of Windows, to change the setting to show extensions for all files.

Figure 7-2: Windows and Outlook warn you about the attachment but offer only ways to save it or open it—which is worse? Why not cancel it?

Macs are considerably better than Windows machines at dealing with email attachments and making subterfuge less simple. Unlike Windows, the Mac operating systems past and present use a file system that embeds the file type into a *resource fork* of the file. A hacker can't get away with changing a file's extension to an innocuous .jpg or .doc to make an executable program file look like a photo or Word document. If the file is something else, the Mac operating system knows it by its resource fork.

Even if you open an attachment or file on a Mac that contains executable code, OS X displays a dialog that requests the application to use with it, and you can cancel the operation easily, as shown in Figure 7-3. And if you proceed with running the attached program, it still can't install anything in OS X without displaying a dialog asking for an administrator password (see Figure 7-4). Somebody would have to be incredibly naïve to ignore all the warnings and proceed anyway.

Figure 7-3: If Mac OS X doesn't recognize the attachment or its application, it asks you first and gives you a chance to choose an application or cancel. Much safer.

Figure 7-4: If some attachment or program tries to install anything with Mac OS X, it asks you for a password first. You can, of course, cancel it.

As a result, viruses and worms do not propagate in the Mac world. The news of a successful attack would be all over the Net before a worm would have a chance to spread. Of course, there is always the possibility that Trojan horses could be disguised in Mac applications offered for free on the Internet. No operating system is completely invulnerable, and no sensible person would claim otherwise. But the underlying design principles of OS X make it more secure than Windows.

Linux is also a far more secure world for email attachments. Opening an attachment requires far more steps and far greater effort than in Windows. You have to save the attached file, give the attachment executable permissions, and then run the executable file. Linux separates normal users from the privileged root user, and you'd have to be running Linux as a root user to do any real damage to the system. You could damage your /home directory, but that's about it.

By comparison, running as a root user in Windows (a.k.a., the administrator) is common. Windows XP automatically makes the first named user of the system an administrator and gives him the power to do anything. People who are the sole users of their PCs typically know nothing about this. And even programs installed by a non-administrative user can still add dynamic link libraries (DLLs) and other system files that can damage the system itself.

To mess up a Linux box, you need to work at it; to mess up your Windows box, you just need to work on it.
—Scott Granneman[3]

With Outlook and Outlook Express as the dominant email clients, the Windows world presents a mono-cultural environment that a virus writer can infiltrate with evil attachments, knowing full well that millions of other systems have the same vulnerabilities. Linux, on the other hand, supports a wide variety of email clients and address books such as KMail, Mozilla Mail, Evolution, pine, mutt, emacs, and so on. A virus targeted to a specific vulnerability in one of those clients might affect some people, but it could never affect everyone using Linux.

Avoid Infections, Part 2: Don't Look at Emails from Strangers

As mentioned earlier, some email clients (and, of course, Outlook and Outlook Express) let you automatically see the contents of a selected email header in a preview pane. This is not good. Many users falsely believe messages aren't really "open" if they are only "previewing" them. In fact, a virus or worm could be hidden inside an email message formatted with HTML and infect your computer when the message appears *just* in the preview pane.

For example, the Wscript.KakWorm uses the automatic signature feature of Outlook Express and the Internet Explorer newsgroup reader to attach itself to all outgoing messages. No need to open an attachment for this one—simply reading the email, which is formatted in HTML, activates the worm.

This problem is more complex in Windows when using Outlook or Outlook Express, because these programs use the code in the consistently buggy Internet Explorer browser to view HTML-based emails, and a security hole in Internet Explorer can affect your email protection. This is true even if you use an alternative browser, because Outlook and Outlook Express rely on Internet Explorer code.

A suspicious email could use HTML formatting to disguise a virus that plants *spyware* in your system, which is software that gathers information from your machine and relays it to an interested party, such as an advertiser or an identity thief. It could also disguise a worm that could turn your Windows PC into a spam machine without your knowledge. Cyber-criminals sell lists of the IP addresses of infected PCs to spammers who can then use the infected machines as mail zombies.

Such emails use "social engineering" techniques to get you to open the email—subject lines that coax you or email address names that sound familiar. You may even fall prey to an Internet hoax that, simply by your reading the HTML-formatted message, infects your Windows PC.

Instead, consider not using HTML to format your outgoing emails. HTML is great for formatting web pages but is far less efficient for email. It can make an email message three times as long as it would be as plain text and sometimes considerably longer. HTML-formatted messages may also be rendered poorly when received in older email programs. Nearly all email programs send formatted HTML email by default, but you can turn off this feature and send plain text, which every email program can read without a problem.

TIP *Turn off HTML formatting for composing email: In Outlook, choose **Tools ▶ Options** and click the **Mail Format** tab. Outlook offers Plain Text, Rich Text, or HTML for sending email—choose Plain Text. In Thunderbird or Mozilla Mail, the option to send in plain text or HTML is tied to individual email accounts—view the settings for a particular account and then turn* off *the option to compose in HTML format.*

If you eliminate the HTML formatting, people who receive messages from you can read them without fear!

LIMIT OUTLOOK'S POTENTIAL DAMAGE

If you insist on using Outlook, you must, at a minimum, try to stem the flow of worms and viruses into (and out from) your system by securing Outlook as best you can. You must also keep up with all Windows security updates, learn how to Google-search for virus information, and speed-read Microsoft technical notes.

Start by making sure ActiveX is turned off for HTML email in Outlook. For whatever reasons, Outlook processes HTML-formatted email in one of the so-called "security zones" associated with Internet Explorer (see Chapter 9). Older versions of Outlook are set to use the Internet zone, a kind of "anything goes," "Wild West" type of security (as in none). Outlook Express 6, Outlook 2002, and Outlook 2003 open HTML email messages in the Restricted Sites zone by default, which is a better choice. To double-check or change the zone for emails, choose **Tools** ▸ **Options** ▸ **Security**. Next, click the **Zone Setting** button and click your way through Custom and Settings to the Security Settings dialog box (shown in Figure 7-5), where you can disable all options for ActiveX Controls and plug-ins and scripting.

Figure 7-5: If you can find your way through this complex set of dialog boxes in Outlook, you can disable ActiveX and other notorious security holes for "restricted zones" on the Internet, and by doing so, stem the tide of viruses and worms traipsing through Outlook to your system.

Microsoft's focus on restricting HTML email is a stop-gap measure that also deflects any criticism of the way it ties applications together and to the Windows system. HTML itself is harmless—it's the *scripts* embedded in the HTML-formatted text that are harmful, precisely because they can interact with programmable applications through Microsoft's ActiveX and VBScript scripting features. Turn these scripting features off, and you stand a chance of protecting your system. Microsoft's security zones feature, shared by Outlook and Internet Explorer, seem less like a convenience and more like a corner-cutting ploy by the company to use the same software to display HTML (and maybe even to more tightly link the applications). With security zones, you have to enter each website you want to restrict access to, or simply declare the entire Internet off-limits—hardly a convenience for you.

(continued)

Worms are clever enough to work if your message appears in Outlook's preview panel, so you should also disable that option. Choose **View** ▸ **Layout** and make sure that the Show Preview pane option is turned off.

Outlook offers an inconvenient brute force method of protecting against viruses and worms embedded in file attachments. With Level 1 security, Outlook simply bans certain file types as attachments. Outlook disables the interface elements that would otherwise let you open or save them, and it rather coldly informs you that the attachments were blocked. If you try to forward the message to someone else, it strips out the attachment. Funny thing, though—if you also have Outlook Express, you can export the messages from Outlook and open them with Outlook Express. Another funny thing—the suspicious attachments disappear from view, but they remain attached to the email message and take up space in your mailbox. If you've been saving email for a number of years, you may now have a virtual museum of viruses, worms, and Trojan horses silently occupying space on your hard disk.

With Level 2 security, attachments defined by your network administrator are blocked, but you can still save them to disk and open them from outside of Outlook.

If you have no IT department at your command and you use Outlook 98, 2000, or 2002, you can still block attachments by installing the Outlook Email Security Update. This update disables some of Outlook's features that allow viruses and worms to spread quickly. Unfortunately, it also disables functionality in other programs that interact with Outlook. The update makes it more difficult to open Visual Basic script (VBS) files, notorious for hiding bad stuff, and it fixes flaws that enable worms to use Outlook to transmit themselves by email. The update also modifies Outlook to use the restricted zone (rather than the Internet setting) and disables the use of Active Scripting in that zone.

The security update is integrated into Office 2000 Service Pack 2; Outlook 2002 and newer releases have the features of the patch built in. If you use Outlook 97 or a version of Outlook 98 older than v8.5.7806, you're out of luck. To find out whether your copy of Outlook includes the security update, check the version number by choosing **Help** ▸ **About Microsoft Outlook**.

You can also configure Outlook to block attachment filename extensions that Outlook 2003 or the Outlook Email Security Update does not block by default. If you're queasy about editing the Windows Registry, don't try it; but if you really want to do this, read the appropriate Microsoft technical note[*] so that you don't cripple your system with Registry errors that might bring other applications to their knees or even crash Windows entirely.

---

[*] "How to configure Outlook to block additional attachment file name extensions" at http://support.microsoft.com/?id=837388.

Avoid Infections, Part 3: Don't Get Fooled Again

If it sounds too good to be true, it probably is. The Internet is Hoax Central. It's April Fools Day *every* day, especially for people who use Outlook or Outlook Express.

You get emails from Nigerian bankers in exile looking to transfer large sums of money to your account. You find out that you just won the lottery in Kazakhstan, although you've never been there. As you open the message itself, you're careful not to open any attachments . . . but there are no attachments. Nothing to worry about, right? Not quite. The hoax message *itself* is loaded with scripts that fool your Windows system into doing something behind your back.

Don't believe anything you read from a stranger. Even a friend might be susceptible to a hoax and pass it on to you. For example, have you ever received a message like this one?

Subject: E-MAIL VIRUS!!!!! -- THIS IS NOT A JOKE!!!!!!
Anyone who receives this must send it to as many people as you can. It is essential that this problem be reconciled as soon as possible. A few hours ago, someone opened an E-mail that had the subject heading of "AOL4FREE.COM" . . .

The AOL4FREE virus described in this message is a hoax. However, after the emergence of the original harmless hoax email, someone added a Trojan horse virus to it; thus, the hoax about a virus became a real virus in disguise. So obviously, if you send it to your friends, you are unwittingly putting them in danger. Or how about this message?

This is very real, and I may have passed it on to you. Check it out as below right now. Your drive may crash!!
I had a virus which apparently attaches itself to everyone in my address book. I deleted it successfully. you may have it as well. Follow these instructions to see if you have it. It lies dormant for 14 days, then kills your hard drive. If you've got it send these instructions to everyone in your address book . . .

Don't believe messages about viruses unless you can verify that it came from someone you know, that the person really *was* the email's sender, and that the virus was real. Viruses that attack Outlook typically send email to address book contacts that appear to come from you, so be sure your friend or associate actually did send that message and that a virus hadn't just hijacked his or her address book.

NOTE *If you're not sure about a message, first check websites that track hoaxes, such as the ones hosted by McAfee Associates (http://vil.mcafee.com/hoax.asp) or Symantec (http://securityresponse.symantec.com/avcenter/hoax.html). Or, if you like to read about hoaxes, check out Hoaxbusters (http://hoaxbusters.ciac.org), hosted by the U.S. Department of Energy.*

One of the more perplexing hoaxes is a false message that tells you how to secure your Windows PC. The tip may actually harm your computer or lull you into a false sense of security. For example, a hoax message has circulated that explains how to protect against email-borne viruses by adding a contact to your address book with the name "!0000" and no email address—or your own email address. This technique does *not* protect your computer. Such a contact name would not appear in the Outlook Address Book, so the virus or worm would never see it. Adding your own address merely ensures that you'll get a copy of whatever message the virus sends—if it indeed uses the address book. Some don't bother with address books; they grab addresses from other sources on your system, such as cached web pages.

An even more insidious hoax virus was an email discovered January 9, 2004, supposedly from Microsoft Windows Update (windowsupdate@ microsoft.com), asking recipients to run an attachment that was supposed to be a revision to XP Service Pack 1. It was actually Trojan.Xombe, a small Trojan horse that downloaded an even larger Trojan horse from a predetermined website (since closed down). The Trojan horse's behavior could change depending on the scripts provided from the website.

And don't fall for the one about getting $800 from Microsoft. It goes something like this:

```
Netscape and AOL have recently merged to form the largest internet company in
the world. In an effort to remain at pace with this giant, Microsoft has
introduced a new email tracking system as a way to keep Internet Explorer as
the most popular browser on the market. This email is a beta test of the new
software and Microsoft has generously offered to compensate who participate in
the testing process. For each person you send this email to, you will be given
$5 . . .
```

Believe me, if Microsoft wanted to track the email activity of a Windows PC running Outlook, it could do so without paying anyone anything.

Avoid Infections, Part 4: Don't Get Mad, Get Alternatives

Don't let viruses ruin your PC. Say no to Outlook or Outlook Express. Say no to any email program that, like Outlook, hooks into Microsoft Word to read and write messages. You may not even know you're using Word, but the email program could automatically launch Word and the message could run Word macros when you open it. It is very important that you know the characteristics of the email program you use.

"If you've lately taken to cursing at your current email program, then I suggest you give Thunderbird a try," wrote Arik Hesseldahl in *Forbes*.[*] Thunderbird (www.mozilla.org/products/thunderbird) is an excellent free alternative, especially for older PCs. It currently runs on Windows 95, 98, Me, 2000, and XP, as well as on Linux, Mac OS X, OS/2, and Solaris. Produced by the Mozilla open source software project as a companion to the Firefox browser, Thunderbird offers intelligent spam filters, a quick search feature, and a built-in spell checker. It also includes a Usenet newsgroup reader and a reader for RSS (Really Simple Syndication) feeds such as blogs (web logs) and news updates. Figure 7-6 shows Thunderbird running on Windows XP.

---

[*] Hesseldahl, Arik. "Mozilla's Thunderbird Takes Off." *Forbes*. February 7. 2005. See www.forbes.com/technology/2005/02/07/cx_ah_0207tentech.html.

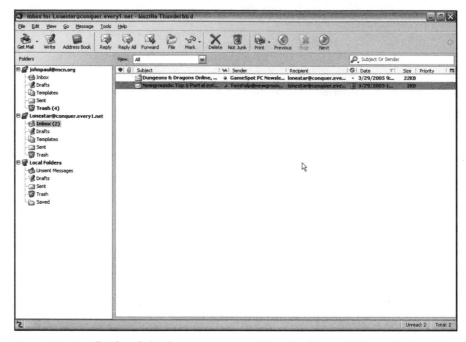

Figure 7-6: Mozilla Thunderbird, an open source alternative for email (shown here running on Windows XP), is far more secure than Outlook and runs on a variety of operating systems, including older versions of Windows.

NOTE *Like many open source applications, Thunderbird's look and feel can change according to themes. Sources for Thunderbird themes include Mozilla Update (http://update .mozilla.org/themes/?application=thunderbird), Sboulema's Extensions Mirror (www.extensionsmirror.nl/index.php?showforum=25), which offers both themes and Thunderbird extensions, and Mozdev (http://themes.mozdev.org/themeSites.html), which offers links to Thunderbird theme authors. The themes forum at MozillaZine (http://forums.mozillazine.org/viewforum.php?f=18) is also a good place to check out themes under development.*

A simpler free alternative is Pegasus Mail (www.pmail.com), which runs on Windows 95, 98, NT4, 2000, and XP, and even older versions such as Windows 3.1 (there's even a DOS version). Pegasus Mail, introduced in 1990 and updated continually ever since, can act as a complete internal mail system on its own without servers or components and supports the standard email protocols. It offers encryption, text glossaries, strong filtering, and circulation messages (to send messages or documents to successive people for comment or review). It's fast and requires very little hard drive space.

Perhaps the most widely used commercial alternative for Windows and Macintosh is Eudora (www.eudora.com) from Qualcomm. It offers a comprehensive set of standard email functions and includes excellent filtering tools that can even alert you when an outgoing or incoming message might be deemed offensive. You can use Eudora for free if you don't mind seeing banner ads on your desktop as you send and receive email. Fortunately, these ads do not appear in your messages. Or, you can buy the commercial version for about $50. Besides its SpamWatch junk mail quarantine filter, the commercial version includes ScamWatch that fights "phishing," schemes that use forged branded emails, and websites to trick you into divulging personal information.

NOTE *Currently, the electronic crime with the greatest impact is phishing, which has cost consumers an estimated $500M worldwide.[*] Financial institutions are the most heavily targeted, averaging 75 percent of all phishing scams in October 2004. By hijacking the trusted brands of well-known banks, online retailers, credit card companies, and even government agencies, phishers are able to convince up to five percent of recipients to respond to them.[†]*

Apple's Mail application is bundled with OS X, but Mac users can also opt for alternatives like Eudora and Thunderbird. Those who need extensive text-manipulation and message-filtering capabilities might want to try Mailsmith from Bare Bones (www.barebones.com/index.shtml), which is exceptionally scriptable and customizable.

Many believe that the Mac is virus-proof, and if any system comes close to being virus-proof, the Mac OS X is it. Ironically, the only malware attack reported on a Mac was through Microsoft software. An AppleScript worm released in May 2001 spread *only* with the use of—you guessed it!—Microsoft Outlook Express (or Microsoft Entourage) for the Mac. Entourage is sold as part of the Mac version of Microsoft Office. It includes all of the features that were previously in the (free) Mac version of Outlook Express, while also incorporating many features from the Windows Outlook program, such as its calendar and address book that integrate with Office applications. Those Windows-related features created the security hole, making the program's address book available for worm-hopping.

Linux folks have it nice, with lots of choices, including Thunderbird, GNUmail, KMail, Pine, VM, XCMail, XFMail, and so on. Evolution is one of the most popular Linux email clients, included with distributions such as Fedora and Novell Linux Desktop. It started out its life as Ximian Evolution, an open source personal and workgroup information management solution for Linux and Unix systems that was bought by Novell. Evolution 2 integrates email, calendaring, tasks, and contact management; as part of Novell Linux Desktop, Novell Evolution connects to corporate servers including Novell GroupWise and Microsoft Exchange.

Linux and the Mac OS are the best choices, regardless of what email program you use (although you definitely should not use Microsoft's email programs). That's because alternatives to Outlook are not enough to keep a Windows PC safe; you need to get away from Windows itself.

While Microsoft says it is making strides to improve the security of its software, especially through its Trustworthy Computing Initiative[‡] that promises to make PCs safe some day, the company's real aim is to secure its hold on

---

[*] TowerGroup study, sponsored by Truste, a nonprofit privacy group, and NACHA, an electronics payment association, reported in *Internet Week*, December 1, 2004.
[†] "Phishing Activity Report" by the Anti Phishing Working Group. October 2004. See www.antiphishing.org.
[‡] See the "Trustworthy Computing Initiative" page for Microsoft's propaganda on how PCs will one day be secure. See www.microsoft.com/mscorp/twc/default.mspx.

the desktop and laptop. The Trustworthy Computing Initiative is as much about restricting consumers and pleasing Hollywood with its copy protection schemes as it is about securing PCs. While the company uses the initiative to fix the notorious security holes in its web servers and virus-prone desktop clients like Outlook and Word, the company is also pushing hard on digital rights management (DRM). It's no coincidence that the proposed antitrust settlement cooked up by Microsoft and the U.S. Department of Justice conveniently excuses Microsoft from having to share any information related to digital rights management and encryption technology with its competitors.

Why is Microsoft using the smoke screen of anti-virus security to advance digital rights management? Because downloadable movies might be the biggest boon to PC sales since the Web caught on over a decade ago. Microsoft hopes to ride the drive for greater security, privacy, and protection of intellectual property as profitably as it rode the initial Internet boom half a decade ago. And while Microsoft fiddles with copy protection for Hollywood blockbusters, your PC continues to burn up with viruses, worms, and Trojan horses.

Keep in mind the lessons of the Melissa virus/worm: mono-cultures are more susceptible to attack. Most of the people who reported an infestation of Melissa (and its variants) worked for corporations and government agencies that had enforced a single standard for computing within their confines. The problem is not that hackers, thieves, and con artists exist (alas, we can't get rid of them). The problem is that organizations mandate a certain operating system, word processor, and email program for all of their users.

New viruses targeting Windows and Outlook still appear often, even six years after Melissa. In late March 2005, a new set of highly critical flaws were discovered in Internet Explorer and Outlook, according to research company eEye Digital Security.[*] The flaws enable attackers to install backdoor Trojans without your knowledge.

Still want to continue using Outlook?

Microsoft expends a significant portion of its monopoly power . . . on imposing burdensome restrictions on its customers and inducing them to behave in ways that augment and prolong that monopoly power. —Judge Thomas Penfield Jackson[4]

Shoot This Messenger

The next time you communicate with instant messaging software, check your system for viruses. Instant messaging software lets you maintain a list of people—often called your *buddy list*—to "talk" with online. Sending a message opens up a small window where you and your friend can type in messages you both can see. These folks will not be your buddies any longer, however, if they get infected from your computer.

Microsoft's MSN Messenger and the newer version included with Windows XP called Windows Messenger—a hybrid of instant messaging, videoconferencing, Internet telephone calling, and application sharing—are the latest examples of Microsoft's monopoly marketing. MSN Messenger is arguably the worst instant messaging software available. With its relentless solicitations for premium, fee-based services, MSN Messenger is more like a

---

[*] Kawamoto. Dawn. "Critical flaws in IE and Outlook discovered." CNETNews.com. April 1, 2005. See http://news.com.com/Critical+flaws+in+IE+and+Outlook+discovered/2100-1002_3-5650238.html.

big advertisement than a useful communication tool. To use it, you need to sign up for Passport, the latest in Orwellian Internet-tracking software (more about this madness in Chapter 9). Not only has Passport has been proven insecure, but MSN Messenger itself has turned out to be buggy and full of privacy holes. Both MSN Messenger and Windows Messenger have been heavily targeted for viruses and worms since 2001. New viruses with names like Bropia, Kelvir, Serflog, and Crog are propagating themselves through MSN Messenger and Windows Messenger by automatically initiating file transfers.

Variants of the Bropia virus have appeared as recently as March 2005, including one that plays on concerns about Bropia itself with this hoax message:

```
*** URGENT *** Download the latest patch from http://msnupdate.**.com/ to
prevent getting infected by W32.Bropia.C.
```

Don't download any files from the above site, as they all contain viruses. If you think you've been infected, run your virus-scanning program and use the Bropia Removal Tool.[*]

Alternatives to MSN Messenger and Windows Messenger include AOL Instant Messenger (AIM), ICQ Messenger (as in "I seek you"), Yahoo Messenger, and GAIM.

ICQ Messenger (www.icq.com) offers the most free features, including video/audio chat, email, SMS and wireless pager messages, and the ability to transfer files and URLs. When you're away from your own computer, you can also communicate with the web-based ICQ2Go service that works from any computer using any browser. ICQphone incorporates IP telephony functions so that you can engage in PC-to-PC and PC-to-phone calls. Used in multiple-user mode, groups can conduct conferences or play games.

GAIM for Linux, BSD, Mac OS X, and Windows (http://gaim.sourceforge .net) is a free multi-protocol instant messaging client compatible with AOL Instant Messenger and ICQ (Oscar protocol), MSN Messenger, Yahoo Messenger, IRC, Jabber, Gadu-Gadu, SILC, GroupWise Messenger, and Zephyr networks. With GAIM you can log into accounts on multiple IM networks simultaneously, chatting with friends on AOL Instant Messenger, Yahoo Messenger, and an IRC channel all at the same time.

AOL Instant Messenger is a free and versatile instant messenger that's best suited for AOL people (you know who you are). It supports voice conferencing and web collaboration and includes standard chat functions, streaming video, and online games. It also annoys you with plenty of ads, which is just what you would expect from a free program from America Online, the major domo of mass mailers. (And how many promo CD mailers from AOL have *you* received this year?)

Microsoft hasn't ignored the virus problem with MSN Messenger, but it hasn't overlooked potential ways of exploiting the problem for its own gain either. Forcing its users to upgrade to a newer version, Microsoft blocked

---

[*] See http://securityresponse.symantec.com/avcenter/venc/data/w32.bropia.removal.tool.html.

older versions from logging on to the service. Seems like a reasonable security measure, right? However, Microsoft went a bit further than was strictly necessary. As you install the update, Microsoft offers several options unrelated to security, one of which is `Make MSN My Home Page`—turned on, of course, by default. If you ignore this option, the next time you start Internet Explorer, your home page changes to MSN.com, which is akin to browser hijacking, a characteristic of many spyware programs. "Microsoft should be ashamed of itself for trying to turn its own security flaw to its commercial gain," wrote Stephen Wildstrom in *BusinessWeek*.[*] "There's no reason to believe that customers installing a mandatory security fix also want to change their browser home page to an MSN portal, and there's even less excuse for trying to spring a change on the unwary."

So don't be unwary. Shoot MSN Messenger and Windows Messenger, and say no MSN.

---

[*] Wildstrom, Stephen H. "Microsoft Slips a Plug in a Patch." *BusinessWeek*. February 24, 2005. See www.businessweek.com/technology/content/feb2005/tc20050224_8905_tc205.htm.

8

THIS LAN IS YOUR LAN

In the famous TV commercial of 1984 to introduce the new Apple Macintosh, aired during the Super Bowl, a woman athlete hurls a hammer at a giant display image of Big Brother, signifying how the Mac (and, by extension, all personal computers) will smash "the state" of mainframe computers. This commercial, designed by the advertising agency Chiat/Day and directed by Ridley Scott, fresh off his science fiction classic *Blade Runner*, has never been run again since. But few commercials have ever been more influential. "With the 1984 ad, Apple identified the Macintosh with an ideology of 'empowerment'," said Ted Friedman, author of *Electric Dreams: Computers in American Culture*,[*] "a vision of the PC as a tool for combating conformity and asserting individuality."

One personal computer couldn't replace the mainframe. It took a *village* of PCs—the local area network (LAN)—to turn isolated PCs into an office computing resource that rivaled the mainframe-slave terminal arrangement by offering faster processing and greater individual productivity.

---

[*] Friedman, Ted. "Apple's 1984: The Introduction of the Macintosh in the Cultural History of Personal Computers." A paper presented at the Society for the History of Technology Convention. Pasadena, California. October 1997.

A LAN consists of client computers, connection methods with hubs or devices (cable with Ethernet hub, wireless hub, etc.), and a server operating system such as Windows Server, Novell NetWare, Mac OS X Server, or Linux. Typically, a LAN connects computers within an office or building, but a LAN can also span multiple buildings in close proximity (within a few kilometers). Within a LAN, computers can share files, devices like laser printers and file servers, and services like broadband Internet access.

While no real smashing occurred, these smaller, more intelligent productivity machines were like the earliest mammals, eating the eggs of the mainframe dinosaurs. A new model emerged, dubbed *client-server* because it needed to accommodate both intelligent, independent computers (*clients*) and shared resources like filesystems on hard disks (*servers*). As the old mainframes were relegated to serving up ancient code and storing large databases, LANs took over the office.

Microsoft took a back seat in the 1980s while companies like Apple and Novell created the first LANs, but Microsoft eventually co-opted the new wave of client-server networks by tying in Windows. Microsoft herded businesses into its Office encampment and circled the wagons by promoting its proprietary formats and protocols as standards. Corporate LANs were designed to accommodate PCs running Windows, without much thought for other types of systems. Who cared if the marketing department's creative group used a network of Macs for graphics and desktop publishing, or the engineering department connected Unix workstations to an Ethernet? New recruits to the office were typically required to use a PC because, in the words of many an IT professional, "The network doesn't support Macs." The reason given for this lack of support was that the Mac platform (which, coincidentally, included the industry's leading laptop) didn't represent a significant market share.

What happened to empowerment, combating conformity, and asserting individuality? The mistaken assumption that Microsoft's office computing platform was good for the industry led to the grand fallacy we live with today: LANs that are way too complicated to manage and not democratic enough to support all types of systems. The pre-1984 mainframe regime morphed by the year 2000 into the conformist, totalitarian regime of the Microsoft Windows–dominated LAN. Perhaps Apple should run a new version of the same commercial, substituting the face of Bill Gates for Big Brother.

How do individual, non-conformist, empowered computer folks deal with the Microsoft regime? As *client* systems, Mac OS X and Linux systems have no trouble connecting to a Microsoft-dominated LAN and sharing its resources. Even if you just give Macs and Linux systems equal footing in a Microsoft-dominated LAN, you'll find that they work better than Windows machines and can often share LAN resources like printers and file servers more easily.

Given Microsoft's dominance of the workplace, client computers are consistently exposed to Word, Excel, and PowerPoint files—all of which are huge and potentially virus-infected. Given Microsoft's copy protection appeasement of the entertainment business, you can expect some resistance to streaming protected media across a LAN. But there are alternatives. You can deal with

Word, Excel, and PowerPoint files using the safer alternatives described in Chapter 4 and Chapter 5. You can use digital media alternatives described in Chapter 6, such as Apple's iTunes, which lets you share a music library across a LAN.

As *servers* on a LAN, Mac OS X and Linux systems cannot only connect but also improve performance, security, reliability, and *scalability*, i.e., the ability to grow the network quickly without sacrificing performance, security, or reliability. In a very small LAN, you can use Macs and Linux machines as file and web servers without centralized control. Larger LANs typically include hardware dedicated to running server software. Very large LANs may offer a mix of Microsoft Windows servers, Linux servers, and even Mac OS X servers (still a very small segment of the market), but as you can imagine, dealing with Windows Server (and older Windows-based servers) in a mixed LAN makes configuration a nightmare.

There are lots of excellent alternatives to Windows Server for home and office LANs—in particular, Novell Netware, Apple Mac OS X Server, and various flavors of Linux. In fact, many corporate LANs are controlled by Linux servers that manage resources and files for Windows and Mac clients, but Microsoft Windows standards still apply, forcing the other machines to deal with its filesystem and methods of communicating.

Gotta Serve Everybody

In an office setting, your LAN is your connection not only to other workers but also to the outside world.

Therein lies the rub: The outside world is dangerous to an office network—a massive security risk. As Microsoft grew to dominate office computing and LANs, it presented a big fat target for mischief and mayhem. Networks based on Microsoft software are notoriously insecure. Client computers are exposed to a potential propagation of viruses, Trojan horses, and worms, as well as other security threats. In fact, Microsoft Windows Server, which includes Microsoft Internet Information Server (IIS), is responsible for two of the most damaging worms in the history of computing—Code Red and its spinoff Nimda.[*]

Microsoft turned Windows-based servers into selfish bullies on the network playground when it centralized security and locked its systems into a technology called Active Directory. Active Directory gives organizations the power to manage and share information centrally about network resources and users, and provides a central authority for network security. But it can also require companies to have every computer on the LAN run Windows in order to function properly. Microsoft designed Active Directory to be the foundation for Windows enterprise deployments, leading to many dependencies. In most corporate LANs that use it, numerous business functions are tied into it, locking the business into continuing to deploy Windows Server on more CPUs. The price for Windows Server goes up as a business scales up with more CPUs, which is how Microsoft makes its money.

[*] Lemos, Rob. "Virulent worm calls into doubt our ability to protect the Net." CNET News.com. July 27, 2001. See http://news.com.com/Code+Red+for+security/2009-1001_3-270471.html.

THE HYPERACTIVE DIRECTORY

Microsoft's Active Directory acts as the central authority for network security, letting the operating system readily verify a user's identity and control his or her access to network resources. Equally important, Active Directory acts as an integration point for bringing systems together and consolidating management tasks.

Active Directory enables administrators to install Windows on multiple client computers without having to physically visit each computer. It provides a way to manage user accounts with defined group policies that control how programs, network resources, and the operating system operate for users and computers in an organization. It controls log-in and authentication and supports certificates and public key infrastructure (PKI) for interoperability with and deployment of extranet and e-commerce applications. Active Directory is designed to be a consolidation point for isolating, migrating, centrally managing, and reducing the number of directories that companies require.

Unfortunately, Active Directory is also a big fat target for malicious as well as mischievous attacks. Active Directory is a lot like the Windows Registry, except that the directory exists on the network, and a Windows network depends on the directory to function. Any tweaking, mischievous or otherwise, of a normal Windows Registry can render a Windows system unusable. By the same token, any tweaking of the Active Directory can render a network unusable.

As an example of how powerful it is and how dangerous it can be, consider just one feature—automated software distribution—that lets administrators automatically distribute applications to users based on their role in the company. For example, all accountants could automatically receive spreadsheet software. All an administrator would need to do is select the wrong group of PCs to receive a new software package rollout, and if the new software was incompatible with the configurations of those PCs, it could blow those machines away, sending them into an infinite reboot loop. Imagine if such a "mistake" was committed intentionally. The Active Directory could theoretically be used for quietly and effectively distributing attacks, as one very large Trojan horse. This Trojan horse would be particularly nasty, because removing it would risk corrupting the directory and bringing down an entire network.

Another unfortunate aspect of Microsoft's monopoly is that so many LAN and server vendors and solution providers accept it and offer no alternatives. The technology helps them lock in customers as well, following the Microsoft plan. The most common recommendation for an open source alternative to Active Directory involves a combination of OpenLDAP and Samba. OpenLDAP is an open source implementation of the standard LDAP (Lightweight Directory Access Protocol), and Samba is an open source suite that offers file and print services. Although it may seem like a hurdle, it's really not that difficult to migrate from Windows Active Directory to Linux using OpenLDAP and Samba—and still get the directory and authentication features needed by most organizations. The key challenge is first to identify and then to find suitable replacements for applications and services that depend on Active Directory—such as a company's telephony infrastructure, which can be replaced by a new Voice over IP (VoIP) infrastructure. But that's a subject for another book.[*]

---

[*] See Mark A. Miller, *Voice Over IP Technologies: Building the Converged Network,* (Wiley, 2002) or Timothy V. Kelly, *VoIP For Dummies,* (Wiley, 2005).

To take advantage of the benefits of Linux, companies using Windows exclusively must plan a migration carefully. With any migration comes challenges, and getting off Active Directory can be the biggest one for companies jettisoning Windows.

Guess Who's Coming to Network?

The Mac is a bit player in the PC marketplace but a potent one. While new PCs have to be set up by the IT department to work with the corporate LAN (mostly because networking options are so confusing, unless you can get by with the Microsoft networking wizard), Macs typically don't have to be set up or reconfigured—just plug and play—even if the IT technician informs you solemnly that "The network doesn't support Macs."

It's a tribute to the Mac's design that every time I was told that Macs were not supported, I connected my Mac PowerBook to the LAN, and it worked fine, without any need for support. Mac OS X has no trouble connecting to and working with Active Directory in a Microsoft-dominated LAN. At one company, I used my Mac PowerBook in place of a Windows PC for more than two months before anyone noticed. Even then, the Mac delivered a few unexpected bonuses. I could access the so-called "protected" internal servers directly without logging into anything, and I could use the laser printers sequestered in marketing's creative department, where graphic artists used Macs.

Apple has always made networking easy. The company has been at the forefront since it first enabled Macs to share laser printers using the newly invented AppleTalk network in 1985. Macs are perhaps the easiest type of computer to add to a network—any network. In fact, much of the file- and printer-sharing capabilities of Windows mimic the pioneering work done on Macs back in the mid-1980s, when only Macs, NetWare servers, and Unix machines could effectively talk over a LAN.

People who opt out of using Windows will find it easier to connect a Mac to a LAN than any other type of computer, even easier than an equivalent PC running Windows (without pre-installation or support from the corporate IT department). Macs make the best choice for graphic artists, publishers, and multimedia professionals for a lot of reasons, and networking with PCs and Linux machines is never an obstacle.

Apple provides a server version of OS X that competes with the best Linux servers on the market as an alternative to Windows Server, supporting all industry standards and even proprietary "standards" such as Active Directory. In fact, Mac OS X Server can access account records stored in Active Directory without requiring any modifications to the Active Directory schema. Based on open source BSD and Mach kernel, Mac OS X Server includes a number of open source projects, including Mailman, Tomcat, JBoss, Apache, Postfix, Perl, Samba, and BIND, and integrates many of them into a central console application to make the entire system easier to use. It provides Mac-easy file management, user management, and print, Internet, and mail services for small business settings. It is a capable website server, grouping together simple hosting, broadcasting, and streaming controls.

NetWare: A Well-Respected LAN

Novell started the LAN business for PCs. In the 1980s, the name Novell was synonymous with fast, reliable filesharing. Its flagship NetWare system became the de facto standard for LANs in enterprises, linking DOS PCs in a straightforward way never seen before or since.

With remarkable simplicity, Novell developed a PC networking system that designated one machine to manage the network and control access to shared devices, such as disk drives and printers. Through the 1980s, corporate requirements for networks grew significantly, with LANs giving way to WANs (wide area networks) to unify large corporate environments. By the early 1990s, NetWare was updated to add key features for distributed enterprises, and it led this market with a nearly 70 percent share. When Novell introduced NetWare Directory Services (NDS), it represented a quantum leap above the competition in directory technology at the time, which was Microsoft's directory service in Windows NT 4.0.

But Microsoft narrowed the gap with Active Directory Services in Windows 2000 and truly caught up with Windows .NET Server 2003. By integrating Exchange and SQL Server products with its own directory service, and by garnering broad industry support for other server products (such as IBM/Lotus Notes), Microsoft turned Active Directory into the *de facto* directory standard. Novell was simply outmuscled by monopoly power, and its technical superiority was no match for the vendor lock-in tactics of Microsoft. Under relentless attack from Microsoft, Novell saw its share of the server operating system market shrivel away. Then the company itself nearly self-destructed.

Journey to Linux LAN

Novell found new life as a Linux vendor, emerging from the wreckage of the 1990s to acquire SuSE Linux, Europe's leading vendor. Novell, like some other Linux vendors, offers a full range of mixed open source and proprietary solutions from server to desktop. In fact, Novell is releasing its Linux Desktop 10 in 2005 to compete head on with Windows on the desktop. It includes Novell's edition of the OpenOffice.org suite, Mozilla Firefox for browsing, an instant-messaging client, and the Novell Evolution open source collaboration client. Combined with a photo management application and a powerful search function, Linux Desktop is an attractive alternative to Windows and obviously works well with a Novell LAN.

APPLETALK: BALLAD OF A THIN LAN

AppleTalk, developed by Apple in the early 1980s in conjunction with the Mac, enabled multiple users to connect to files and printers more easily than any other LAN. It is one of the earliest implementations of a distributed client-server networking system for personal computers. AppleShare, which appeared in 1986, provided filesharing features that anyone could learn to use over a LAN that could include Macs, DOS PCs, Windows PCs, and Apple II computers. By 1987, Macs were used as front-end terminal connections for mainframes and minicomputers and for transferring files with any type of system on the market. The potent combination of a network of Macs, laser printers, and page layout software fueled the desktop publishing explosion of the late 1980s.

Eventually, Apple developed EtherTalk, organizing a LAN exactly as an IEEE 802.3 network, supporting the same speeds and segment lengths, as well as the same number of active network nodes, so that you could use AppleTalk with any of the thousands of Ethernet-based networks in existence at that time, including the relatively inexpensive "thin" Ethernet cabling. One could easily outfit a house or small office with this type of network and offer connectivity for dozens of Macs and PCs.

While AppleTalk is still supported by Macs to this day, the emphasis has shifted to TCP/IP and other standard Internet protocols. What's remarkable is that I can still use decades-old AppleTalk-compatible laser printers and AppleShare file servers with today's version of Mac OS X. It's easy to create small, nearly self-sufficient, and even somewhat isolated and protected Mac OS X and AppleTalk networks that can be linked up to larger Ethernet and wireless LANs to access the Internet. A creative department working inside a large corporation and using a Microsoft-dominated corporate LAN could keep its Macs, file servers, and printers secure, no matter how badly the rest of the LAN is infected.

Linux is already the preferred system for file and web servers shared on a LAN. The top four server hardware sellers—IBM, Hewlett-Packard, Sun Microsystems, and Dell—all support Linux. Linux distributions differ considerably at the enterprise server level, not only in price, but in ease of installation, included features and software, and particularly in ease of administration. Besides the two market leaders, Novell's SuSE-based distribution and Red Hat's distribution, Debian and Gentoo are worthy contenders too. While free distributions are available, pricey ones (which vary based on the type of support and the type of CPU, as well as other options) offer easier administration and better overall support. For example, Red Hat's Enterprise Server is basically the same code as the Fedora kernel, which is free; however, the Red Hat distribution includes the Red Hat Enterprise version of the Linux kernel, which is specially optimized for server situations. You also get the Red Hat Network, which automates the installation of new packages, updates, and bug fixes.

Microsoft long ago recognized the threat of open source software, in general, and of Linux, in particular, in the server market. According to the so-called Halloween memo,[*] an internal strategy memorandum on Microsoft's possible responses to the Linux phenomenon, "Open source software poses a direct, short-term revenue and platform threat to Microsoft, particularly in server space. Additionally, the intrinsic parallelism and free idea exchange in open source software has benefits that are not replicable with our current licensing model and therefore present a long-term developer mindshare threat."

AIRPORT 2005: LAN ON THE RUN

With the widespread adoption of wireless connectivity, you can now dispense with cabling and wander the corridors of your office or home while staying connected to your LAN and the Internet. Mac PowerBooks offer integrated, built-in wireless LAN support—there's no need for an extra card. Dubbed AirPort, Apple introduced the technology in 1999 as one of the first affordable and easy-to-use solutions for getting on the Internet from a coffee shop or WiFi hotspot—before hotspots started to proliferate.

In 2003, AirPort Extreme took this unwired connection to the next level with the 802.11g wireless standard, offering data rates nearly five times those of the older 802.11b standard that many wireless networking devices (and hotspots) still use. Apple then introduced AirPort Express, the first device to pack wireless networking, streaming music, printer sharing, and network-bridging capabilities into a pocket device that can plug into any hotel room socket and turn it into a wireless office.

The AirPort Base Station is an inexpensive wireless access point that includes an Ethernet port, a V.90 modem, and a PCI card for Windows computers. Its configuration software runs Mac OS X, but you can also configure it from a Windows computer with freeware called FreeBase (http://freebase.sourceforge.net). Combined with Mac OS X, AirPort presents the most effective solution for adding a wireless LAN to any other type of LAN or an Ethernet connection.

That so-called "intrinsic parallelism" is part of the open source culture in which developers—because they have access to the source code—can improve the software in different ways, including making it run on different machines. As developers make modifications available, they are legally bound by the General Public License (GPL) to distribute the source for those modifications. As a result, Linux can operate on a variety of hardware platforms, even older computers, and with a variety of devices such as display cards and mass storage drives. It can run without a graphical user interface if you wish, so it needs less hardware horsepower than Windows. It can even run nicely on Intel 486-based machines. Nationwide pizza chain Papa John's converted 2,900 of its

---

[*] See www.opensource.org/halloween/halloween1.php.

franchises to Linux. Linux can also run on IBM mainframes (the Z series) and high-end IBM servers. eBay runs its operation on Linux, as does Google.

Linux has an edge over other systems for working in clusters of servers—even enormous clusters that can provide supercomputer-type performance at a fraction of the expense. "Linux now has become so technically powerful that it lays claim to a prestigious title—it runs more of the world's top supercomputers than any other operating system," wrote Daniel Lyons in *Forbes* magazine.* Lawrence Livermore National Laboratory uses Linux for nuclear weapons simulations, and NASA uses it for space shuttle simulations.

When *Forbes* asked Linux inventor Linus Torvalds why Linux has an advantage over other systems for supercomputers and servers, Torvalds pointed out that "Linux is easy to get, has no licensing costs, has all the infrastructure in place, and runs on pretty much every single relevant piece of hardware out there."

One of the most attractive features of using Linux servers on a LAN is the ability to remotely control the servers. Since Linux includes a Telnet server, you can use virtually any computer, regardless of operating system, and use Telnet to log into the servers to do all administrative tasks. By comparison, to administer a Windows NT server remotely, you need to buy a separate application that offers remote control (such as PCAnywhere by Symantec)—a costly approach because you need a copy for the server to act as the host and a copy for each computer that needs to control the server remotely.

With all this flexibility in hardware platforms and support for industry standards, Linux is a natural for running servers in an office LAN—especially for sharing files with Windows and Mac computers on a LAN.

We Can Share with Windows, We Can Copy Files

An important concern for many people switching from Windows to another system is whether it will be easy to copy files to and from Windows PCs and use those files on, say, a Mac or Linux machine. The files themselves are quite usable on all these systems. "I switch between Windows PCs and Macs all day, every day," wrote Walt Mossberg in Mossberg's Mailbox in *The Wall Street Journal*, in reply to a typical query from someone wanting to switch from Windows to a Mac, "and find these file-compatibility problems to be nonexistent."†

In fact, the problems with sharing files are not due as much to incompatible formats or different systems as they are to the difficulties in moving around very large files. Attaching a file to an email message is the most popular method of transferring a file to someone else, but there is a limit to what you can get away with. As the saying goes, "If the file is over four, it won't go through the door." Four megabytes, that is; and the door is the network's email server. Most email servers won't accept an attachment larger

---

* Lyons, Daniel. "Linux Rules Supercomputers." *Forbes.* March 15, 2005. See www.forbes.com/ 2005/03/15/cz_dl_0315linux.html?partner=tentech_newsletter.

† Mossberg, Walter S. "Transferring Files to a Mac." Mossberg's Mailbox. *The Wall Street Journal.* May 5, 2005. See http://ptech.wsj.com/archive/mailbox-20050505.html.

than five megabytes; some won't accept larger than four. Digital media files are bigger than that—a song is typically five or ten megabytes; a slideshow might be at least that large; and a digital video movie is way up there at about one gigabyte for five minutes. A LAN is the best way to share large files among the computers connected to it.

While a Windows machine requires log-in accounts, you can still access a Windows shared folder (set up for public access over a network) from a Mac without one. But if you *do* have a valid user ID and password for an account on the Windows computer, you can also browse that account's Home directory, using the Mac to copy, rename, and delete folders and files.

To access any shared folders or accounts on the Windows machine from a Mac, follow these steps:

1. Set the Windows computer to share one or more folders. In Windows XP, open My Computer and browse for the folder, choose **File ▸ Sharing and Security**, and turn on the options for Network sharing and security, as shown in Figure 8-1.

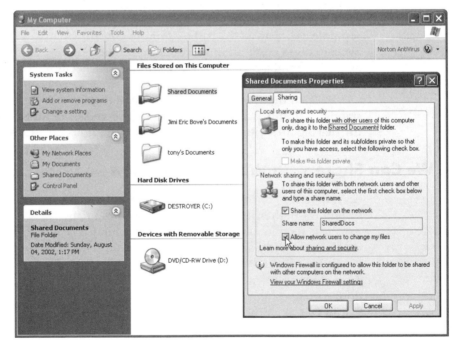

Figure 8-1: Turn on sharing for folders in Windows XP so that other computers on the LAN can access them.

2. Choose **Go ▸ Connect to Server** on the Mac if using OS X version 10.2.8 or earlier, or click the Network icon in the Finder Sidebar if using OS X 10.3 or newer, as shown in Figure 8-2.

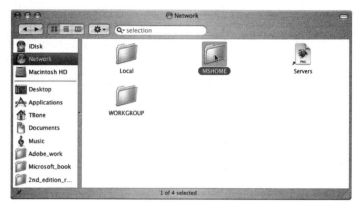

Figure 8-2: Choose a network server on a Mac. The Windows machines
are located in the MSHOME workgroup folder.

3. Choose the name of the Microsoft Windows workgroup. The names of any
   Windows-based PCs on the LAN appear after selecting the workgroup.

4. Select a Windows-based PC by name and log in if you have an account
   name and password, or simply choose one of the shared folders, as shown
   in Figure 8-3. The Windows folder appears just like a Mac hard drive in
   the Finder.

Figure 8-3: Choose a shared folder on the Windows machine for access
by other computers on the WAN.

You can also turn the tables on any Windows user who doesn't know the
first thing about turning on filesharing, and share your Mac folders. It sounds
creepy, inviting all sorts of mischief and voyeurism, but you maintain control
over what others can access.

In Mac OS X, open System Preferences and click the Sharing icon. The
Sharing preferences should appear as in Figure 8-4, with the Services pane
front and center. Turn on the Personal File Sharing and Windows File
Sharing options in the list and click the **Start** button. Sharing takes just a

moment to set up, and when it's ready, a check mark appears next to Personal File Sharing and the Start button turns into a Stop button. From that point on, guests on the LAN can access the Mac's Public folder and anything inside it.

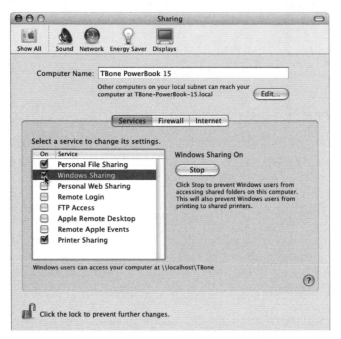

Figure 8-4: Turn on personal filesharing, with Windows compatibility, on a Mac, so that the Mac's folders can be shared on a LAN.

What others can do in a Mac's shared folders and files depends entirely on how you've set up the Ownership & Permissions section of the folder's Info window. Select the folder, choose **File** ▶ **Get Info**, and click the arrow next to Ownership & Permissions to open the section. Pop-up menus provide access capabilities you can assign to others, including defined groups. "Read only" means files can be copied *from* the folder, but not *to* it. "Write only" provides a drop-box where people can copy *to* but not *from*. "Read & Write" provides full access.

Linux users can use Samba (http://us1.samba.org/samba), a free open source suite that provides filesharing and print services with Windows on a network. Samba uses the TCP/IP protocol to interact with a Windows client or server as if it were a Windows file and print server. It enables a Linux or Unix system to move into a Windows Network Neighborhood without causing a stir. Windows users can access file and print services without knowing or caring that those services are being offered by a Linux host.

Samba can not only share directories on a Linux machine on a Windows network, but it can also manage a Windows domain as its domain controller. Samba uses a protocol suite called CIFS (Common Internet File System), at the heart of which is a protocol called SMB (Server Message Block). One of the cool things you can do with a Windows PC is use a shared SMB directory as if it were a hard disk on your own machine. The N: drive can look, smell, feel, and act like your own disk, but it's really space on some other computer somewhere else on the network. Linux systems can do this too, using the smbfs filesystem. Built from Samba code, smbfs (which stands for SMB Filesystem) allows Linux to map a remote SMB directory into its directory structure.

Microsoft's LAN and server protocols are still a moving target for maintaining interoperability. Linux vendors and Apple have to keep a foot in the door, so to speak, to continue to get information from Microsoft. Once again, it's the European Union that is challenging Microsoft to make networks interoperable at a reasonable price.

SAMBA NETWORKING, EUROPEAN STYLE

In the 2004 European Commission (EC) antitrust ruling against Microsoft, the software giant agreed to create a server interoperability license that would allow rival server software makers to write applications that can "achieve full interoperability" with Windows client and server operating systems on "reasonable and non-discriminatory terms."

Fat chance that Microsoft would play fair with its new enemies in the open source world. In March 2005, the Commission rejected Microsoft's proposed server interoperability license, saying that it contained a number of serious flaws, including unjustifiably high royalty fees and the exclusion of open source vendors. According to Samba co-creator Jeremy Allison,[*] "The royalty payments are really high. They have been set as if you were creating a premium product. . . . There is no flexibility in the monstrous fixed fee you must pay." Without access to the protocol documentation, the Samba team has to work longer and harder to make the application interoperate with Microsoft servers. "They make changes to the protocol all the time," he pointed out to the Commission. "It is usually some new wrinkle placed on top of things we already have working."

As Microsoft refuses to play fair and the U.S. Justice Department looks the other way, Europe is once again taking responsibility for sticking up for the rights of open source vendors. Microsoft, in responding to the requirement to publish withheld information, is actually taking the opportunity to extend its abuse of power. The implication is that if vendors don't sign up and pay high royalties, they'll be open to patent suits. The EC ruling forced Microsoft to pay a fine, but still, it would have been more effective if it had, instead, forced the company to make the server protocols freely available.

[*] Marson, Ingrid. "Microsoft's EU proposal is monstrous, says Samba." ZDNet UK. February 4, 2005. See http://news.zdnet.co.uk/software/applications/0,39020384,39186884,00.htm.

There is only one way out of this LAN interoperability madness: Just say no to Microsoft's system and server upgrades. Use what you have now, if you can—older Windows machines and servers, Linux and Unix servers, Macs, PCs running Linux, and so on. Your LAN will be free and most likely easier to keep safe from virus attacks.

9

BROWSERS AND YOUR OWN PRIVATE IDENTITY

The concept of privacy is not new. It can be traced back to the Athenian society in ancient Greece, long before the emergence of tabloids, limousine-chasing paparazzi, and dinner-time phone solicitations. No one would have followed you around the Athenian markets noting your purchases and annoying you with suggestions for other products. On the other hand, the corner grocer in Athens probably knew in advance that you preferred retsina to ouzo—but only because you told him yourself.

This is the difference between invasion of privacy and a personalized service. The right to privacy is the right to be left alone, the right to exercise autonomy or control over your personal matters, and the right to limit access to yourself. Microsoft is committed to protecting your privacy; it says so right in the company's Privacy Statement. But if you were to test Microsoft Internet Explorer, the standard web browser for Windows, for its compliance with these rights, it would fail all three.

Gaping security holes in Windows and Internet Explorer open your computer up to adware and spyware that won't leave you alone. And while it provides security settings to stem the flow of malware into your computer,

Internet Explorer's settings are so complex that most people don't understand them. Moreover, its interactions with websites are unpredictable and its treatment of website activity is confusing, irritating both website developers and consumers looking for the convenience of personalized service.

While the best alternative is to switch to either a Mac or Linux, even those stuck with Windows can still use something better than Internet Explorer for browsing the Web safely. With Internet Explorer, people *do* have the *right* to exercise autonomy and control—they just can't figure out *how* to *do* it, and Microsoft places the onus on people to do it for themselves. And since people don't (or can't) spend the time learning the Byzantine intricacies of security policies, they fail to protect themselves adequately from the worst form of malware you can catch while surfing the Web—*spyware*.

Spyware: The Enemy Within

Spyware is a form of malware that gathers and reports information about your system without your knowledge or consent. It ranges from ads that pop up on your system desktop (called *adware*) to Trojan horses that harvest private information, re-route web page requests to send you to other sites, and install stealth phone dialers. For virtually everyone surfing the Internet, spyware and adware are a nuisance, but if you don't take steps to remove spyware from a PC, it can lead to more serious consequences, such as identity theft. It comes as no surprise that the spyware that causes the most damage and incurs the most risk is the code that targets Windows systems, using Internet Explorer as its vector of entry.

*You may know spyware by one of its many names: adware, malware, trackware, scumware, thiefware, snoopware, or sneakware.
—Webroot.com, "Spyware Information Center"[1]*

Some spyware is legitimate, even if somewhat annoying, such as a web browser toolbar that can track the sites you visit in order to suggest other sites or count clicks for web advertisers. Spyware is often used to track online behavior to target pop-up ads more effectively. But some spyware is clearly not legitimate, such as a Trojan horse that secretly monitors everything that is typed, hoping to snare a log-in ID and password or capture confidential emails. The files associated with tracking behavior sneak into your system through security holes in Internet Explorer and Outlook, and they hide on your hard drive. Once there, these barnacles can drastically impair system performance, and they frequently abuse network resources. To make matters worse, they are difficult or nearly impossible to remove from a Windows system.

Even though spyware has been a recognized threat within the general IT community for well over 15 years, it's a bigger problem now than ever before. Despite improvements in protective technologies and loads of security patches over the years from Microsoft, many companies and users do not implement these patches and technologies effectively because the system protection mechanisms are too complex. Like putting fingers into the holes of a leaking dike, Microsoft issues security updates that don't reach enough people fast enough to stem the flow of malware. Older, unpatched systems are left vulnerable to new strains and clever hackers. One example, Phatbot, a Trojan horse that repetitively installed spyware, encoded Windows vulnerabilities from as far back as early 2003 into its payload.

Vulnerabilities in Internet Explorer, discovered as recently as April 2005,[*] allow remote code execution that can install Trojan horses without your knowledge. You can be tricked into going to a site carrying malicious code just by surfing across a banner ad. CoolWebSearch, for example, is probably the most vicious piece of spyware you might encounter, because it completely hijacks your browser.

COOLWEBSEARCH: HIJACKING FOR FUN AND PROFIT

If you find Internet Explorer straying to websites you don't intend to visit, you may have an unwelcome soul in your machine. CoolWebSearch is an infamous set of spyware browser hijackers that exploits holes in Internet Explorer and Windows.[*] Introduced in May 2003, variants have been released every few weeks since, with countless competing groups writing and distributing them, many of whom operate pay-per-click sites in Russia and Eastern Europe.[†] The reason why this particular set of browser hijackers keeps proliferating into new variants is that the perpetrators have a tasty incentive—converting browser clicks into cash.

One early variant converted the PC into a source of revenue for fly-by-night pornographers by installing dozens of bookmarks for porn sites, adding a new spyware toolbar to Internet Explorer, and changing your home page. It also significantly slowed down a PC's performance and introduced some modifications that could cause Windows to freeze, crash, or randomly reboot. Other variants dropped a CSS (cascading style sheet) file in the Windows folder and set it to be used as the stylesheet for all web pages viewed in Internet Explorer. The stylesheet included embedded JavaScript code that spied on browsing activity, just like a stalker hiding a listening device inside your home.

The vast majority of CoolWebSearch variants (but not all of them) target Internet Explorer and its Microsoft Java virtual machine. They can hide in blind links, message boards, and pop-up advertisements (even on mainstream web pages). These variants have grown increasingly aggressive and complicated and are virtually impossible to remove, short of reinstalling the operating system or restoring a previous version of the Windows Registry. Some variants target the very sites that offer anti-spyware software! Others have been known to disable anti-spyware applications and utilities such as Bazooka, Ad-Aware, Spyware Blaster, and Spybot, and even prevent you from visiting anti-spyware sites.

CWShredder (www.intermute.com/products/cwshredder.html) can locate and remove most variants.[‡] To prevent reinfection, your best bet is to use a better browser such as Firefox (or a better system than Windows, of course). If you use Internet Explorer, you must disable the Microsoft Java virtual machine in Internet Explorer, since there have been reports of infections even on fully patched systems. Also, disable ActiveX downloads and install Microsoft security patches.

[*] For details, see the CoolWebSearch Chronicles (http://cwshredder.net/cwshredder/cwschronicles.html) and doxdesk.com (www.doxdesk.com/parasite/CoolWebSearch.html).

[†] Libbenga, Jan. "CoolWebSearch is winning Trojan war." *The Register*. June 29, 2004. See www.theregister.co.uk/2004/06/29/cws_shredder.

[‡] Since the site might be blocked by the Trojan horse on your system, try a mirror site to download the software, such as http://209.133.47.200/~merijn/index.html.

[*] Kawamoto, Dawn. "Critical flaws in IE and Outlook discovered." CNET News.com. April 1, 2005. See http://news.com.com/Critical+flaws+in+IE+and+Outlook+discovered/2100-1002_3-5650238.html?part=rss&tag=5650238&subj=news.

While CoolWebSearch tops the list of the most dangerous examples of spyware targeting Internet Explorer and Windows,[*] there are plenty of other threats as well as adware annoyances. BlazeFind, for example, can hijack web searches and change your home page and other Internet Explorer settings. And watch out for Perfect Keylogger, a monitoring tool that records websites visited, keystrokes, and mouse clicks. You might also want to clean your system of KeenValue, an adware program that collects personal information and sends advertisements back to you. Some spyware hooks its victims by claiming to eliminate spyware itself. For example, PurityScan displays pop-up ads and claims that it can delete pornographic images (don't believe it), and Transponder, an Internet Explorer "browser helper object," monitors web browsing and sends relevant advertisements.

A recent spy audit report published by Earthlink and Webroot Software[†] found an average of 26.5 spyware traces are present on any given PC. In a six-month period, two million scans found 55 million pieces of spyware.

NOTE *According to a report issued in June 2003 by the National Cyber Security Alliance, 9 out of 10 PCs connected to the Internet are infected with spyware (from a report by the National Cyber Security Alliance, a nonprofit commissioned by America Online to study home computer security, available at www.post-gazette.com/pg/04300/401798.stm).*

As a result of Microsoft's concerted effort to fortify and expand its monopolies by tightly integrating applications with its operating system and its success in achieving near ubiquity in personal computing, our computer networks are now susceptible to massive, cascading failures.
—*Computer and Communications Industry Association report[2]*

What can average Windows users do to rid themselves of spyware, adware, and other malware? The same companies that offer anti-virus software also offer spyware detection and eradication products. You can try the commercial offerings from Symantec (www.symantec.com) and McAfee (www.mcafee.com), which provide updates for new spyware variants. Figure 9-1 shows Symantec's Norton AntiVirus software at work on one of my PC laptops. Another program, McAfee AntiSpyware, detects keystroke loggers before they have a chance to record keystrokes and removes the spyware programs and files that otherwise may take over the hard drive.

Plugging security holes in the Windows dike is a profitable business. There will always be security breaches due to the sluggish implementation of Microsoft security patches and the onslaught of attacks that, in and of themselves, are turning profits for cyber-criminals. The Mafia couldn't have thought up a better protection racket than the platform Microsoft has provided: an architecture loaded with loopholes that criminals and crime-stoppers can both exploit for profit.

Security, of course, is a grave concern for Microsoft. Released in early 2005, Windows AntiSpyware is Microsoft's answer to malicious spyware, although it remains to be seen how much adware and other annoyances will be blocked by it. But even admirers were concerned that the company might charge consumers for this anti-spyware tool. Bill Gates ended the speculation by announcing that the tool would be free.[‡]

---

[*] Check out Webroot's list of the 10 worst spyware and adware threats at www.webroot.com/spywareinformation/spywaretopthreats.

[†] The complete report is available at www.earthlink.net/spyaudit/press.

[‡] Kawamoto, Dawn. "Windows anti-spyware to come free of charge." CNET News.com. February 15, 2005. See http://news.com.com/Windows+anti-spyware+to+come+free+of+charge/2100-7355_3-5577202.html.

Security companies are nevertheless cautious about the company's expansion into security software. Simply by entering the security market, Microsoft could stall innovation by freezing the venture capital spent on Windows security, which, in the long run, will lead to less security against spyware, not more.

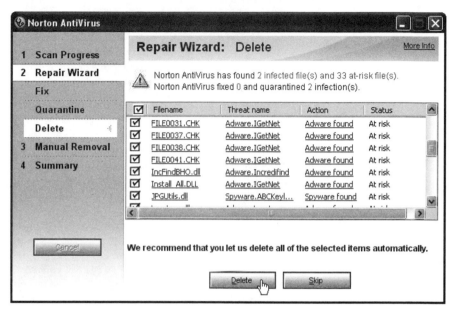

Figure 9-1: Norton AntiVirus detects some spyware variants on Windows PCs and gives you a chance to quarantine them before they steal information.

Privacy and Internet Explorer

Like most browsers, Internet Explorer keeps track of every site you visit in a history file. It saves identifying information about your computer. It saves a cache in memory of graphics and web pages for quicker access. It saves bookmarks you assign for your own convenience. Put it all together, and your browser could make interesting suggestions about where to go next—or it could simply report its findings to advertisers.

Browsers save history and bookmark files and create and manage cookies on your hard disk to carry this information. A *cookie* is a small piece of information sent to a browser along with an HTML page or created dynamically by a script in a language such as JavaScript. Sites with "shopping carts" use cookies to keep track of your selections for purchase. Some sites use cookies to store your log-in name and password in an encrypted format so that you don't need to re-enter them when you switch pages within the site. A cookie might contain a unique tracking number to reveal how many times you've accessed a site. Advertisers often set cookies whenever your browser loads one of their banners. Some websites distribute cookies to other servers or use them to send spam.

MICROSOFT'S PROTECTION RACKET:
CALL THE UNTOUCHABLES

Is Microsoft guilty of perpetuating a protection racket? The question seems as out-landish as the speculation that anti-virus software vendors started the virus craze to sell more software. But there is a ring of truth to it.

Microsoft has a history of using the monopoly power of its operating system to stomp the competition. The company has succeeded in designing its software in ever more complex ways so as to illegally shut out efforts by others to interoperate or compete with its products. Over the years, Microsoft has deliberately added more and more features to its operating system in such a way that people can't easily remove them. Even when the company makes a seemingly magnanimous gesture of giving away software for free, as with Internet Explorer and its new spyware tool, the distribution is part of an scenario designed to lock customers into its products.

Most people believe that the inclusion of Internet Explorer in Windows 95 all but killed Netscape Navigator, but that the company did so without malice. Micro-soft's sins were sins of omission and neglect, as when it delayed giving Netscape technical data on Windows 95 until after the operating system hit the market. The business press scoffed at speculation that the operating system actually contained booby traps to cause conflicts with Netscape Navigator. It just seemed ridiculous that the Justice Department might have to call in Eliot Ness and the Untouchables.

But Ness would probably have concluded that Microsoft did act with some malice, causing applications from competitors to cease working. Windows 95 included software that disabled other pieces of Internet connection software, notably the *winsock,* which provides an interface between Windows applications and TCP/IP (Transmission Control Protocol/Internet Protocol), and is used to make network con-nections. Many vendors put their version of winsock into the Windows directory as a convenience so that other programs could use it, but when Windows 95 detected a non-Microsoft winsock, it carefully and deliberately replaced it. Folks who had installed the Netscape browser and then tried Internet Explorer discovered that Netscape would no longer work. The same problem affected users of CompuServe's Internet in a Box software.

With a history of such activities and no accountability, what would stop Microsoft from using its spyware tool to disable any competing spyware detectors? Indeed, what would stop Microsoft from turning into the largest protection racket ever seen, in which the company compels billions of people to pay fees to protect themselves from the bad effects of Microsoft's own software?

Perhaps nothing can stop it: Microsoft announced on Friday the 13th of May 2005 that it is testing a subscription security service called OneCare that guards against spyware and virus attacks that plague Windows. Microsoft's acquisition of several anti-virus and anti-spyware companies in 2004 and 2005 indicates that this service may allow Microsoft to compete directly with (as in, put out of business) Symantec and McAfee, which have built entire businesses based on Windows' weaknesses.

In a report by CRN,[*] David Friedlander, senior analyst with Forrester Research, questioned whether customers would be happy with such a service. "Will customers trust Microsoft enough to buy a security product from them as well as an operating system that needs to be protected?" Only if the company made an offer they couldn't refuse. The CRN report noted that Microsoft is signing up major cable providers to offer this service at what will probably be a $10 per month incremental fee above and beyond the usual broadband charges.

---

[*] Darrow, Barbara. "Microsoft Starts Testing Windows OneCare Security Subscription Service." CRN, May 13, 2005. See www.crn.com/sections/breakingnews/breakingnews.jhtml?articleId= 163101740.

All browsers let you toss your cookies (sorry for the pun!) or have the browser prompt you before saving a cookie. But cookies are a fact of web life. If you turn all of them off, you won't be able to make purchases on most sites, and if you set your browser to prompt you for each cookie, you'll be accepting or rejecting cookies on every page you visit, without ever really knowing whether the cookies are dangerous or not.

Internet Explorer offers a Privacy tab, shown in Figure 9-2, that is actually Microsoft's implementation of the Platform for Privacy Preferences (P3P) developed by the World Wide Web Consortium. The tab lets online visitors decide what general rules will be established for accepting cookies from websites or third parties (such as vendors running banner ads). These choices range from accepting everything to accepting nothing. But the problem with Microsoft's implementation is that a website that makes extensive use of cookies must implement what are known as *compact* cookie policies or risk having Internet Explorer users turn their cookies off—simply because they're ignorant of the site's cookie policies. The implementation favors larger sites that can afford extensive recoding.

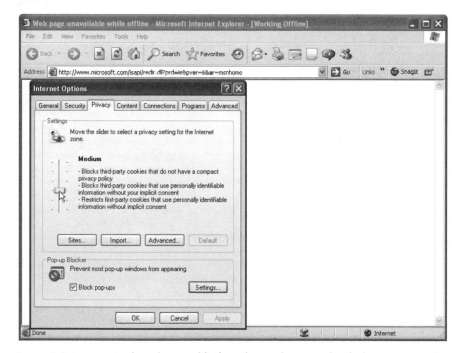

Figure 9-2: Internet Explorer lets you block cookies with privacy levels that correspond roughly to P3P preferences.

Protecting yourself from malicious cookies is a chore with any browser, only more so with Internet Explorer. In Explorer, you have to open each cookie manually, whereas browsers such as Firefox offer an easier way—you can browse through your cookies graphically, delete them as you go along, and tell your browser not to accept another cookie from those sources.

The security problem with Explorer is tied to how Explorer deals with HTML, JavaScript, Java, Visual Basic, and ActiveX—all vectors for virus attacks and Trojan horses and, not coincidentally, conduits for nasty cookies. For example, a design flaw in versions of Windows Media Player (fixed in version 9) enabled an unscrupulous website to use simple JavaScript code on a web page to grab the unique ID number of the visitor's copy of Windows Media Player. This ID number could then be used like a "super cookie" to track the visitor's travels around the Web—bypassing cookie blockers and the new privacy and P3P protections that Microsoft has added to Internet Explorer version 6.[*]

One might stop and wonder about a company that champions digital rights management while at the same time putting out an application that leaks data in spite of its own security settings.

GUARD YOUR COOKIES

P3P, the Platform for Privacy Preferences, is a new Internet standard that theoretically allows browsers to interpret website privacy policies. The technology has been praised as efficient and criticized as confusing.

One of the biggest drawbacks is that P3P doesn't take into account the Fair Information Practices espoused by the Federal Trade Commission (FTC)[*] or other existing privacy legislation, such as the Health Insurance Portability and Accountability Act of 1996 (HIPAA), nor does it provide an enforcement mechanism to ensure that websites are doing what their P3P policies indicate. As a technical solution only, there is the all-too-likely possibility that webmasters will simply make P3P policies work as necessary to ensure that the site continues to function properly, without getting its legal department involved. Some critics of P3P point out that sites could add disclaimers to P3P policies, stating that they are not legally binding or are still subject to review.

P3P makes the naïve assumption that consumers are willing to take the initiative to learn about the P3P platform and set their preferences accordingly. Even if they spend the considerable time it takes to adjust cookie choices, they may not understand why Internet Explorer is blocking a particular site's cookies. The privacy icon gives no clue, nor does the privacy report explain why the cookie was blocked. Consumers might think a perfectly legitimate website is mishandling their personal data when the site actually has excellent privacy practices.

Even worse, consumers could be lulled into a false sense of security by P3P, for there is no reason to believe that the privacy practices of a P3P-compliant website are any more protective of a user's privacy than a non–P3P-compliant website.

P3P is a means of expressing a site's online privacy practices in a standard language that can then be automatically interpreted by P3P-enabled software agents. But adopting P3P is a costly and time-consuming endeavor. Translating existing policies into P3P's XML-based language requires additional and extensive coordination with a company's IT department. Large websites can have hundreds or even thousands of pages, often with multiple cookies on each page, requiring a great deal of work and expense to make it P3P-compliant.

(continued)

_____

[*] See www.ftc.gov/os/2000/05/index.htm#22.

_____

[*] Greene, Thomas C. "Windows Media Player must be patched to fix IE." *The Register.* January 16, 2002. See www.theregister.co.uk/2002/01/16/windows_media_player_must.

With P3P, sites can define *long-form* policies that express privacy practices with respect to cookies—if a site sets a cookie to recognize its customers and observe their surfing behavior while at the site and this cookie is linked to the customer billing information, the privacy policy associated with that cookie must disclose what information is made available by that cookie. Many sites already have long-form policies in place.

But Internet Explorer doesn't use the long-form policies—it makes decisions about accepting or blocking cookies based only on compact policies, which are intended to be used in conjunction with full policies as a way of enhancing a site's performance. If a site hasn't yet implemented the compact-form policies, Internet Explorer interprets the site's cookies as not having *any* privacy policy associated with them, even if the site has a long-form policy or has otherwise has posted its privacy policy online. These compact cookie policies need to be revised each time a site wants to add new features or alter its current data-collection practices. As a result, website providers don't really know exactly how cookies will be treated by people using Internet Explorer.

The European Union rejected P3P in 1998 as a sole means of implementing privacy protections,[*] insisting that a technical platform by itself is not sufficient. Rather, technical measures must be applied in the context of enforceable data-protection rules, instead of putting the onus on individual users to protect themselves. Although politicians and the public continue to hope for simple, silver-bullet solution to privacy concerns, P3P and its implementation in Internet Explorer doesn't provide it.

[*] Harvey, James A. and Karen M. Sanzaro. "P3P and IE 6: Raising More Privacy Issues Than They Resolve?" GigaLaw.com. (www.gigalaw.com/articles/2002-all/harvey-2002-02-all.html). See also Lorrie Faith Cranor and Rigo Wenning. "Why P3P is a Good Privacy Tool for Consumers and Companies." GigaLaw.com. See www.gigalaw.com/articles/2002-all/cranor-2002-04-all.html.

NOTE *Back in the day, the registration wizard for Windows 95 scanned your hard drive and transmitted information about all your programs (including competing programs) to Microsoft. When this became public knowledge, Microsoft tried to justify its policy as a way to inform its customers about updates, though this did not explain why the registration wizard looked for non-Microsoft products—even software for children and games, which can't be updated.*

The Heterogeneous Zone

Microsoft organizes its security features in Internet Explorer around the idea of a security zone. These days, the security zone is more like the demilitarized zone in Korea at the 38th Parallel. The war between profiteering Internet pirates and the typical Microsoft Windows user has never been more heated. Most people think they're safe with the security zone in Internet Explorer, if, in fact, they can locate it and manage it, but most people would be wrong.

When Internet Explorer opens an HTML-formatted web page, it places restrictions on what the page can do, based on the page's location and assigned security zone. There are several security zones—Internet, Local Intranet, Trusted, Restricted, Local Machine, and so on—each with a different set of restrictions. Pages located on the Internet are opened in the more restrictive Internet zone, while pages on a corporate network are opened in the Local Intranet security zone, with fewer restrictions. You can pick a zone and set your own custom restrictions, which is fine, except that it is a complicated procedure for a typical consumer.

PASSPORT TO INSECURITY

How about this for an idea: Let's give Microsoft *all* of our personal information to make sure it stays secure. Yeah, great idea . . . Given Microsoft's track record with its Passport authentication system, you'd have to be crazy.

In 2001, software flaws in the security of Microsoft's Passport authentication system left consumers' financial data wide open. The company got slapped on the wrist for this security lapse. As part of a settlement agreement with the FTC, the company agreed to make "sweeping changes," which were, in reality, just changes to the company's privacy statements and promises to submit to audits.* Fortunately, real punishment was meted out to Microsoft by the industry itself, which, for once, decided to say no.

At issue is Microsoft's Passport, a set of technologies that acts as a center-piece for web services. Passport accounts are central repositories for a person's online data and can include personal information such as birthdays and credit card numbers. They can also act as a single key to access many online accounts. Microsoft uses Passport authentication for its Hotmail email service and its MSN Messenger instant messaging service. Other e-commerce services also rely on Passport; it's used in transactions in online gaming and for purchases of Microsoft Reader e-books.

Another flaw, discovered in 2003, could have allowed attackers armed only with a Passport user's email address to get that user's name, address, and credit card number. Passport lost its credibility quickly. Privacy organizations galore rejected it outright. The European Union demanded changes to give users more control over how their personal data is shared with partner sites. Then, in early 2005, eBay officially notified customers that it would no longer let them log on through Passport. As I write this, Passport use is limited to Microsoft-owned sites and a handful of close partners.

The big promise of Passport was that it would simplify shopping by allowing folks to use the same sign-on for multiple shopping sites. "It proved to be far more complicated than Microsoft imagined," said Matt Rosoff, an analyst for research firm Directions on Microsoft, to CNET.† "Passport became this poisoned service under a lot of scrutiny from regulators."

---

* Wilcox, Joe. "Microsoft, FTC reach privacy settlement." CNET News.com. August 8, 2002. See http://news.com.com/Microsoft%2C+FTC+reach+privacy+settlement/2100-1001_3-948922.html?tag=nl.

† Becker, David. "Passport to nowhere?" CNET News.com. March 23, 2004. See http://news.com.com/2100-7345_3-5177192.html?tag=cd_lede.

To configure settings in Internet Explorer, you need to follow these steps:

1. Select the **Tools** menu, choose **Internet Options**, and then click the **Security** tab.

2. Click a security zone to select it and view its current settings, as shown in Figure 9-3.

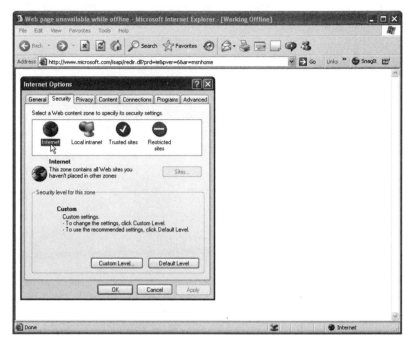

Figure 9-3: Internet Explorer offers this confusing Security panel that separates security settings into different zones—certainly not comfort zones.

To change settings, you have to follow the rest of these steps *for each zone*:

1. To change the security level for the selected zone to High, Medium, Medium-Low, or Low, drag the slider.

2. To add or remove websites from the zone, click the **Sites** button, and then click the **Add** button or the **Remove** button to customize your list of sites for the selected zone.

3. For more precise control of your security settings, click the **Custom Level** button, and then select the options you want, such as Run ActiveX controls and plug-ins, as shown in Figure 9-4. Note that there are several options for warning you about ActiveX and so on, but only one option—the one in Figure 9-4—that actually disables it.

As you can see, the process is complex and time-consuming. People generally make do with the default settings and occasionally add a site to the Restricted or Trusted zones. But the default settings, before Windows XP Service Pack 2 (SP2), assumed that content on your local filesystem was secure and assigned those pages to the Local Machine security zone with very few restrictions. Sensing a vulnerability overlooked by some Jolt-addled programmer in Redmond, hackers can take advantage of the Local Machine zone to set up worms and virus attacks or install spyware.

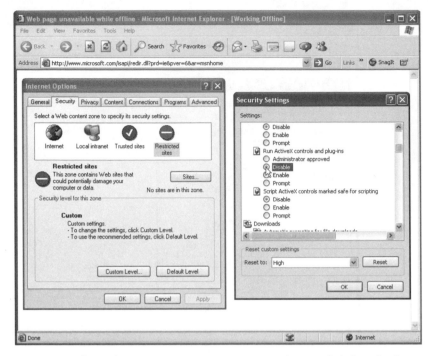

Figure 9-4: After picking a security zone in Internet Explorer and clicking the **Custom Level** button, you finally get to change some useful security settings, such as turning off ActiveX.

SP2 places more restrictions on the Local Machine zone, but lots of people still haven't upgraded more than six months after its release. And if you're one of about 200 million people using older versions of Windows and you want the latest security enhancements to Internet Explorer, you need to spend at least $99 to upgrade to XP (or $199 to start from scratch).

The Danger of an ActiveX Life

The most important security setting for Microsoft's security zones is the ability to turn off ActiveX controls. ActiveX has been implicated in a wide array of security scenarios, including the surreptitious installation of adware, spyware, and viruses.

ActiveX refers to portable, executable COM (Component Object Model) controls for Windows. These powerful controls run natively on a local machine rather than in a protected environment—they can be accepted or rejected, but they can't be assigned specific restrictions.

With this all-or-nothing approach, if an ActiveX control is accepted, it simply runs, doing whatever useful or destructive act it was designed to perform. You might assume that ActiveX controls from a trusted source are secure, but the problem is that a trusted source is still perfectly capable of writing appallingly bad code. Hackers can exploit flaws in authorized controls rather than writing new controls or cracking encrypted signatures to modify existing controls. In short, if you allow ActiveX to run in any security zone used for web pages or email, you are gambling with your privacy and security.

Even though Microsoft's long-delayed and glitchy SP2 update stuck more warning labels and alert dialogs in the way of ActiveX controls, the mechanism is still a favorite for phishing scams that use legitimate-looking but fake sites to try to con people into handing over personal information such as credit card numbers. Even after SP2, phishers have found ways to exploit the flaws in ActiveX and other security zone features.

BAIT FOR PHISHING SCAMS

A vulnerability in Internet Explorer version 6 enables scammers to launch a phishing attack against Windows PCs, even those updated with Windows XP Service Pack 2 (SP2). Making use of a flaw in the browser's handling of an ActiveX control, phishers can hijack cookies from any website and create fake sites that are difficult to distinguish from the real thing. Some even use forged signature padlock certificates. You can't trust what you see in your browser window.

"The problem is that certain input that is supplied to the ActiveX control isn't properly validated before it is returned to the browser," said Thomas Kristensen, CTO of Secunia, which reported the problem.[*] The flaw can be exploited to place code that controls the browser window so that the browser believes it is actually visiting a trusted website.

More flaws have been discovered since after SP2 shipped, including one that had been fixed in older versions of Internet Explorer but has reappeared in the latest version.[†] "It's a concern that a company like Microsoft has a problem that's already been fixed in older versions but that resurfaces in newer ones," said Kristensen. When multiple Explorer windows open, a pop-up ad unleashes a Trojan horse that collects keystrokes and passwords when people visit any of nearly 50 legitimate banking sites. Through one of the open browser windows, hackers can change the content of another website without users ever knowing about it. Links that seem to come from legitimate and trusted sites might redirect victims to harmful sites.

It's a bummer when you can't trust what you see in your browser window. It's more than a bummer when someone online steals your identity.

[*] Kawamoto, Dawn. "Phishing hole discovered in IE." CNET News.com. December 17, 2004. See http://news.zdnet.com/2100-1009_22-5495719.html.

[†] Reardon, Marguerite. "Microsoft haunted by old IE security flaw." CNET News.com. June 30, 2004. See http://news.zdnet.com/2100-1009_22-5253112.html.

Service Pack 2 (SP2), the security-focused update for Windows XP, has alarmed vendors and site developers as well as users. With SP2, Microsoft blocks ActiveX controls from running and flashes an explicit warning that unknown software can cause harm to a PC. People who still want to install a plug-in must now take a series of complex steps to override the protection scheme.

These changes aroused suspicion among vendors who use ActiveX for plug-ins. Was Microsoft exploiting security imperatives and public concern to further its own nefarious ends? People might be alarmed and confused by a warning about a legitimate plug-in and cancel its installation. "This destroys all business models associated with being able to play content in the browser," said Alex St. John, who helped create Microsoft's DirectX graphics software as an employee and who now runs the WildTangent 3D games site.[*]

---

[*] Festa, Paul. "SP2 vs. the plug-ins." CNET News.com. September 3, 2004. See http://news.com.com/2100-1032-5345881.html.

Microsoft defended its update by pointing out that people need more warning. "What we found was that most users were becoming accustomed to saying, 'OK' and not reading the [ActiveX warning] dialog," said Doug Stamper, an Internet Explorer group program manager who worked on SP2. "We made these changes in the ActiveX user experience because users were getting drive-by downloads."

Microsoft's new *information bar*, a thin strip just below the web address bar that carries warning messages, flashes a variety of warnings such as This site might require the following ActiveX control . . . Click here to install. But for some plug-ins—notably the free RealPlayer software that competes with Windows Media Player—the bar reads, To help protect your security, Internet Explorer blocked this site from downloading files to your computer. Click here for options. Understandably, Real was unhappy with being off-handedly branded an insecure site.

Microsoft's critics have suggested that the company's security measures have been implemented in that bolster its own businesses at the expense of others. You think? How about the fact, also pointed out by Alex St. John, that site developers can successfully bypass the ActiveX security protocol if they switch from common web technologies to Microsoft's .NET framework and the C# programming language? "Maybe breaking ActiveX forces a look at .NET," St. John said. "And it's all done with the pretext of security."

The Big Chill

Unleashed, Microsoft is going to ensure that its monopoly grows stronger and stronger, and as it does so, running Windows is going to become rougher and rougher for users, who have no choice but to play by Microsoft's rules.
—Stewart Alsop[4]

Indeed, whatever Microsoft does to its ActiveX plug-in handling affects many Microsoft competitors, from Real's RealPlayer to Macromedia's Flash, Apple's QuickTime, and Adobe Systems' Reader for PDF files. Microsoft could easily use ActiveX security to squeeze out other plug-ins. For example, if Microsoft's new warnings scare off users from loading ActiveX controls, people might stick with the pre-installed Windows Media Player.

It's a pattern Microsoft knows well. Fear, uncertainty, and doubt (FUD) keep people from moving away from the pre-installed Microsoft software and keep competitors from challenging any piece of the puzzle. While the press characterized the Browser Wars of the late 1990s as between Internet Explorer and Netscape Navigator, the real battle was between Microsoft and *any* other browser. Microsoft has even insisted that the browser should be integrated with Windows, with web-browsing functions embedded deeply within applications, placing Windows at the center of the computing experience.

The "smoking gun" that signaled Microsoft's intention to leverage its Windows monopoly against browsers was an internal document written by Jim Allchin, a Microsoft vice-president, to his boss Paul Maritz in 1996, titled "Concerns for Our Future"* "I don't understand how IE [Internet Explorer] is going to win. The current path is simply to copy everything that Netscape does packaging and product wise. . . . My conclusion is that we must leverage

---

* Naughton, John. "Why Microsoft is fighting a free and open exchange." *Observer* (*Guardian*, U.K.). February 25, 2001. See http://observer.guardian.co.uk/business/story/0,6903,442476,00.html.

Windows more. Treating IE as just an add-on to Windows which is cross-platform [is] losing our biggest advantage—Windows market share. We should dedicate a cross-group team to come up with ways to leverage Windows technically more."

And yet, despite an antitrust conviction for dealing a death blow to Netscape, Microsoft emerged from its courtroom ordeal at the end of 2001 with its browser strategy essentially intact.

The last full release of Internet Explorer was in 2001, with the launch of the 6.0 version. It was updated slightly with the Windows XP Service Pack 1 release in 2002. The software is woefully outdated as of this writing, and site developers are unhappy about the browser's lack of support for basic web standards like CSS and the PNG (Portable Network Graphics) image format, and for its lack of popular features like tabbed browsing.

DON'T CATCH A WEB BUG

Yet another example of the kind of problems caused by the mono-culture of Internet Explorer is the web bug—invisible pieces of code that can be used for everything from secretly tracking your web travels to pilfering computer files. You can catch a web bug by simply surfing a web page with a browser. It may not do any harm unless, of course, it contains malicious code that takes advantage of Internet Explorer and Windows vulnerabilities.

Site operators and advertising companies place web bugs on their pages to collect information about surfing habits. Web bugs are often invisible because they are typically only one-by-one pixel in size and represented as HTML image tags. But these bugs can also capture your IP address or install nasty Trojan horses. The bugs can also be matched with cookies to grab personal information such as log-in IDs and passwords.

Web bugs can easily be confused with invisible GIF files used for alignment purposes on web pages, except that a web bug typically loads from a different web server than the rest of the page. Your best defense against illegitimate web bugs wreaking havoc on your system or stealing personal information is to ditch Internet Explorer. Firefox, for example, lets you block images that come from any site other than the web page's originating site.

Of course, the need for security is yet another powerful motivator to get people to upgrade. But bowing to public pressure, Microsoft eased off its position that these features and Internet Explorer "improvements" would have to wait until Longhorn, the next version of Windows. Bill Gates announced on February 15, 2005 that the company would ship an update to its browser separately from the next major version of Windows.[*]

Competition, for once, has lit a fire under Microsoft, coming in the form of the free Firefox browser from the open source Mozilla Foundation. People are flocking to it in order to gain some measure of security in their Windows systems. "It's not about the features," Chris Hofmann, Mozilla's director of

---

[*] Festa, Paul. "Microsoft yielding to IE standards pressure?" CNET News.com. March 16, 2005. See http://news.com.com/Microsoft+yielding+to+IE+standards+pressure/2100-1032_3-5620988.html.

engineering, told CNET.[*] What's driving people away from Internet Explorer is security. "If we were in a world where there were less of a mono-culture for browsers, it would make it harder to design [malware] exploits that would affect that much of the marketplace. That's one of the driving forces of the Mozilla Foundation—to provide choices so that someone can't come up with an exploit that affects nearly the whole population."

Security groups advise switching from Internet Explorer to something else to avoid attacks. One such group is the U.S. Computer Emergency Readiness Team (US-CERT), the official government body responsible for defending against online threats. CERT noted, however, that people who choose another browser but continue to run Windows are still at risk, because Windows itself relies to some degree on Internet Explorer functionality.

ZOMBIE PCS: SPAMMING BEHIND YOUR BACK

You thought it might be safe to use those ActiveX controls on your Windows PC with certain "trusted sites," but when you weren't looking, a Trojan horse entered your system and turned it into a *zombie PC*—a compromised system that sends out junk email or attacks without your knowledge. The Honeynet Project[*] estimates that a worldwide population of more than one million ungrateful dead PCs are under the control of computer crackers.

The zombie PCs are silently linked to networks called *botnets* that can distribute spam, mount distributed denial-of-service (DoS) attacks to bring down sites, sniff network traffic for unencrypted passwords, log keystrokes, install spyware, and perform click fraud. Botnets launched 226 distributed denial-of-service attacks on 99 different targets in a three-month period from November 2004 to January 2005, according to the Honeynet Project, which tracked more than 100 active botnets, some with up to 50,000 zombie PCs.

And at least 80 percent of the spam you receive emanates from zombie PCs, according to a study by network management firm Sandvine.[†] Some security experts think that many of the infamous worm attacks of 2004 (such as MyDoom and Bagle) were launched expressly to install spam Trojan horses on PCs in order to use them later as zombie PCs. According to Sandvine, the most active Trojan horses for spamming purposes were the Migmaf and SoBig variants.

Once you have removed such Trojan horses from your Windows system, switch to another browser and make sure ActiveX is not used by that browser. (If it is, turn it off.) You may also want to turn off JavaScript and cookies. Another solution, obviously, is . . . get a Mac! There is no evidence that Macs have been used as zombies to date.

---

[*] The Honeynet Project. "Know your Enemy: Tracking Botnets." March 13, 2005. See http://project.honeynet.org/papers/bots.

[†] Leyden, John. "Zombie PCs spew out 80% of spam." *The Register*. June 4, 2004. See www.theregister.co.uk/2004/06/04/trojan_spam_study.

Browsers from the Counterculture

In 1998, Netscape took an idea popularized once before by the Diggers in San Francisco's Haight-Ashbury community during the Summer of Love in 1967. The Diggers popularized the notion of "free" by giving away food and

---

[*] Lemos, Robert and Paul Festa. "IE flaw may boost rival browsers." CNET News.com. June 28, 2004. See http://news.zdnet.com/2100-1009_22-5250697.html.

clothing in order to nurture a counterculture. Netscape wanted to nurture the development of its browser technology, so it gave away the source code to its Navigator browser. "By giving away the source code for future versions, we can ignite the creative energies of the entire Net community and fuel unprecedented levels of innovation in the browser market," said Jim Barksdale, Netscape's president and chief executive officer.[*]

Today, free open source browsers, including Firefox, the highly evolved descendant of the Netscape browser whose development was continued by the Mozilla Foundation, challenge Internet Explorer on its own turf—Windows. In addition, the Mac has its own browser, Safari, that has replaced the Mac version of Internet Explorer. Safari improves on Explorer with a pop-up blocker to stop unwanted pop-up ads and tabbed browsing to help with screen clutter; it even runs faster. Linux folks have a plethora of browsers to choose from, including Firefox, Opera, KDE file manager (kfm), Grail, ICE, Jazilla, and JoZilla.[†]

Even if you still use Windows, you can surf more securely without Internet Explorer. Non-Microsoft browsers, such as the Opera browser and the Mozilla and Firefox browsers (see Figure 9-5), don't have many of the vulnerable technologies inherent to Microsoft's browser. The amount of code for these browsers is less than Internet Explorer, because the developers focus more on providing Internet-browsing features and ignore ActiveX controls and whatnot for linking together Microsoft applications and Windows. By actively addressing problems that arise, open source developers end up with a highly secure browser.

Figure 9-5: Web pages look pretty much the same in Firefox as they do in Internet Explorer—only your PC is more secure.

[*] Netscape press release, January 22, 1998. See http://wp.netscape.com/newsref/pr/newsrelease558.html.

[†] For list of Linux browsers, see www.itp.uni-hannover.de/~kreutzm/en/lin_browser.html.

THE FIREFOX NETWORK

Firefox is the best-known open source challenger to Internet Explorer, surpassing 10 million downloads in a little more than a month after its release in November 2004. By February 2005, more than 25 million copies had been downloaded.

The Mozilla Foundation, spun off from AOL Time Warner as a nonprofit, carries on the open source development work launched in 1998 by Netscape Communications and its Mozilla.org wing. It developed the browser as an alternative to Internet Explorer, relying on donations and an army of volunteer programmers.

Firefox on a Windows system is not much more secure than Internet Explorer, due to Firefox's own popularity and the vulnerabilities of Windows. But the vulnerabilities in Internet Explorer are more severe, and Microsoft takes longer than the open source community to fix the problems.

According to the Symantec's security response team,[*] "The average time between when a vulnerability is publicly announced and when a patch comes out is 43 days for Internet Explorer, only 26 days for Firefox." And Internet Explorer still leads Firefox—leads every Windows application, in fact—in the total number of vulnerabilities. Symantec's count has Internet Explorer as having more than 300 known vulnerabilities. Mozilla's base code for Firefox, which preceded Internet Explorer and Netscape Navigator, has fewer than 100.

Firefox provides a more secure browsing environment out of the box, although no browser is bulletproof. Firefox makes it easier to set and change security options, compared to Internet Explorer, by putting all the security settings in one place—the Privacy panel (see Figure 9-6), which you can display by choosing **Tools ▶ Options**. You can clear each category in the Privacy panel individually or click the **Clear All** button to wipe out all privacy-related data in one fell swoop.

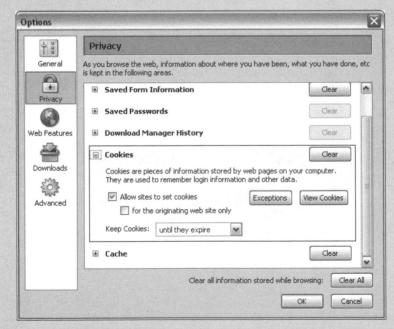

Figure 9-6: Firefox puts all its privacy settings in one place and doesn't allow ActiveX controls to gain a foothold in your PC.

(continued)

---

[*] Keizer, Gregg. "New Firefox Version Heightens Debate Over Browser Security." *TechWeb News.* March 24, 2005. See www.techweb.com/wire/security/159905537.

Firefox steers clear of ActiveX completely, which is one of the main attack vectors for gaining unauthorized access to a Windows PC. The tradeoff is that sites that use ActiveX won't work as well with Firefox. You can also control the use of Java and JavaScript, disable common JavaScript techniques that hide the true origins of a website or the true destination of a web link, and control the use of SSL (Secure Sockets Layer) for secure connections and for managing and validating certificates.

Firefox offers everything else you may be looking for in a browser—pop-up ad blocking, tabbed browsing for quick access to multiple web pages without having to open multiple windows, and cookie controls. With Internet Explorer, you have to open each cookie manually to see what data it carries. Firefox lets you browse through your cookies, delete any you don't like, and tell the browser to ignore cookies from the sites you don't like. For example, if you don't want anything from doubleclick.net stored on your computer, you can simply tell Firefox to ignore all doubleclick.net cookies.

When you browse the Internet with a Windows PC, you put your digital life on the line. If your primary purpose in using a computer is to browse the Web, collect and send email, and use typical productivity software (such as word processing, spreadsheets, and presentations), you are much better off with a Mac or Linux machine. As a person who does all his banking and most of his work on the Internet, I can testify that my Mac has protected me from everything described previously in this chapter (and in other chapters as well). My Linux PC is equally safe. No spam issues forth, no viruses wreak havoc, no worms burrow deeply into the system's psyche, and no Trojan horses unleash armies of crawling bots. All is quiet on the Internet front.

PART IV

GETTING ON WITH YOUR COMPUTER LIFE

10

TWELVE STEPS TO FREEDOM FROM MICROSOFT

If you're serious about quitting your Microsoft addiction, you *can* get help. But anyone who has battled addictive behaviors knows that recovery can be anything but simple. It can be difficult, frustrating, confusing, and sometimes work-threatening or even lethal to your documents and data files as you battle the sly ways of Microsoft addiction. Armed with enough information and useful tools, however, you can bring some order, simplicity, and clarity to the recovery process and make it easier to achieve the serenity and strength that comes from full detox—a completely Microsoft-free system that is more reliable and more productive.

The 12-step program model pioneered by Alcoholics Anonymous (A.A.) in the 1930s has gone on to be the most widely used and successful approach to dealing with addictive behaviors, and it serves as a useful guide for weaning yourself of Microsoft software.

Steps 1 to 3: The Problem Is Yours, Not Microsoft's

It's not your fault, but it is your problem. You have to take the first step:

1. **Admit you are powerless over your addiction—and that your computer system and software have become unmanageable.**

    Windows, Office, Outlook, and Internet Explorer have all become unmanageable due to their vulnerabilities to malware attacks. Besides, why let a single company in Redmond, Washington control your computer's destiny—even when, or *especially* when, that company is the largest software company in the world? Windows upgrades are worked on by nerdy elves strung out on Jolt Cola who spend half their time skateboarding the parking lots of the Big Green campus and the other half under the watchful eye of millionaire managers protecting their portfolios from Change. Once you've acknowledged that change must come from *you*, you can embark on the path to recovery.

2. **Believe that a set of technologies greater than Microsoft's can restore your computing life to sanity.**

    As scary as it is to recognize your problem, it needn't be a cause for panic. Microsoft may employ a *few* of the best programmers on the planet, but it certainly hasn't captured *all* of them. Its development efforts are saddled with compatibility issues with legacy systems, applications, and hardware. The mono-culture of Microsoft code in nearly every computer presents an irresistible target for hackers looking to exploit weaknesses for fun or profit— worms carrying malware are nearly always successful at propagating themselves. A key lesson from nature we should never forget is that diversity is mandatory for species to adapt successfully to a changing environment. To foster innovation, the computer and software industries needs vigorous competition. Rejecting Microsoft is not the end of your computing world; there are higher powers.

3. **Make a decision to open your computer life up to accept the free, unfettered market of ideas and innovations.**

    Don't be afraid of the Mac, Linux, or open source software. Look how unstable your computer is now. How could it possibly get any worse?

    Erase the myth from your mind that you need Microsoft software because everyone else uses it. Actually, only about 95 percent of the computing world uses it. The other 5 percent is composed of the free thinkers who are willing to try new things; the artists, writers, and musicians who shape our culture; the software geniuses and inventors who brings us new innovations; the scientists and engineers that make everything work; the desktop publishers, multimedia professionals, video editors, and graphic artists who make communication happen; and just about all the actors and celebrities in Hollywood. If you feel yourself to be a part of this group (or at least want to be invited to their parties), get off Microsoft as soon as you can.

Steps 4 to 6: Take Stock of Your Computer Life

Consider your hardware, software, and applications from top to bottom: What applications and utility programs do you really use? What interfaces do your devices connect to?

4.   Make a searching and fearless inventory of your devices, applications, documents, and data files.

Start with the Windows Start menu, as shown in Figure 10-1: Do you really use all those applications? Some were supplied by the hardware manufacturer, and you may have no real use for them. Others might be useful, but you were just so bewildered by your Windows system that you never got around to trying them. Make a list of applications that you use regularly, and then in a lower priority, add applications or categories of applications you still want to investigate.

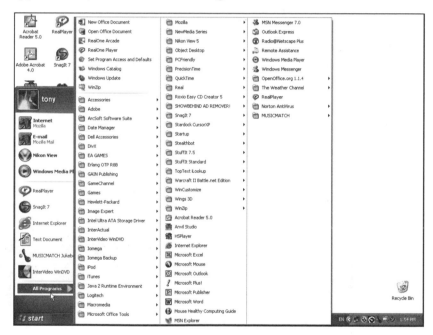

Figure 10-1: Start something? The Windows Start menu lists all your applications, even ones supplied with the system that you've never tried before nor want to.

Locate all the documents and data files that you want to migrate to the new system. Most people keep all of them inside the My Documents folder of their user folder. But don't forget music files, photos, movies, and other types of files you've created or captured from the Internet. There is no reason not to expect that most everything you have will migrate smoothly to the new system.

Do a visual inspection to see how devices are connected to your computer. Many connect via the USB connector, which is standard on all machines, including Macs, but some may connect through other methods, such as

FireWire (IEEE 1394). Macs and Linux distributions support USB and IEEE 1394, and even Bluetooth wireless connections. However, you may need to update the software drivers that are supplied with your devices. Start by making a list of the devices defined in your Windows system:

a.   Open My Computer and click **View System Information** in the list of System Tasks. The System Properties window appears, as shown in Figure 10-2.

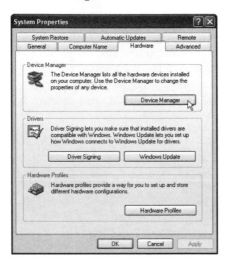

Figure 10-2: The System Properties window gives
you access to the Windows Device Manager.

b.   Click the **Device Manager** button in the System Properties window. The Device Manager window appears, as shown in Figure 10-3.

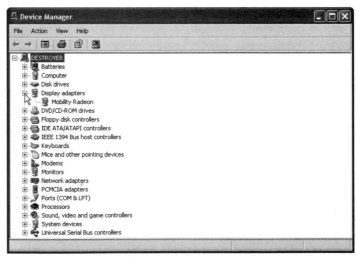

Figure 10-3: The Device Manager window provides a list of all devices
defined in your Windows system and information about each device.

c. Click the plus (+) sign next to each category of devices to see a list of the devices in your system.

Select a device and right-click your mouse to select Properties for the device. The Properties window provides information about the device and its software driver version. You can go directly to the device manufacturer's website to get the latest updated drivers for the operating system you use.

5. **Admit to yourself (and others) the exact nature of what is wrong with your Windows PC and its applications.**

Upgrading the operating system of a Windows personal computer is somewhat like ripping a house off its foundation and moving the structure to a new one that is almost—but not quite—the same size . . . The relocated house sits uneasily on this new foundation. You can still live there, but you never know when a wrong step will drop you through the floorboards. —Mike Langberg[1]

Besides the buggy nature of Windows itself and Microsoft's applications, the chief complaint is malware and related adware and spyware. People don't like having the machine they paid for clogged up with stuff they didn't want, slowing it down and making it unstable. Even if you could upgrade and fine-tune your Windows system to be relatively safe, secure, and productive, you'll still spend a lot of time and effort keeping it that way. And why should you? Don't you have a life? Admit that the Microsoft mono-culture causes the problem and move on. It was never your fault.

6. **Make yourself ready to embrace new technologies from the free market that would replace the buggy and vulnerable Microsoft code.**

To paraphrase Bay Area radio jockey/pundit Scoop Nisker, if you don't like the research you read, do some of your own. If you type "Microsoft alternatives" into Google, you'll find hundreds of websites describing or offering alternatives among the 2,890,000 search results. Not all of these people are Microsoft haters—many of them simply want better options (or any options!). Visit the Apple site (www.apple.com) to learn all about Macs, and visit Linux Online (www.linux.org) for comprehensive information and resources about Linux.

Step 7: Get Support for Your New Habit

Having made your decision to leave Microsoft behind, stick with that decision. If you need help, get help—an entire industry of help is ready and waiting.

7. **Humbly ask for support in reconfiguring Linux to run with your hardware, or for money to buy a Mac.**

Macs are simple to set up and use and require no support unless the hardware itself is malfunctioning; but Macs cost more than PCs. The least expensive model, the Mac mini, is designed to replace a desktop PC chassis and saves you money by working with your existing display monitor, keyboard, and mouse. But even if you're willing to shell out big bucks for the best laptop on the market (the Mac PowerBook), remember that time is money—and you'll be saving a lot of time by avoiding the complexities and malware plagues of Windows.

WINDOWS XP SP2: UPGRADE OR QUIT?

Microsoft recently issued an upgrade to Windows to meet security concerns and is promising to deliver yet another new version in 2006—dubbed Longhorn—that will once again change computing forever. Microsoft says the party will go on. Should you stay or should you go?

Many Windows XP users can't take advantage of the upgrade—known as Windows XP Service Pack 2 (SP2)—until their applications support it. Microsoft has issued a list of nearly 50 applications and games that may encounter problems with SP2.[*] Among the primary issues are glitches related to the relationship between the Windows firewall, which is automatically turned on as a security default by SP2, and many of the listed programs. The updated firewall can prevent applications from properly connecting to outside networks, limiting their ability to receive data. Some of the problems caused by the SP2 update include issues with remote desktops, filesharing, email notifications, and online multi-player games. Among the most high-profile, widely used products listed are anti-virus applications from Symantec, network management software made by Computer Associates International, and multimedia tools from Macromedia.

Windows systems upgraded with SP2 seem to be more secure than those without it. But the SP2 upgrade may instill a false sense of security in administrators who install it on their users' desktops and laptops. In many cases, when a warning appears about the Windows firewall blocking an unknown application, people click the Unblock button just to get rid of the warning message and move on with their work, defeating the purpose of the firewall in the first place. The SP2 problems related to anti-virus applications are disconcerting, because these applications are the first line of defense against virus attacks. Perhaps Microsoft hasn't moved fast enough to help the vendors of anti-virus applications, because Microsoft is looking to expand into this area with its own anti-virus products. If that's the case, Microsoft has put its own profits above the goal of improving system security.

People have reported other problems over the course of the torturous two-hour installation procedure for SP2.[†] For many, the service pack dramatically impacts system performance and stability—such as getting the Blue Screen of Death every time the system starts up or running so slowly that the system is unusable. If you haven't scanned and deleted spyware in advance of installing SP2, you stand a good chance of losing your network and Internet connectivity. And while Windows XP offers a System Restore feature that lets you revert back to previous restore points should something go wrong, once you install SP2, you lose the ability to revert back to before the installation.

If these problems aren't enough to convince you to quit Windows entirely, consider that Microsoft has based Longhorn on this inconvenient and incompatible SP2 code. Microsoft will make Longhorn prettier than the current version of Windows, using technology called Avalon that improves on the visual look of windows and applications, and it will make data sharing among applications easier with technology called Indigo that implements web services. But most of these new capabilities won't be useful until applications support them, which is not likely to happen until after Longhorn becomes widely available.

---

[*] See Microsoft help and support pages at http://support.microsoft.com/default.aspx?kbid= 884130&product=windowsxpsp2 and http://support.microsoft.com/default.aspx?kbid=842242.

[†] See the ZDNet UK review of Windows XP Service Pack 2 at http://reviews.zdnet.co.uk/ software/os/0,39024183,39163261,00.htm.

If you look at the
history of
Microsoft in the
operating system
business, you
might conclude
that the company
doesn't like its
own products. It
always seems to
be saying it has
some new
operating system
that will solve the
problems of
whatever it is
selling at the time.
—Stewart Alsop[2]

The cheaper route is to use the free Linux operating system on inexpensive PC hardware. Older PCs that can't run the latest version of Windows can still run Linux, so you'll save money by using hardware that would otherwise be obsolete. However, Linux can be tough to set up for specific hardware devices such as older display and sound cards. Without help, you could end up spending considerable time getting your Linux system up and running with an appropriate desktop environment and a set of applications that rivals Microsoft's.

For a relatively new model PC, commercial Linux distributions[*] from companies such as Red Hat and Novell (SuSE Linux) are a breeze to install and configure. There are also free Linux distributions that work well with modern hardware, and all you need is a good Linux book.[†] There are possibly hundreds of different Linux distributions available on the Internet—since it is an open source project, anybody can build a complete Linux distribution and release it for download. All a distributor needs is to get hold of the Linux kernel and a few dozen other software packages, all of which are freely available and distributable. Some of the Linux distributions have established growing user bases and have increased in popularity over time, while others have come and gone rather quickly. According to various surveys and statistics, the five most popular Linux distributions are:

- Red Hat
- Mandrake
- SuSE (Novell)
- Debian
- Slackware

Linux is very popular as a server operating system, so it makes sense for server hardware vendors to offer support specific to their hardware offerings. Thus, large, established server vendors such as IBM, Hewlett-Packard, and Sun Microsystems all offer comprehensive support for Linux running on their hardware. HP, for example, offers end-to-end Linux solutions that meet specific enterprise requirements—including a suite of porting services to move your custom software and data into the Linux environment. Many of these server vendors also offer 24-7 disaster recovery services that can keep a large business running no matter what happens to its servers—with daily backup and automatic fail-over systems.

As more businesses standardize on Linux with servers and desktops, independent service vendors have emerged to provide fee-based support for Linux and open source software. The leading distributors of Linux offer various levels of commercial support. For example, Red Hat's wide range of support services is a principal reason why the company and its Linux distribution are successful in the professional IT world. Its software packages are

---

[*] DistroWatch.com keeps track of Linux distributions and provides reviews and comparisons. See http://distrowatch.com.

[†] For a hands-on, project-based, take-it-slow approach to learning Linux, see Rickford Grant's *Linux for Non-Geeks*, No Starch Press, 2004.

easy to update via Red Hat Network, and the company offers training certification programs in most parts of the world. But you don't have to pay for Linux support—*free* support is available from the Free Linux Support community (http://support.marko.net).

Another way to get Linux support is to ask Doctor Tux (www.doctortux .com) or another similar free service that lets you enter questions and view answers from its knowledge base. Doctor Tux also provides expert installation and technical support services on all major Linux distributions, including Red Hat, Fedora, Debian-GNU, SuSE, Mandrake, and Slackware. Doctor Tux works with small companies, including hotels, property management firms, and home builders, as well as folks with home computers, to set up wireless networks of Linux machines.

EVALUATING TECH SUPPORT

With Windows on a desktop or laptop PC, chances are your support was limited to the geek down the hall (or in my case, my 15-year-old son, who seemed to know more about PCs than anyone else in my extended circle of family and friends). For the odd time when you needed additional tech support—other than training to learn how to use Windows security features—your first call was to the hardware vendor. As a software company only, Microsoft typically referred customers with problems to their hardware vendors. Thus, support for a Windows PC has been largely the province of Dell, Sony, Toshiba, Gateway, or your local computer fixer who put together PCs from parts. And you would bounce back and forth like a pinball between the flippers of the manufacturer's support department and the Microsoft support department as they pointed accusing fingers at each other.

Apple offers decent support for its hardware *and* software, so getting a Mac fixed is an easier process, though not any faster—for hardware issues, you'll still either have to mail the machine back to Apple or drop it at an Apple retail store.

Linux support is comparable to Windows—you get software support only. But support and training are serious and costly issues for large organizations with thousands of desktops and laptops. Microsoft points out that the total cost of ownership with Windows for large organizations—including training and support—is lower than Linux, even though Linux is free.[*] However, some of the studies that purport to show that Windows is more cost-effective have not been credible due to Microsoft's unabashed funding for the studies. If you work in a large organization that has standardized on Windows, you may want to point out to its IT department that independent studies have shown that Linux, even with very expensive 24-7 support, can be more cost-effective than Windows. Even a Microsoft-sponsored study by BearingPoint[†] found licensing and support costs of Windows Server 2003 to be only "comparable" to Novell's SuSE Linux 8 and Red Hat Inc.'s Enterprise Linux 3, with Windows being less expensive only in some cases.

(continued)

[*] Foley, John. "Ballmer's Linux Spin." InformationWeek. November 1, 2004.
See www.informationweek.com/story/showArticle.jhtml?articleID=51201703&pgno=1.

[†] "Licensing and Support Acquisition Costs Comparable for Windows Server, SuSE Linux, and Red Hat Enterprise Linux." May 5, 2004. See www.microsoft.com/windowsserversystem/facts/analyses/comparable.mspx.

It's difficult to trust any of the studies when they are funded either by Microsoft or by an open source advocacy group or support organization—both of whom have clear agendas to push.[*] Sometimes the media report a study's findings straight from the Microsoft press release without having access to the entire text of the study—and the fine print tells a different story. For example, in one white paper sponsored by Microsoft, tech industry analyst firm International Data Corp. (IDC) makes at least three observations that are not favorable and were not reported by the press: Linux is more reliable, Linux is cheaper for web hosting, and Microsoft enjoys only a temporary advantage in support staffing.[†] But Microsoft neglected to include these key findings in its official press announcement, so most people never read about them.

Since you can't rely on industry studies and analyst reports, try this anecdotal evidence: A group of programmers working with Microsoft Access and other Microsoft software decided to call Microsoft tech support about the software's ability to connect with servers. After charging them $55 for the call, the tech support person left the programmers on hold for a while and then suggested that they use the company's online help, which was no help at all.

The callers then, as a lark, tried asking the Psychic Friends Network the same questions—technical questions about connecting Microsoft Access to servers. The Psychic Friends Network person sensed that there was a real problem with some connection, that something wasn't being fulfilled either in a sexual, spiritual, or emotional way—and identified that there was some sort of physical failure that was causing the problem. "In terms of technical expertise," reported the programmers, "we found that a Microsoft technician using Knowledge Base was about as helpful as a Psychic Friends reader using tarot cards. All in all, however, the Psychic Friends Network proved to be a much friendlier organization than Microsoft Technical Support."[‡]

[*] Hamm, Steve. "The Truth about Linux and Windows." *BusinessWeek*. April 22, 2005. See www.businessweek.com/the_thread/techbeat/archives/2005/04/the_truth_about_1.html.

[†] Scavo, Frank. "Microsoft-sponsored study on Win2K vs. Linux is NOT all good news for Microsoft." *The Enterprise System Spectator*. December 17, 2002. See http://fscavo.blogspot.com/2002/12/microsoft-sponsored-study-on-win2k-vs.html.

[‡] Ellard, Michael Patrick, and Daniel Albert Wright. "Microsoft Technical Support vs. The Psychic Friends Network: Which Provides Better Support for Microsoft Products?" August 19, 1998. See www.netscrap.com/netscrap_detail.cfm?scrap_id=704.

Steps 8 to 9: Get Your Data Together

It's time to move your data. Whether you are literally moving everything to a new computer, or simply replacing Windows with Linux on your current machine, you need to make a backup first. Pack up all your data, including those folders stuffed with music and video files, and don't forget the emails you want to save. And the documents. And the spreadsheets and presentations. And so on. What you *won't* need are the Windows applications or system files. You are replacing them with Linux and open source software, or simply moving on to a Mac.

8. **Make a backup copy of all documents, data files, and communication settings that may be ignored or harmed in the process of moving to the new system, and be willing to use backups to restore your documents and data files.**

Back up your documents and files using a standard backup medium, such as an external USB hard drive, or burn a standard CD-ROM or DVD data disc. You can use these types of backup media with Macs and Linux PCs to restore your documents and data. Also, write down your communication settings such as TCP/IP and modem settings for your ISP or LAN connection to the Internet. After switching to the new system, transcribe your communications settings into the new system's network settings to get reconnected to the Internet.

TIP *If you're moving to a Mac, remember that most Windows applications—including Microsoft Office—have Mac counterparts. Save versions of your documents and data files in formats you can use with Mac applications first and then copy those new versions to the Mac.*

Linux runs on PC hardware and recognizes PC hard drives and backup media such as writable CDs and DVDs. It is also just as easy to transfer files from PCs to Macs. Any recent model Mac can recognize a PC-formatted portable hard drive, portable Zip drive, floppy disk, recordable CD or DVD, and just about any other removable or portable media you can throw at it. Here are a few options for backing up your files:

Use a portable USB drive.
These things come in pocket-sized models for under $200, even for one as small as a keychain fob. They connect directly to the USB port of any PC or Mac. You can transfer files at will from one type of computer to another. Macs recognize Mac and Windows formats; Windows and Linux recognize only the Windows format.

Use removable media compatible with your Mac.
You might use Iomega Zip drives at work and at home; if so, you can copy files to a removable Zip disk formatted for Windows that works in either a Mac or a Linux-based PC.

Transfer the files over the Internet.
You can copy the files to a website (such as those offered by paid online storage services such as .Mac, or free ones like Yahoo! Briefcase) and put links to the files on a web page. Access the page using a browser and click the links to download the files. You can also use an FTP utility to transfer files to and from a website or FTP site on the Internet.

Mac folks: Use the Mac's iDisk.
Apple offers the .Mac service for copying files to your own secure hard disk on the Internet and set up a web page specifically for dropping off files you can download later. (See the section ".Mac the Knife" in Chapter 2 for details.)

Send files as email attachments to yourself (or to another email address for yourself).

Attaching a document to an email message is the most popular method, not to mention the easiest method, for transferring a file to another computer user or computer. I attached several chapters of this book to a single email to send to the publisher—not because I'm lazy, but because it is convenient for the publisher to receive the files that way. I don't even know what kind of computer the publisher uses; it doesn't matter.

Transfer files through a local area network (LAN).

You may already use a LAN to share an Internet connection with another computer, especially a broadband connection. Set your Windows folders to be shared over the LAN so that you can copy their contents to any other computers on the LAN. (See Chapter 8 for details on using LANs.)

Switching from one system to another is a defining moment of your computer life. The move gives you a chance to standardize your digital life and make it ready for the future. With that in mind,

9. **Switch to using non-Microsoft document and data standards wherever possible, except when to do so would injure your productivity.**

The most troublesome document format is the Word doc—but many folks simply *must* be able to work with these types of files to do their jobs. However, every alternative to Word listed in Chapter 4 can open the Word docs you receive from other people. If possible, don't *send* Word docs—use PDF if you want to protect the document while also offering the ability for reviewers to add comments. Use the RTF format to transfer Word doc files to other formats, or save Word docs directly into alternative formats such as OpenOffice.org or WordPerfect. Use XML for spreadsheets, plain vanilla HTML for presentations, and plain text or HTML for email messages. Use MP3 for music files and MPEG for video files.

In short, use open source formats and standards whenever possible. In the future, when your descendants are still able to open these files on whatever computer they've got on the Starship Enterprise, they'll be thankful you followed this advice.

Step 10: Test Everything First

Test everything from the ground up, just like the "level 1 diagnostic" on those *Star Trek* reruns.

10. **Continue to question the usefulness of software functions and to test software before committing to using it, and when you're wrong about some new piece of software, promptly admit it.**

The brave new world of open source software includes the bad and the good—but if you stay tuned in to the open source community, you'll find out quickly how to distinguish between them. See this book's appendix for a list of sources for Linux and Mac information.

Commercial applications might seem more reliable simply because they're backed by established companies, but just look at Microsoft. Its products illustrate perfectly how commercial offerings can perform worse than their open source counterparts. Don't believe any hype. Test applications thoroughly before committing your next project to them.

Step 11: Learn All You Can

You've had enough of watching screens of bug-ridden, virus-riddled, crash-provoking Windows apps. No billion-dollar, jive-talking, power-hungry, boyish nerd is going to stop your productivity with the Blue Screen of Death. All you want is the truth (with apologies to John Lennon).

11. **Through research and continued web searching, improve your knowledge of computer technologies and alternatives to Microsoft systems and software.**

You might want to start with websites that offer information about alternative software:

Microsoft has had clear competitors in the past. It's a good thing we have museums to document that.
—Bill Gates, joking to an audience at the Computer History Museum[3]

MSBC Alternatives (www.msboycott.com/thealt)
This section of the Microsoft Boycott Campaign (MSBC) site includes a directory of products that replace similar items from Microsoft. The software and hardware products in this directory are for multiple platforms and run on a variety of operating systems and computer types.

The Anti-Microsoft Web Ring (http://e.webring.com/hub?ring=antims)
This page links to a "ring" of interconnected sites that all provide topical information about Microsoft or Bill Gates (such as jokes and essays), plus alternatives to Microsoft systems and software.

Computer Gripes (www.computergripes.com)
This site is, according to its author, Michael Horowitz, "devoted to what stinks about computer products" and goes into the specific horrors that Horowitz has experienced. "It exists because the errors, bugs, poor documentation, and occasional stupidity in the field drive me nuts," according

to Horowitz. It lists just about all Microsoft systems and software products and quite a few offerings from other vendors. Rather than offering straight product reviews, which typically describe features and benefits, Horowitz focuses exclusively on what's bad about these products, which is far more useful as well as entertaining.

Step 12: Tell Everyone You Know

You've seen the light—spread the word!

12. **Now that you've moved on to a better computer life, carry the message of this book to other Microsoft addicts and urge them to practice these principles to free themselves.**

Tell others how to get by on a no-Microsoft diet. They'll thank you when their systems act in a more regular fashion. And you'll thank them for switching out of Outlook—as a result, their address books will no longer be surreptitiously used for flooding email servers with viruses. And you'll thank them for not attaching Word docs to emails that would compromise other PCs. And you'll thank them for cleaning up the malware that had turned their PCs into spam zombies in the middle of the night.

Mitchell Kapor, Lotus founder, co-founder of the Electronic Frontier Foundation, is a man who, by fighting the ultimate spreadsheet war with Lotus 1-2-3 against Excel, gave Bill Gates the most competition Microsoft ever had. As Kapor put it:[*] "Ultimately, positive action to rein in Microsoft will be taken when the general public realizes they're being had; that as a society we're being forced to pay huge costs in lost productivity due to the unnecessary difficulty of using computers; and when the basically amoral and ruthless character of Microsoft's leadership is graphically revealed."

---

[*] Mitchell Kapor's blog at http://blogs.osafoundation.org/mitch.

11

WHERE DO YOU WANT TO GO TOMORROW?

In 1996, Microsoft posed a question to the public in TV commercials to highlight its Internet capabilities: "Where do you want to go today?" It became the butt of a thousand jokes. A false rumor spread through the Internet that Microsoft had been subsequently deluged with responses by email, fax, and postcard with answers such as "Chicago," "the corner of Fourth and Elm," "Egypt," "Tahiti," "Anywhere but Redmond," "Ulaan Baator," and so on. In a humorous retelling of the fable by Denounce,[*] a satirical website, people called Microsoft's 800 number at all hours of the day and night to deliver a brief statement and then hang up. "I was just answering their own question," said one caller.

Just where *is* Microsoft going? Straight back to its customers to further entrench them in Windows technology. The brand is continually boosted by PR blitzes and media campaigns. Its recent "Start Something" advertising campaign for Windows XP in April 2005 celebrated how people can use Windows to follow their dreams and pursue what they are passionate about.

---

[*] "Microsoft to Drop Its 'Where Do you Want to Go Today?' Campaign." Denounce. 2003. See www.denounce.com/mswhere.html. Denounce is a satire website specializing in false press releases that are meant neither to inform nor to educate.

It's clear what Microsoft is passionate about: branding. Advertising trade publication *Adweek* estimated the cost of the campaign at about $100 million, including the production of more than 50 versions of television commercials for 11 countries.[*] Until the company can corral its forces and unleash Longhorn, the next version of Windows, it has to keep its customers transfixed on the Windows brand some other way.

Never mind that Microsoft didn't start anything new back in 1996. Ironically, Microsoft also had a credibility problem the last time it used "Start" in a campaign. In 1995, the company launched Windows 95 with the Rolling Stones song "Start Me Up," which, as Douglas Adams, author of *The Hitchhiker's Guide to the Galaxy,* noted at the time, "is better known for its catchy refrain 'You make a grown man cry.' This is a phrase you may hear a lot of over the next few days as millions of people start trying to install Windows."[†]

Microsoft is like a religion in that it asks you—the consumer or business—to make a leap of faith. Ignore all those other new developments ("false idols" like Firefox and the Tiger version of Mac OS X) and remember that Windows—and only Windows—can bring you the future, can "start something." The problem with this leap of faith, and indeed with some religions, is that it is promoted in a language of vague promises that leave you feeling uncertain about the competition and fearful of the unknown.

Microsoft and the Press: The Road to Perdition

A mass of Latin words falls upon the facts like soft snow, blurring the outlines and covering up all the details . . . The great enemy of clear language is insincerity. When there is a gap between one's real and one's declared aims, one turns as it were instinctively to long words and exhausted idioms, like a cuttlefish spurting out ink.
—George Orwell[1]

Never before has truth been so commoditized in the service of a monopoly. Microsoft uses a language of plausible deniability and spin control, which James Gleick called *Microspeak* and compared to George Orwell's description of a debased language consisting of "euphemism, question-begging, and sheer cloudy vagueness." Gleick wrote,[‡] "Microspeak is language with a purpose, and it works, in a way . . . It is what Orwell saw as language of orthodoxy, of concealment, of the party line."

For example, Microsoft releases information that Longhorn's desktop system will be based on an upgrade of the Windows Server 2003 code base, not on the Windows XP code, and claims that this will make Longhorn "notably more stable"[**] than Windows XP. More stable? At what point in the future will it actually *be* stable? With a full year to go before Longhorn's release, who really knows? And how is it that the "upgrade" of the Windows Server 2003 code base is better? Has anyone used it? Information about the supposed capabilities of Longhorn have been leaking out of Microsoft for more than two years.

And what better way is there to stifle competition than to imply the power of a monopoly and sow seeds of fear and doubt in the investment community? Who would want to invest in a company that might get trampled?

---

[*] "Microsoft Launches New Ad Campaign for Windows." Reuters. April 18, 2005. See www.reuters.com/newsArticle.jhtml?type=technologyNews&storyID=8215113.

[†] Adams, Douglas. "Beyond the Hype." Guardian, U.K. August 25, 1995. See http://users.aol.com/machcu/dawin95.html.

[‡] Gleick, James. "A Bug By Any Other Name." See www.around.com/microspeak.html.

[**] Finnie, Scot. "The Lowdown On Longhorn." TechWeb. May 2, 2005. See www.techweb.com/wire/software/162100427.

"Google is interesting," Bill Gates told *Fortune* magazine,[*] "not just because of web search, but because they're going to try to take that and use it to get into other parts of software." Bill's real message is between the lines: Google is treading on Microsoft territory, and Microsoft intends to fight back by adding new search capabilities to Windows. And when Microsoft announced Windows Mobile 5.0 for handhelds and cell phones, Bill Gates gave reporters a neat sound bite that could be interpreted as a threat: "Essentially, you find us in every device where software makes a big difference; Microsoft comes in and sees how we can make a contribution." Indeed, it becomes an offer you can't refuse.

Microsoft has a history of using Microspeak to manipulate the press—such as the announcement on April 16, 1997 that it would continue to make its email service more useful by doubling its servers. In reality, the company was doubling its servers in order to recover from a failure that caused emails to be lost.[†] America Online had similar email problems at that time and was skewered in the press, while Microsoft got off without even having to offer a refund, as AOL did.

The press generally accommodates Microsoft's bum steers about Longhorn (sorry for the pun) as if they were facts. Case in point: When Apple introduced Tiger (version 10.4 of Mac OS X) at the end of April 2005, a fanfare of stories appeared that compared it to Microsoft's future Longhorn. CNET News even ran the headline "Longhorn on Tiger's tail" and described some of the new features of Longhorn, many of which are supposedly Tiger-like. And yet, Longhorn won't be available until the end of 2006! Some of the features Gates demonstrated in April 2005 won't even be in the first release. Gates said himself at the press conference, "When I see those demos, I think, 'Gosh, let's get Longhorn done.'"[‡] Gee whiz, Bill! The press awaits with bated breath.

How does Microsoft get away with manipulating the press? The same way presidents get away with it: by restricting press access to the Oval Office, or as Microsoft plays it, by playing favorites with journalists and reporters. Obey the rules, and you receive carrot-like access to previews and demos; ask too many pesky questions or express too much criticism, and you get the stick. "Getting time with Microsoft's [third most important executive] Jim Allchin used to be as easy as gaining an audience with the pope," admitted Charles Cooper, a journalist[**] with CNET who was eventually granted an interview.

Journalists are mostly in awe of Bill Gates. When *Time* magazine published a cover story on January 13, 1997 about the private life of Bill Gates, the piece was too important to be done by a reporter who might have asked annoying questions. Time's highest-ranking editorial staff member, managing editor Walter Isaacson, waxed superlative about the man so many

---

[*] Vogelstein, Fred. "Gates vs. Google: Search and Destroy." *Fortune.* May 2, 2005. See www.fortune.com/fortune/technology/articles/0,15114,1050065-1,00.html.

[†] Gleick, James. "A Bug By Any Other Name." See www.around.com/microspeak.html.

[‡] Fried, Ina. "Gates offers Longhorn appetizer." CNET News.com. April 25, 2005. See http://news.com.com/Gates+offers+Longhorn+appetizer/2100-1016_3-5683686.html?tag=nl.e496&tag=nl.e496).

[**] Cooper, Charles. "Going long on Longhorn." CNET News.com. April 22, 2005. (http://news.com.com/Going+long+on+Longhorn/2010-1071_3-5680345.html?tag=nl).

entrepreneurs love to hate. "[Gates] has become the Edison and Ford of our age," the piece reverently intoned. "A technologist turned entrepreneur, he embodies the digital era." Reporter Jon Katz in *The Netizen*[*] questioned why trees would even be wasted in publishing a story about Bill's private life: "The guy is the biggest bore in the history of legends. He doesn't have it in him to utter a stirring word or inspiring thought . . . In fact, as many reporters as have flocked in awe to Redmond (oddly enough, the more skeptical ones don't seem to get through), not one has ever come up with a single memorable utterance from 'the man who is shaping our future.'"

MAPPOINT: CAN'T GET THERE FROM HERE

Another paper Bill Gates found interesting during his Think Week of 2005 came from Microsoft's MapPoint unit. It described mapping services that would deliver travel directions with live images of destinations and details on traffic conditions and other information. Some of the ideas he later dismissed as "overly Jetsons," according to *The Wall Street Journal* staff reporter Guth, but Gates said he loved the vision. Later, back at the MapPoint unit, Microsofties brainstormed on comments from Bill, canceled some plans that Bill didn't like, and welcomed other groups who had heard about Bill's endorsement. Eventually, Bill himself dropped by for two hours to give the team some guidance. And that's how funding increases for a project at Microsoft.

Let's hope Microsoft's MapPoint unit gets its live images from the right satellites. A bug in Microsoft's current MapPoint software and web service sends those looking to travel between two Norwegian cities on a trip across much of Western Europe. The suggested quickest route between Haugesund and Trondheim is a 1,685-mile journey through Belgium, England, France, Germany, and Sweden. The site estimates the journey will take some 47 hours and 31 minutes.[*]

---

[*] Fried, Ina. "MapPoint users in for long and winding road." CNET News.com. January 26, 2005. See http://news.com.com/MapPoint+users+in+for+long+and+winding+road/2100-1012-5552305.html?part=dtx&tag=ntop&tag=nl.e703.

The Microsoft PR machine cranks Bill Gates up to monstrous proportions as the Ford and Edison of our times, even though he hasn't actually invented anything as startlingly innovative as the light bulb or the Model-T factory. But all these media circus acts are diversions. All the reports about viruses, zombie PCs, and systems that always crash also miss the forest for the trees. No one effectively takes on Microsoft's monopoly power—the elephant in the room.[†]

Or is it a Longhorn in a china closet? Just how successful will Microsoft's future technology be?

---

[*] Katz, Jon. "Big-Media Blow Jobs." *The Netizen*—Media Rant. January 12, 1997. See http://webmonkey.wired.com/netizen/97/02/katz0a.html.

[†] See Terry Kettering's poem, "The Elephant in the Room," at www.walkthroughlife.com/personal/pqv/poem/elephant.htm.

BILL GATES: THE GREAT HELMSMAN

With the fate of most of the world's computers in Microsoft's hands, you'd think that the company would employ a team of the top computer scientists in the world to help guide it into the future. You'd be wrong. Never before in the history of technology has so much power rested in the hands of one person, who for the last few years has also been the world's richest: Bill Gates.

A top journalist in the computer industry once noted that you can figure out where Microsoft is going next by reading Bill's lips in interviews, speeches, and press conferences. Like Babe Ruth, Gates points in the direction of his next home run and gets ready to swing at the pitch. He then leaves it up to the spin controllers at Microsoft to remove any ballplayers who might get in his way.

No matter what title he now has at Microsoft, it is Bill Gates who calls the shots for the future. Twice a year Bill Gates goes into seclusion for a week and reads thousands of pages of research reports, emails, product plans, and white papers. In February 2005, Bill went off again on his Think Week. "The effects of this Think Week are rippling through Microsoft," wrote *The Wall Street Journal* staff reporter Robert A. Guth,[*] who is the only journalist ever to be allowed to visit Gates during these sojourns. "Yusuf Mehdi, vice president in the MSN online group, says he lugged a six-inch-thick printout of Mr. Gates's Think Week comments on a business trip. In the Office software division, one group says it used Mr. Gates's comments to change direction on whether to team up with or acquire certain companies . . . Mr. Gates is well aware of the potential impact of his comments and doesn't take writing them lightly. 'If I write a comment that says, "We should do this," things will be re-orged, engineers will move,' he says. 'It's not like I can just read this paper and say, "Hey, cool, looks good." They'll assign 20 people to it then.'"

What papers did Bill Gates find particularly interesting at his recent Think Week? One, titled "Can We Contain Internet Worms?" described a novel way for Microsoft to stop the spread of worms that have taken advantage of Microsoft systems and applications for many years. According to Guth, in late-night emails to Microsoft executives, "[Gates] mused that the approach seemed almost too good to be true and might have a flaw. But if it doesn't, he explained out loud, 'We've got to deploy this thing.' By morning, he had email responses from as far away as Cambridge, England."

What's interesting about *The Wall Street Journal*'s coverage of Bill's Think Week is the amount of Microsoft PR that went into setting up the story, to the point of providing a nice graphic outlining the topics Bill read about—computer trends, education, languages, Office, security, speech, and video games. Missing from this list are some really important topics that Bill must have thought about, if not read papers on. There is no discussion of the future of search technologies, for example, at a time when Google is encroaching on Microsoft territory. There are no ruminations on mobile computing, server-based consumer applications, or web services, no talks about the future of the iPod and other music distribution methods.

And, of course, there was no discussion at all of the power of Microsoft's monopoly over the ecosystem of technology.

---

[*] Guth, Robert A. "In Secret Hideaway, Bill Gates Ponders Microsoft's Future." *The Wall Street Journal.* March 28, 2005. See http://online.wsj.com/article_email/article_print/ 0,,SB111196625830690477-lzjgYNklaB4o52sbHmla62Im4,00.html.

Microsoft's Future: Uncertainty and Doubt

"Many people consider Microsoft to be this all-powerful entity that always gets its way and succeeds in whatever it attempts," said former Microsoft employee Adam Barr, author of *Proudly Serving My Corporate Masters,*[*] in an interview with kuro5hin.org.[†] "But in fact, if you look back at all the initiatives Microsoft has attempted, most of them have failed. Remember Windows at Work, an attempt to unify all office machines on a network? Or TrueImage, a clone of the PostScript page description language? Or ACE, the Advanced Computing Environment, designed to replace the Intel PC architecture? If you look at all the things that Microsoft has boldly announced with a gaggle of industry partners, the success rate is maybe 10 to 20 percent."

That estimate may be too low heading into the future. Microsoft might have a considerably higher success rate, because Microsoft's monopoly power has grown by virtue of being unchallenged, and there are many more ways than ever that the company can leverage that power. Microsoft's challenge is to make the same sort of quantum leap that it made with Windows 95, something that could lock in its 90+ percent market share of the desktop computing world into a more comprehensive Microsoft-dominated technology ecosystem. Microsoft hopes Longhorn will precipitate that quantum leap.

Longhorn will eventually dominate the computing landscape, but it will not produce a quantum leap. For one thing, it is a fairly minor change to the bulk of the Windows operating system, just as Windows XP was a fairly minor change from Windows 2000. And today's Windows XP indicates where Microsoft is going with Longhorn, and why consumers may find it unappetizing. Windows XP is arguably the first operating system that takes control *away* from people. The various automatic installations and software updates that happen without your explicit permission challenge the idea that you should be in control of what goes into and out of your computer.

"Microsoft Windows XP connects with other computers, or expects to be allowed through the user's network protection firewall, in more than 16 ways," wrote Michael Jennings of Futurepower.[‡] "The issue is not that the connections are always bad for the user. The issue is that Microsoft has moved from making operating systems that are independent to making operating systems that try to connect to Microsoft's own computers, and are somewhat dependent on new ways of having access through the software firewall." One important reason for automatic installations is that Microsoft needs to continually upgrade the system software to guard against new malware attacks. Automatic installation of upgrades is regarded as convenient, but Microsoft has used security upgrades to change the operation of other components of its software too, or to change the licensing terms—leaving you between a rock and a hard place if you don't agree with these licensing terms.

---

[*] Barr, Adam. *Proudly Serving My Corporate Masters.* Writers Club Press. December 1, 2000.

[†] Barr, Adam. "What the Future Holds for Microsoft." kuro5hin.org. See www.kuro5hin.org/?op=displaystory;sid=2003/1/2/153157/7696.

[‡] Jennings, Michael. "Windows XP Shows the Direction Microsoft is Going." See www.futurepower.net/microsoft.htm.

WINDOWS IN 2006: LONGHORN AND MORE BULL

Longhorn, the next version of Windows, is Microsoft's most important bet of this decade. The company started spinning news about it in fall 2003, but has had to delay it to concentrate on near-term security-based solutions. The commercial part of the software industry not connected to open source sincerely wants to believe in Longhorn. "Every segment of the PC food chain is desperate for a megahit out of Microsoft," wrote CNET reporter Cooper about Longhorn.[*] "With memories of the go-go days a fading memory, they would like nothing better than a killer operating system that ignites a furious upgrade cycle—if not a mad spree of impulse buying." As Randy Newman sings, "It's money that matters."

Unfortunately, you probably won't need many of the bells and whistles of Longhorn—you just need an operating system that is reliable and not so vulnerable to malware.

Steve Jobs had this to say about Longhorn at the Apple shareholder's meeting immediately after launching Tiger: "They are shamelessly copying us . . . They can't even copy fast."[†] And yet the press is willing to be steered into describing Longhorn in the present tense; perhaps it's wishful thinking on their part that Longhorn will be an improvement over Windows XP and will go a long way toward answering lingering complaints about ease-of-use and computer security. But the net effect of Microsoft's demo and press blitz is the spreading of FUD: fear that Longhorn will be the better system, uncertainty that Apple will be able to stay competitive as Longhorn rises, and doubt that there is any need to switch from Microsoft's system, because its next version addresses all your needs.

[*] Cooper, Charles. "Going long on Longhorn." CNET News.com. April 22, 2005. See http://news.com.com/Going+long+on+Longhorn/2010-1071_3-5680345.html?tag=nl.

[†] Fried, Ina. "Apple's Jobs swipes at Longhorn." CNET News.com. April 21, 2005. See http://news.com.com/2061-10794_3-5680232.html.

It's not even clear that Microsoft can fix problems with these security upgrades. No matter how pretty Microsoft makes it, the code for Longhorn will be so complex that Microsoft won't be able to tell what makes it crash—which is why the company announced that it will be adding the PC equivalent of a flight data recorder or "black box" to the next version of Windows, in an effort to better understand and prevent computer crashes.[*] The "black box" will report detailed information about the crash, including what programs were running at the time and the contents of documents that were being created. IT managers in corporations could set up the "black box" to retrieve even more information, such as any web pages you were browsing or any video feeds you were watching. IT managers could even discover that a worker was using Instant Messenger to chat with a co-worker about finding a new job. Even airline pilots have more privacy—the real "black box" in airplanes keeps routine in-flight dialog confidential.

So Microsoft has put mechanisms in place for the system to detect failures and report them back to Microsoft, and these mechanisms also allow Microsoft applications to communicate back to the mother ship in Redmond—for example, Windows Media Player can report which DVDs you watched today.

[*] Fried, Ina. "Microsoft to add 'black box' to Windows." CNET News.com. April 26, 2005. See http://news.zdnet.com/2100-9588_22-5684051.html.

Even if Microsoft says it never uses that information or doesn't even bother to retrieve it, there is no guarantee that its policies won't change. Longhorn will only strengthen these mechanisms by making them essential for the operation of any computer.

Even though the computer industry has conceded the desktop to Microsoft, it hasn't thrown in the towel in other areas related to computing. In areas Microsoft hasn't yet penetrated, such as the smart cell phone industry, Microsoft intends to "make a contribution" and take market share away from Nokia and others using rival system software.

MICROSOFT TO TURN OLD PCS INTO DUMB TERMINALS

If you think Windows is dumb, try this: paying for a new, stripped-down version of Windows that turns old PCs into even dumber terminals.

Microsoft won't abandon the millions of people who use old PCs that can't run Windows XP or Longhorn. The company smells an opportunity to make money by offering an "upgrade" that combines parts of Windows XP with the SP2 upgrade. According to news reports, this version of Windows, code-named Eiger, will turn older PCs into a *thin client*—a dumb terminal that gets most of its information from a central server. Unlike traditional dumb terminals and thin clients, it will still be able to run Internet Explorer, Windows Media Player, and anti-virus software.

Older PCs running Windows 95 or 98 are so insecure and vulnerable to viruses and malware that they are an embarrassment to Microsoft and could dampen consumer enthusiasm for the Windows brand. "From a security perspective, there are a lot of unhappy customers out there because they are running older machines that can't be patched," admitted a group product manager in Microsoft's Windows client unit to CNET.* "If they wanted to run Windows XP, it really doesn't run very well [on older PCs]; it might take 20 minutes to boot."

An "older PC" is really any PC that's not capable of running Windows XP. To run Eiger, Microsoft will most likely recommend a Pentium II processor and 128 MB of memory, but it should also run on machines with an older Pentium processor and as little as 64 MB of memory.

Eiger dumbs down the PC, making it less capable than the version of Windows you'd be replacing. Microsoft won't guarantee that it will run any Windows programs and won't even promise support for Office, except as a server application—with Eiger as a thin client. Since you can already turn an old PC running an old version of Windows into a dumb terminal without buying Eiger, the project confirms my suspicions that older versions of Windows are a hazard to everyone, and the only way to fix the problem is to replace Windows itself. Microsoft is cynically asking consumers to pay more to fix up Microsoft's mess.

If you have an old PC running a version of Windows pre-XP, now is the time to consider Linux. It's not a dumb choice.

_____

* Fried, Ina. "Microsoft tries to breathe life into older PCs." CNET News.com. May 12, 2005. See http://news.com.com/Microsoft+tries+to+breathe+life+into+older+PCs/2100-1016_3-5705456.html?part=rss&tag=5705456&subj=news.

"The mobile space," Bill Gates told CNET News,* "there are so many neat things that can go on if—for example—you use Outlook and our phone, if you use Office and a phone, if you use our mobile format and a phone . . . We see

_____

* Fried, Ina. "Gates sees big dollars in little devices." CNET News.com. May 10, 2005. See http://news.com.com/Gates+sees+big+dollars+in+little+devices/2008-1016_3-5701477.html.

certainly a decade's worth of work, where mobile devices can get richer and richer." Reading between the lines, Microsoft's strategy is to leverage its Windows, Office, and Outlook monopolies to compete not only against other versions of smart phones but also against the popular BlackBerry from Research In Motion (RIM).

But past failures and investigations haunt Microsoft as it prepares to do battle in these new areas, and competitors are likely to spring up at every new turn of the technology cycle. One can only imagine how the TV commercials for mobile phones will change from "Can you hear me now?" to "Can you stop my phone from crashing?" Once you've married your mobile phone to your Windows PC, there would be no escaping the use of Outlook and Office, whether you want to use them or not.

By designing systems that connect and automatically install software without your knowledge or consent, Microsoft is trying to assemble an ecosystem of devices and PCs that relies on core, proprietary Microsoft code. If you want to go where no Microsoft code has gone before, you need to be wary of new devices and technologies such as smart phones, tablet-sized PCs, digital TV cable boxes, game machines, and even social networks built around blogs and RSS feeds. With Microsoft software running in every digital device, as the company would like to see happen, you may have no choice over where Microsoft takes you tomorrow—unless you make choices that bolster Microsoft's competition.

And that is what scares Bill Gates: a backlash that has competitors adding all sorts of new features to the current version of Windows XP, and to Mac OS X and Linux, that would make Longhorn irrelevant.

So what's Microsoft's single greatest innovation? Take your time. It's a trick question. There aren't any. All that money Microsoft spends on research; what have they got to show for it? Nothing! —Larry Ellison, Oracle Corp. Chairman[3]

Google Your World

Anything that scares Bill Gates is okay by me—that means software innovation must be happening outside of Microsoft's control. It has been a while since Bill Gates ran scared—the last time was in the mid-1990s when he overlooked the importance of the Internet. But Bill is scared again, and this time it's Google putting the fear into him.

Google is, as most of you know, the place to go when you want information and you don't know where it is on the Internet. Type a phrase into Google and click **Google Search** for a complete list of web pages that match the search, or click **I'm Feeling Lucky** for a single result. Google's complex, automated methods make human tampering with its results extremely unlikely. And though the company annoys you with ads, the ads can be seen as relevant to your search and are clearly marked as ads. Google does not sell placement within the results themselves.

Whether you like Google or not, the company has nearly singlehandedly invented a new market for digital advertising worth billions. Microsoft has only a minuscule part of this market, and its teeth are bared for battle. According to Fred Vogelstein at *Fortune* magazine, Bill Gates browsed the Google site's employment pages—not looking for a job, of course, but looking to see what kind of people Google wanted to hire for future projects. Why, he wondered, were the qualifications for so many of them identical to Microsoft job specs?

Microsoft was already gearing up to compete with Google for search engine advertising, but now Gates wondered whether his company might be facing much more than a war in search. He sent an email to Microsoft executives saying, in effect, "We have to watch these guys. It looks like they are building something to compete with us."[*]

Bill Gates typically takes any competition personally. You can glean quite a bit about which companies and technologies get under his skin from listening to his occasional slips in interviews and off-the-cuff answers to reporters' questions. Vogelstein got this one from a relaxed Gates after prodding him with Google's success in the stock market: "There are companies that are just so cool that you just can't even deal with it," Gates said sarcastically, according to Vogelstein, suggesting that Google was nothing more than the latest fad. Gates then added, "At least they know to wear black."

But Google is something more than a fad. In 2003, Google moved into Microsoft territory with the Deskbar, a toolbar that runs on Windows. The ability to search is a key component of future operating systems—Longhorn will be designed to appear as a unified interface for a PC's hard drive, its local network, and the Web. For this strategy to work, Longhorn needs to provide a sleek search utility, and acquiring Google has so far been out of the question. (Google allegedly spurned a Microsoft offer in late 2004.)

Microsoft has responded to the threat with a pilot program to sell its own keyword search ads—a first step to owning a commercial search network to rival those of Google and Yahoo. Microsoft Network's adCenter will offer advertisers detailed information on users' responses to certain keywords, as well as demographic and psychographic profile data. This is one search service you would be well advised to avoid. It's also very easy to avoid—Google is already integrated into Apple's Safari browser, and the Google search engine works faster with Firefox and other Mozilla browsers because it can pre-load the top search result into the cache. (Internet Explorer doesn't offer this feature.)

Google represents your first line of defense against Microsoft propaganda. You can use it as a bullshit detector: do a Google search on any phrase involving Microsoft products and the word "problem" or "alternative." See Figure 11-1 for some sample results.

Google's goal is to organize information and make it universally accessible, and that goes far beyond search. It has the potential to move the computing experience forward and a bit away from a Microsoft, making people less reliant on storing information on PCs and more dependent on free web-based email and search functions that can be accessed anywhere from any device regardless of the operating system. "Indeed," wrote Charles H. Ferguson in a special report on Google for *Technology Review*,[†] "if [Google] does everything right, it could become an enormously powerful and profitable company, representing the most serious challenge Microsoft has faced since the Apple Macintosh."

---

[*] Vogelstein, Fred. "Gates vs. Google: Search and Destroy." *Fortune.* May 16, 2005. See www.fortune.com/fortune/technology/articles/0,15114,1050065,00.html.

[†] Ferguson. Charles H. "What's Next for Google" *Technology Review.* January 2005. See www.technologyreview.com/articles/05/01/issue/ferguson0105.asp?p=1.

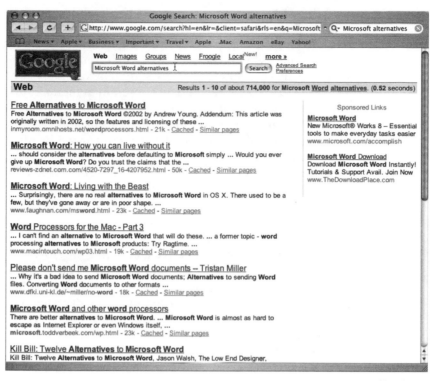

Figure 11-1: Use Google to search for the phrase "Microsoft Word alternatives" in order to get a list of web pages and sites promoting alternatives to Word. If the truth is out there, Google can probably find it.

IN SEARCH OF . . . ALTERNATIVES

You know how Google works: Go to www.google.com (or use the Search field in Apple's Safari) and type in a word or phrase to search. But Google is much more. Its search box is a phone book and a dictionary. It can check stock prices, provide news, track FedEx packages, perform metric conversions, locate airplanes, offer street maps, and supply weather conditions. It'll search retail outlets by zip code and, with Froogle, scour the Web for products.

Google's news section generates stories based on the search engine's perceived relevance of content to a particular term and the time at which any particular piece of data or story is first published online. Google concedes that stories from weirdo hate sites and other disreputable publishers lurk within the thousands of results generated from a news search, but hey, this is the Internet. Google doesn't tell you if the information is worthless.

That's fine with me. I conduct much of my research using Google, which applies no censorship or editorial rules to what I can search for or the results it generates. I find it useful that Google's system for ranking search results relies on the uniquely democratic nature of the Web—it counts the links a page receives, and analyzes the other pages that linked to it, to determine a page's "importance" or value as a search result.

Given Microsoft's track record, I don't believe the company would provide a completely censorship-free search engine. I can't imagine trusting the results of a search for "Microsoft alternatives" using a Microsoft search engine.

Start Something New

What do Google, Linux, OpenOffice.org, iTunes, Firefox, Samba, and the Mac have in common? Besides competing somewhat successfully against Microsoft, these technologies were started by visionaries with modest means who chose to innovate rather than copy or incrementally upgrade an existing product. But these innovators had no choice, really. Microsoft can get away with leveraging a monopoly to maintain its position in the market, but it can't innovate in a timely fashion. There will always be willing competitors and excellent alternatives.

Fortunately, you don't have to simply imagine a world without Microsoft. You can run your digital life without Microsoft code, and run it less expensively and with better security against viruses and malware. You can work productively, collaborating and sharing information with Microsoft-addicted individuals, offices, and businesses without ever having to use the stuff. You can even hide your secret free computing life from them, keeping up a Microsoft-like appearance for your system and importing and exporting Microsoft data formats. Thanks to real competition, you have real choices. You can afford to say no to Microsoft until the day when it loses enough market share to transform itself into a truly innovative company that does not rely on monopoly power.

When cutting-edge fields of knowledge come into contact, new disciplines can be spawned, and progress can go zooming off in unexpected directions.
—Paul Saffo, Institute for the Future[5]

There is hope that even Microsoft will change, and competition in some areas is already having an effect—Linux is so established in the server market that Microsoft has to compete with it on a feature-by-feature basis, and in large server accounts, Microsoft might be willing to go the next step and give Windows away for free with its server technologies in order to remain competitive with Linux. OpenOffice.org is applying pressure to Microsoft to release a new version of Office *before* Longhorn becomes available. The iPod and iTunes are spurring Microsoft to try to come up with the equivalent functions involving video. Free wireless technologies, rival smart phone systems, BlackBerries, handhelds, and game machines are giving Microsoft a run for its money. And Google is poised to take away from Microsoft one of the most important functions of an operating system: the ability to search for information.

There has never been a better time to just say no to Microsoft.

THE TRUTH IS OUT THERE

You too can investigate the strange and unexplained behavior of Windows PCs and Microsoft applications, and you won't need an X file to do it, because there are no hidden forces at work to impede your efforts— it's all right out there on the Internet.

Microsoft can spread fear, uncertainty, and doubt among the population; it can lock up corporate IT departments with dependencies on its file formats and protocols; it can bully developers and software vendors into turning over their trade secrets; it can throw a monkey wrench into the plans of hardware manufacturers; and it can even offer a bedroom in Bill Gates' mansion to U2 frontman Bono while he's on tour. What it can't do is stem the flow of free information.

And people are getting angry. One web page claims that Bill Gates is the focus of evil in the modern world.[*] Others rightly point out that Microsoft systems and software are truly more vulnerable to viruses and malware. This appendix lists a few interesting pages that summarize many of the problems with Microsoft.

---

[*] "I Hate Microsoft" page at www.interstel.net/~jdpaul/microsoft.html.

"Viruses Affecting Microsoft Outlook" (www.slipstick.com/problems/virus.htm)

Look up the most famous viruses and worms and follow links to analysis and recovery information.

"Gripes About Microsoft Word" (www.computergripes.com/Word.html)

Learn how Word documents can be rigged to hijack files from PCs and other mischief.

"We Can Put an End to Word Attachments" (www.gnu.org/philosophy/no-word-attachments.html)

Richard Stallman is one of the founders of the free software movement. "Word attachments are annoying, but worse than that, they impede people from switching to free software. Maybe we can stop this practice with a simple collective effort."

"Windows XP Shows the Direction Microsoft Is Going" (www.hevanet.com/peace/microsoft.htm)

To quote the author, "You have a right to know . . . Windows XP is the first Microsoft operating system to challenge whether the user can have control over his or her own computer."

Anti-Microsoft Conspiracies

Microsoft may or may not have a right to be paranoid, but there *are* companies and organizations trying to bring down the not-so-jolly green giant, either for altruistic or commercial reasons. Sun Microsystems (www.sun.com), Apple (www.apple.com), Oracle Systems (www.oracle.com), Novell (www.novell.com), Adobe Systems (www.adobe.com), and IBM (www.ibm.com) are all eager to eat Microsoft's lunch, even though they also field products that work with Microsoft's systems.

In the late 1990s, as Microsoft rolled out Windows 98 and Windows ME on the system side and Office 97 and Internet Explorer on the applications side, and the U.S. Justice Dept. took over the FTC investigation of the company, loads of web pages and entire sites erupted with anti-Microsoft sentiments. All sorts of scholarly pages were published along with anecdotes and humor from wackos and enraged hackers. Many of these pages are still up on the Web and are entertaining if not informative, drawing attention to bugs and viruses and explaining why Microsoft software is particularly vulnerable:

The Microsoft Boycott Campaign (www.msboycott.com)

Although this site hasn't been significantly updated since 2002, it lists alternatives, both commercial and open source, for every significant Microsoft product—with links to their suppliers.

Boycott Microsoft (www.vcnet.com/bms)

This site stopped producing news in 2000, but it offers an excellent time capsule history of Microsoft's dirty tricks, and an informative collection of reader-submitted outrages.

The Anti-Microsoft Association (http://members.aol.com/machcu/amsa.html)

This site hosts essays on what's wrong with Microsoft, what you can do about it, and what the government should do about it. While it hasn't been updated since December 2001, it offers links to humor pages, books, articles, and reports.

The Gneech's Micro$oft Boycott Page (http://members.aol.com/thegneech/msb.htm#how)

Largely the personal opinion of the author, this page includes a "How do you want to crash today?" section of visual and verbal humor blasting Microsoft and in-depth technical descriptions of why Microsoft software is "just plain shoddy." However, this site hasn't been updated since 1997.

NetAction's Microsoft Archives (www.netaction.org/msoft)

In May 1997, NetAction launched the Consumer Choice Campaign to focus attention on Microsoft's growing monopolization of the Internet. At that time, no other organizations were working to mobilize Internet users to speak up. NetAction published the Micro$oft Monitor, conducted surveys, and researched and published white papers between May 1997 and July 1999—all of which are listed on this page.

Warum ich Microsoft hasse (http://mitglied.lycos.de/sebastianbohle)

A hate-Microsoft page with alternatives, for all you folks who read German.

Life Without Microsoft (www.frogtown.com/~mblake/noms)

The author of this page (like the author of this book) decided once and for all to jettison Microsoft from his computer life and to help others do so, too. This page includes a pledge you can take to make an effort to get Microsoft out of your lives, and a way to add your name to a list of people who have accepted the challenge.

Anti-Microsoft Site (http://pcwar.8m.com)

This site provides an analysis of why Bill Gates is the devil and other satire.

Vrythramax's Microsoft Haters Site (www.kenshi.net/microsloth/index.html)

This site, updated in 2004, starts off with the proclamation that "Microsoft's XP software violates the law and abrogates consumer rights. When you buy XP software, you do not own it; instead Microsoft owns you." It goes on to describe how the Windows XP Activation Wizard works, all the laws it supposedly breaks, and why you should avoid Windows XP.

Proudly Serving My Corporate Masters: Disliking Microsoft (www.proudlyserving.com/archives/2005/03/disliking_micro.html)

A Microsoft employee speaks out. Adam Barr, author of the book *Proudly Serving My Corporate Masters*,[*] describes his 10 years as a software developer for Microsoft.

---

[*] Barr, Adam. *Proudly Serving My Corporate Masters*. Writers Club Press. December 1, 2000.

Resources for the Rehabilitated

You are not alone in your quest to get beyond Microsoft's reach. The resources listed in this section give you information about how to say no to Microsoft.

Alternatives to Microsoft

Whether you use OpenOffice.org as an alternative to Microsoft Office, or Firefox as your browser, or Linux as your operating system, or any other alternative to Microsoft software, you'll find these sites useful:

Get Off Microsoft (www.tonybove.com/getoffmicrosoft)
I offer a site dedicated to helping people make the switch from Microsoft systems and software to alternatives. Included are tips, techniques, reviews, and an extensive set of links to free software downloads and resources, including all the links in this book.

MSBC's The Alternative: Replacements for Word (www.msboycott.com/thealt/alts/word.shtml)
The Microsoft Boycott Campaign offers a comprehensive list of commercial and free alternatives to Microsoft Word, with links to download sites.

MSBC's The Alternative: Replacements for Office (www.msboycott.com/thealt/alts/office.shtml)
The Microsoft Boycott Campaign provides a short list of commercial and free bundled applications that can replace the entire Microsoft Office suite, including Word, Excel, and PowerPoint.

MSBC's The Alternative: Replacements for PowerPoint (www.msboycott.com/thealt/alts/powerpoint.shtml)
The Microsoft Boycott Campaign provides a surprisingly long list of Power-Point alternatives.

MSBC's The Alternative: Replacements for MSN Messenger (www.msboycott.com/thealt/alts/messenger.shtml)
The Microsoft Boycott Campaign again, this time with alternatives for instant messaging.

OpenOffice.org (www.openoffice.org)
Headquarters for the free OpenOffice.org project, an open source alternative to Office that includes replacements for Word, Excel, and PowerPoint.

Firefox—Rediscover the Web (www.mozilla.org/products/firefox)
The Firefox home page provides a great big green Free Download button. Firefox is the most popular alternative web browser.

Outlook Alternatives (www.pcbuyersguide.com/solutions/web/email_alternatives.html)
An in-depth review of alternatives to Microsoft Outlook for email, calendars, and schedules.

Apple and Mac

The following sites provide information about Apple, Mac computers, software and accessories for the Mac, and troubleshooting support:

Apple Computer (www.apple.com)
The official site offers product information and the Apple Store.

VersionTracker software updates and downloads for Mac OS X (www.versiontracker.com/macosx)
This site is the first place to look for free Mac software.

MacFixIt (www.macfixit.com)
This site offers the latest information and troubleshooting solutions for Apple system and software updates.

MacInTouch (www.macintouch.com)
This site and publication has been offering Mac news and information since 1994.

The Mac Night Owl (www.macnightowl.com)
This site is a technical support site for Mac users that also offers an email newsletter.

Mac OS X Hints (www.macosxhints.com)
This site offers tips and troubleshooting solutions for Mac OS X.

iPodlounge (www.ipodlounge.com)
This site offers news and reviews of iPod accessories and software.

Linux, Open Source Software, and Unix

These sites tell you everything you need to know about Linux, Unix, and open source software for your computer:

Samba (http://us1.samba.org/samba)
This site supports the free open source Samba suite for Linux that provides file sharing and print services with Windows on a network.

WINE HQ (www.winehq.com)
Headquarters for the WINE open source implementation of the Windows programming interface on top of X and Unix. WINE is a compatibility layer for running Windows programs that does not require Windows or any Microsoft code.

DesktopLinux (www.desktoplinux.com)
This site focuses on using Linux in enterprises and office desktops. It offers news, opinions, how-to articles, product reviews, a discussion forum, and a resource directory.

DistroWatch (http://distrowatch.com)
This site keeps track of Linux distributions and provides extensive reviews and comparisons.

Doctor Tux (www.doctortux.com)
This site lets you enter questions about Linux and view free answers. It knows about all major Linux distributions including Red Hat, Fedora, Debian-GNU, SuSE, Mandrake, and Slackware.

Edgy Penguins—Linux for Non-Geeks (www.edgy-penguins.org/non-geeks)
Rickford Grant, the author of *Linux for Non-Geeks*,[*] provides information online for those "who want to enter the world of Linux but have been holding back out of fear that it is a system for compu-geeks."

Frank's Corner (www.frankscorner.org)
This site provides just about all the information you need to get some popular Windows applications and games running on Linux using WINE—see WINE HQ (http://www.winehq.com).

Browsers for Linux (www.itp.uni-hannover.de/~kreutzm/en/lin_browser.html)
This page provides an exhaustive list of Linux browsers and links to news and support information about them.

Miscellaneous Useful Websites

The following sites can help you with practical solutions to problems you may encounter while weaning yourself off Microsoft:

ABC Amber Conversion Software (www.thebeatlesforever.com/processtext/index.html)
This commercial vendor provides conversion software for just about every file format for text, documents, and multimedia information.

PDF Research/Links/Troubleshooting and Solutions (www.performancegraphics.com/Pages/linktrbl.html)
This site provides the best collection of links to troubleshooting information for Portable Document Format (PDF) files and Adobe Acrobat products.

DVD FAQ (www.dvddemystified.com/dvdfaq.html)
Frequently asked questions and answers spanning the entire range of DVD technology.

Doom9.net—The Definitive DVD Backup Resource (www.doom9.org/index.html?/codecs-203-1.htm)
An extremely technical site with highly detailed information about making backup copies of DVDs and converting them to formats for playback on Linux and other systems.

MPEG playback technology recommendations (http://xtras.tabuleiro.com/support/technotes/general/gn002.htm)
A technical site that outlines the recommended MPEG playback technologies to use for video projects. See also "MPEG2 playback considerations" (http://xtras.tabuleiro.com/support/technotes/mpeg_advance/ma007.htm) for a technical overview of common MPEG issues.

---

[*] Grant, Rickford. *Linux for Non-Geeks*. No Starch Press. 2004.

Slashdot (http://slashdot.org)
> The venerable site offering news for nerds and "stuff that matters" covers the entire computing industry and in particular, the open source community from the perspective of software developers. See also the Information Technology (IT) subsection, "It is what IT is" (http://it.slashdot.org), for perspectives on enterprise software.

As the Worm Turns: Updated Reports on Infections

These sites provide useful information about viruses, worms, spyware, and other malware affecting Microsoft software:

Symantec Security Response site (http://securityresponse.symantec.com)
> This site provides the latest information on virus and worm attacks with links to detailed information.

F-Secure (www.europe.f-secure.com/virus-info)
> This European site offers new information daily about virus attacks.

Vmyths.com (www.vmyths.com)
> This site provides information about the latest virus hoaxes.

Symantec (www.symantec.com) and McAfee (www.mcafee.com)
> These are the two largest commercial anti-virus software providers.

The National Cyber Security Alliance (www.staysafeonline.info/home-tips.html)
> The NCSA provides tips on how to keep computers secure from outside attacks.

Webroot (www.webroot.com/spywareinformation/spywaretopthreats)
> This page lists the 10 worst spyware and adware threats of the moment.

McAfee Associates (http://vil.mcafee.com/hoax.asp) or Symantec (http://securityresponse.symantec.com/avcenter/hoax.html)
> These sites track virus hoaxes.

Hoaxbusters (http://hoaxbusters.ciac.org)
> This site is both useful and entertaining—it's hosted by the U.S. Department of Energy.

If You Must Use Microsoft . . .

If you just can't wean yourself off Microsoft Windows or Microsoft applications (such as the Mac versions) at this time, at least take steps to make your computer less vulnerable to viruses and malware. For example, you should just say yes to Windows patches and updates. You can't afford to second-guess Microsoft on this; once you are locked into using the Microsoft's code, you have to follow Microsoft's upgrade plan or risk making your computer even more vulnerable than before. While the lock-in is similar on a Mac (i.e., you have to follow Apple's plan), at least with a Mac you have one company responsible for both hardware and software—and a lot less finger-pointing by support when something goes wrong. If you stay with Microsoft, you must also keep up with upgrades and patches from your hardware manufacturer.

Many people need to stay with Microsoft systems, because many enterprises have standardized their IT departments around Microsoft technology. If you work for such an enterprise, you may not realize how much you rely on the nerds in white coats in the IT lab. They have to keep up with an endless stream of server software fixes and security patches to keep the servers running. If you don't work in such an enterprise but still need to stay with Windows, you need to keep up with system patches and updates yourself. For the most up-to-date information about Microsoft system security patches, see Microsoft TechNet's Security Bulletin Search page (www.microsoft.com/technet/security/current.aspx).

Use Windows Update and Office Update regularly to apply the most recent patches. The Windows Update mechanism (http://windowsupdate.microsoft.com) is an ActiveX control downloaded from Microsoft that checks for available updates to system files, device drivers, service packs, and new Windows features. In addition, the patches applied by Windows Update can disable, patch, or remove ActiveX controls that have been found to contain security risks. If you have Microsoft Office, you should use Microsoft's Office Update (http://officeupdate.microsoft.com) as well, because Microsoft Office contains additional ActiveX controls that Windows Update does not maintain.

Since the Windows Update and Office Update product catalogs are tailored for the programs and components you have installed at the time you visit the Update page, you should check Windows Update and Office Update whenever you add additional components to your system. If you re-install Windows or Office, you also need to re-install any components you had previously downloaded through the Update mechanisms.

Many of you can't take advantage of the Windows XP Service Pack 2 (SP2) upgrade until your applications support it. Microsoft has issued a list of nearly 50 applications and games that may encounter problems with SP2—see the Microsoft help and support pages for SP2 (http://support.microsoft.com/default.aspx?kbid=884130&product=windowsxpsp2 and http://support.microsoft.com/default.aspx?kbid=842242).

Besides checking the anti-virus sites listed in this chapter and following instructions associated with reported attacks to remove viruses, worms, adware, and spyware, you may also find these sites useful for helping you deal with Microsoft software:

Excel Oddities (www.j-walk.com/ss/excel/odd/index.htm)
This site's introduction says it best: "Excel is a complex program, and has been around for a long time. Consequently, it has many obscure nooks and crannies to discover. Some of them are described here."

Windows Media Player multimedia file formats (http://support.microsoft .com/default.aspx?scid=kb;en-us;Q316992)
Microsoft's "Help and Support" page provides links to information about each format. It also provides Microsoft-blessed sample files in each format so that you can test your playback application.

Microsoft Office Assistance Page (http://office.microsoft.com/en-us/ assistance/HA011402971033.aspx)
This page provides a list of the file types blocked from use as email attachments by Microsoft Outlook—more than 70 different types of files are blocked by default. For information on how to block additional file types as email attachments, see the page "How to configure Outlook to block additional attachment file name extensions" (http://support .microsoft.com/?id=837388).

CWShredder (www.intermute.com/products/cwshredder.html)
This software can locate and remove most variants of the CoolWebSearch spyware that targets Internet Explorer and its Microsoft Java virtual machine. Since the site might be blocked by the Trojan horse on your system, try a mirror site, such as http://209.133.47.200/~merijn/index.html, to download the software.

Microsoft Word: Living with the Beast (www.faughnan.com/msword.html)
I don't recommend continued use of Word, but this site provides useful information about avoiding Word's pitfalls and vulnerabilities and turning out virus-free Word documents. As the author notes, Word "is to software as the Irish Elk was to mammals. It is an inherently incurable mass of contradictory impulses, which are fully evident in Word's formatting model. It is the single most miserable piece of software that I absolutely must use."

CITATIONS

Chapter 1

1. Emerson, Bo. "Ed Roberts and MITS." *Atlanta Journal-Constitution.* April 27, 1997.
2. Alsop, Stewart. "Just How Bad Is Windows 95?" *Fortune.* November 11, 1996. See http://208.234.7.168/arnspub/old/Macintosh/Apple/Just-How-Bad-W95.html.

Chapter 2

1. Tufte, Edward R. *Envisioning Information.* Cheshire: Graphics Press, 1990.
2. Stephen Manes. "Full Disclosure: Sick of Blue Screens? Get a Mac!" *PC World.* September 2002. See www.pcworld.com/news/article/0,aid,102528,00.asp.

Chapter 5

1. Cassia, Fernando. "OpenOffice 2.0 preview released." *The Inquirer.* December 19, 2004. See www.theinquirer.net/?article=20293.

Chapter 6

1. Cringely, Robert X. "Triumph of the Nerds: The Television Program Transcripts." PBS Online. 1996. See www.pbs.org/nerds/part3.html.
2. Junnarkar, Sandeep. "Glaser, others blast Microsoft." CNET News.com. July 23, 1998. See http://news.com.com/Glaser,+others+blast+Microsoft/2100-1023_3-213667.html.
3. Ibid.

Chapter 7

1. Arthur, Charles. "Microsoft's browser dominance at risk as experts warn of security holes." The Independent. July 5, 2004. See http://news.independent.co.uk/world/science_technology/story.jsp?story=537951.
2. Sanchez-Klein, Jana. "McNealy bashes Microsoft smart card OS, touts Java." InfoWorld Electric. November 4, 1998. See www.infoworld.com/cgi-bin/displayStory.pl?98114.wnmcnealy.htm.
3. Granneman, Scott. "Linux vs. Windows Viruses." SecurityFocus. October 20, 2003. See www.securityfocus.com/columnists/188.

4. Segal, David. "Judge May Issue Findings in Microsoft Case Today." *The Washington Post*. November 5, 1999.

Chapter 8

1. Adams, Douglas. "Beyond the Hype." *Guardian*, U.K. August 25, 1995. See http://users.aol.com/machcu/dawin95.html.

Chapter 9

1. See www.webroot.com/spywareinformation/?WRSID=6bab3d100477 b1dbdc0fe502966fc0a6.
2. Geer, David, et al. "CyberInsecurity: the Cost of Monopoly. How the Dominance of Microsoft's Products Pose a Risk to Security." Computer and Communications Industry Association. See www.ccianet.org/papers/cyberinsecurity.pdf.
3. Lohr, Steve. "Microsoft Gives A Freer Hand To Gateway." *The New York Times* (Business and Financial Desk). May 28, 1998.
4. Alsop, Stewart. "Alsop on InfoTech: The Monopoly Has Just Begun." *Fortune*. July, 2001. See www.fortune.com/fortune/alsop/0,15704,371207,00.html.
5. Fried, Ina and Paul Festa. "Reversal: Next IE divorced from new Windows." CNET News.com. February 15, 2005. See http://news.com.com/Reversal+Next+IE+update+divorced+from+Windows/2100-1032_3-5577263.html.

Chapter 10

1. Langberg, Mike. "Millennium OS upgrade not worth the risk." *San Jose Mercury News*. September 9, 2000.
2. Alsop, Stewart. "Just How Bad Is Windows 95?" *Fortune*. November 11, 1996. See http://208.234.7.168/arnspub/old/Macintosh/Apple/Just-How-Bad-W95.html.
3. Krill, Paul. "Gates undaunted by Linux." *InfoWorld*. October 1, 2004. See www.infoworld.com/article/04/10/01/HNgatestalksmuseum_1.html.

Chapter 11

1. Orwell, George. "Politics and the English Language." First appeared in *Horizon*, London, 1946. Reprinted in *Shooting an Elephant and Other Essays*. Secker and Warburg. 1950. See www.mtholyoke.edu/acad/intrel/orwell46.htm.
2. "The Future of Tech: Speaking Out: Institute for the Future's Paul Saffo." BusinessWeek Online. August 25, 2003. See http://businessweek.com/magazine/content/03_34/b3846640.htm.
3. Symonds, Matthew. *Softwar: An Intimate Portrait of Larry Ellison and Oracle*. Simon & Schuster. 2003. See www.usdoj.gov/atr/cases/f204400/204461.htm.
4. Magee, Mike. "Microsoft says life's simple." *The Register*. September 2, 1999. See www.theregister.co.uk/1999/09/02/microsoft_says_lifes_simple.
5. Saffo, Paul. "Untangling the Future." *Business 2.0*. June 2002. See www.saffo.org/untangling_the_future.html.

INDEX

iPod, 33–35, 128
Iraq war, 105
Isaacson, Walter, 213–214
iTunes Setup Assistant, 126
iTunes software, 33–35
    music sources for, 125–128
    as proprietary platform, 112
    security, 117

J

Jackson, Penfield, 158
Janus technology, 113
Java platform, 23
Jennings, Michael, 216
Jobs, Steve
    on Longhorn, 217
    on Microsoft taste, 112
    and music, 35
    on music industry, 125
Justice Department, 13–14, 16

K

Kaplan, David A., 11, 18
Kaplan, Jerry, 17
Kapor, Mitchell, 209
Katz, Jon, 214
KDE (Kool Desktop Environment), 55
KeenValue adware, 178
Keynote 2 application, 109
Kildall, Gary, 10–11
Knoppix distribution, 55
knowledge for alternative software, 208
KOffice suite, 110
Kool Desktop Environment (KDE), 55
Kpresenter application, 110
Kristensen, Thomas, 187

L

LAME encoder, 131
Langberg, Mike, 201
LANs (local area networks), 161–163
    Linux, 167–169
    Macintosh, 165–166
    for moving data, 207
    NetWare, 166
    risk in, 163–164
    for sharing files, 169–173
Leonhard, Woody, 72
Liberty Alliance, 103
Library tab, 123–124
licenses
    copyleft, 62
    Microsoft, 47–48

Linspire distribution, 54
Linux operating system, 43–44
    applications, 59–61
    attachments in, 150
    bugs, 49
    for desktop, 52–57
    distributions, 54, 203–204
    for email, 157
    for file sharing, 172–173
    free software movement, 44–48
    LANs in, 167–169
    pocket devices, 58–59
    resources for, 227–228
    revolution, 61–63
    servers in, 50–52
    system upgrades in, 48
    for video, 134
litigation
    antitrust, 12–13, 16, 19
    DVD encryption, 138
    Linux, 53
local area networks. *See* LANs (local area
    networks)
Longhorn operating system, 216–217
lossless and lossy compression algorithms,
    128
Lotus 1-2-3 application, 96, 99
Lphoto applications, 59
Lyons, Daniel, 169

M

.Mac service, 36–38
Macintosh computers, 27–28
    attachments in, 149–150
    GarageBand application, 35–36
    identity security and viruses in, 30–31
    iLife package for, 31–33
    iPod, 33–35
    LANs in, 165–166
    .Mac service, 36–38
    operating systems in, 38–42
    resources for, 227
    switching to, 28–30
macros
    viruses in, 144
    in Word, 71
    in Writer, 85
Macrovision, 115
Mailsmith application, 157
Mailtraq, 148
Manes, Stephen, 42
manipulation of press, 212–215
MapPoint unit, 214
markup tools in PDF, 90

trash bins, programming ideas in, 61
Trojan horses, 144
Trojan.Xombe Trojan horse, 155
TrueImage language, 216
TrueType format, 74
trustworthiness, 25
Trustworthy Computing Initiative,
    157–158
Tufte, Edward R., 41, 104
Tuftedal, Ole-Bjorn, 44
Turkel, Sherry, 106
12-step rehabilitation program, 197–209

U

U.S. Computer Emergency Readiness
    Team (US-CERT), 190
Unix
    resources for, 227–228
    SCO, 53
Ussachevsky, Vladimir, 35

V

VBScript, 143
video. *See* digital media
VideoLAN project, 134–135, 137
virtual private networks (VPNs), 166
viruses
    email, 143, 146
    infections. *See* infections
    in Linux, 46
    in Macintosh computers, 30
    macro, 144
    in Word, 71
VisiCalc application, 96
Vogelstein, Fred, 219–220
VPNs (virtual private networks), 166

W

Waitt, Ted, 181
Warnock, John, 89
WAV (Waveform Audio File Format)
    encoders, 128–130
Wayner, Peter, 63
web bugs, 189
web email services, 146
web pages
    for Excel, 101
    .Mac service, 37
Weinberg, Jerry, 141
Weinberg's Law, 141
Wildstrom, Stephen, 160
WinAmp player, 132
Windows Media Audio (WMA) format,
    113, 126

Windows Media Player, 113–114
    for DVDs, 136
    encrypted path in, 116–118
    file associations in, 121–124
    setup for, 118–121
Windows Messenger, 158
Windows systems and applications
    development of, 14–15
    in Linux, 60
    sharing files with, 169–173
Windows Update, 230
WinDVD player, 136
WINE (WINE Is Not an Emulator), 60
wireless LANs, 168
WMA (Windows Media Audio) format,
    113, 126
Wong, Karl, 21
Word application, 67–68
    alternatives to, 80–81
        AbiWord, 86–87
        collaboration in, 86–87
        PDF, 89–92
        WordPerfect, 81–83
        Writer, 83–86
    annoying features in, 68–70
    ASCII text files in, 77–78
    bloated files in, 71
    document format in, 70–71
    HTML files in, 78
    PDF files in, 77
    printing in, 72–75
    RTF files in, 75–76
    special characters in, 78–80
    stealing files with, 72
WordPerfect application, 81–83
world domination agenda, 18
worms, 144, 153
Writer application, 81, 83–86
Wscript.Kak worm, 151

X

X MultiMedia System (XMMS) player, 133
Xandros distribution, 54
xine library, 59
Xine player, 136
XML (Extensible Markup Language)
    with AbiWord, 87
    with Calc, 99
    with Excel, 96, 100
    for spreadsheets, 102–103
XMMS (X MultiMedia System) player, 133

Z

zones, security, 183–186

LINUX MADE EASY
The Official Guide to Xandros 3 for Everyday Users

by RICKFORD GRANT

Based on Xandros 3, arguably one of the most user-friendly versions of Linux available today, *Linux Made Easy* concentrates on the subjects of most interest to the average home user or hobbyist: installation, using the Internet, playing CDs and audio files, using scanners, working with digital cameras and images, games, downloading software and fonts, USB storage devices, PDAs, printing, Internet telephony, and more.

AUGUST 2005, 496 PP. W/CD, $34.95 ($47.95 CAN)
ISBN 1-59327-057-7

STEAL THIS COMPUTER BOOK™ 3
What They Won't Tell You About the Internet

by WALLACE WANG

This offbeat, non-technical book looks at what hackers do, how they do it, and how you can protect yourself. The third edition of this bestseller (over 150,000 copies sold) adopts the same informative, irreverent, and entertaining style that made the first two editions a huge success. Thoroughly updated, this edition also covers rootkits, spyware, web bugs, identity theft, hacktivism, wireless hacking (wardriving), biometrics, and firewalls.

MAY 2003, 384 PP., $24.95 ($37.95 CAN)
ISBN 1-59327-000-3

STEAL THIS FILE SHARING BOOK™
What They Won't Tell You About File Sharing

by WALLACE WANG

Steal This File Sharing Book tackles the thorny issue of file sharing networks such as Kazaa, Morpheus, and Usenet. It explains how these networks work and how to use them. It exposes the dangers of using file sharing networks—including viruses, spyware, and lawsuits—and tells how to avoid them. In addition to covering how people use file sharing networks to share everything from music and video files to books and pornography, it also reveals how people use them to share secrets and censored information banned by their governments. Includes coverage of the ongoing battle between the software, video, and music pirates and the industries that are trying to stop them.

NOVEMBER 2004, 296 PP., $19.95 ($27.95 CAN)
ISBN 1-59327-050-X

THE CULT OF iPOD

by LEANDER KAHNEY

Wired News reporter Leander Kahney follows up his best selling *The Cult of Mac* (No Starch Press) with *The Cult of iPod*, a comprehensive look at how Apple's hit iPod is changing music, culture, and listening behavior. *The Cult of iPod* includes the exclusive back story of the iPod's development; looks at the many ways iPod's users pay homage to their devices; and investigates the quirkier aspects of iPod culture, such as iPod-jacking (strangers plugging into each other's iPods to discover new music) as well as the growing legions of MP3Js (regular folks who use their iPods to become DJs).

NOVEMBER 2005, 256 PP., $24.95 ($33.95 CAN)
ISBN 1-59327-066-6

THE eBAY® SURVIVAL GUIDE
How to Make Money and Avoid Losing Your Shirt

by MICHAEL BANKS

The eBay Survival Guide is a no-holds-barred guide to safe and successful buying and selling on the popular online auction site. This book reveals the strategies of winning bidders and offers tips for beating competitors to get the items you want—without overpaying or becoming the victim of scams. It's filled with practical advice for avoiding frauds, what to do if an item doesn't sell, how to list items effectively, choosing an auction type, how to get the best price and much more. An excellent resource for anyone looking to steer clear of scammers, execute successful transactions, and win good stuff!

SEPTEMBER 2005, 288 PP., $19.95 ($26.95 CAN)
ISBN 1-59327-063-1

PHONE:
800.420.7240 OR
415.863.9900
MONDAY THROUGH FRIDAY,
9 A.M. TO 5 P.M. (PST)

FAX:
415.863.9950
24 HOURS A DAY,
7 DAYS A WEEK

EMAIL:
SALES@NOSTARCH.COM

WEB:
HTTP://WWW.NOSTARCH.COM

MAIL:
NO STARCH PRESS
555 DE HARO ST, SUITE 250
SAN FRANCISCO, CA 94107
USA

 **Electronic Frontier Foundation**
Defending Freedom in the Digital World

Free Speech. Privacy. Innovation. Fair Use. Reverse Engineering. **If you care about these rights in the digital world, then you should join the Electronic Frontier Foundation (EFF). EFF was founded in 1990 to protect the rights of users and developers of technology. EFF is the first to identify threats to basic rights online and to advocate on behalf of free expression in the digital age.**

The Electronic Frontier Foundation Defends Your Rights!
Become a Member Today!
http://www.eff.org/support/

Current EFF projects include:

Protecting your fundamental right to vote. Widely publicized security flaws in computerized voting machines show that, though filled with potential, this technology is far from perfect. EFF is defending the open discussion of e-voting problems and is coordinating a national litigation strategy addressing issues arising from use of poorly developed and tested computerized voting machines.

Ensuring that you are not traceable through your things. Libraries, schools, the government and private sector businesses are adopting radio frequency identification tags, or RFIDs – a technology capable of pinpointing the physical location of whatever item the tags are embedded in. While this may seem like a convenient way to track items, it's also a convenient way to do something less benign: track people and their activities through their belongings. EFF is working to ensure that embrace of this technology does not erode your right to privacy.

Stopping the FBI from creating surveillance backdoors on the Internet. EFF is part of a coalition opposing the FBI's expansion of the Communications Assistance for Law Enforcement Act (CALEA), which would require that the wiretap capabilities built into the phone system be extended to the Internet, forcing ISPs to build backdoors for law enforcement.

Providing you with a means by which you can contact key decision-makers on cyber-liberties issues. EFF maintains an action center that provides alerts on technology, civil liberties issues and pending legislation to more than 50,000 subscribers. EFF also generates a weekly online newsletter, EFFector, and a blog that provides up-to-the-minute information and commentary.

Defending your right to listen to and copy digital music and movies. The entertainment industry has been overzealous in trying to protect its copyrights, often decimating fair use rights in the process. EFF is standing up to the movie and music industries on several fronts.

Check out all of the things we're working on at http://www.eff.org and join today or make a donation to support the fight to defend freedom online.

ELECTRONIC FRONTIER FOUNDATION · 454 SHOTWELL STREET · SAN FRANCISCO, CA 94110 · 415.436.9333

COLOPHON

Just Say No to Microsoft was written in OpenOffice.org and laid out in Adobe FrameMaker. The font families used are New Baskerville for body text, Futura for headings and tables, and Dogma for titles.

The book was printed and bound at Malloy Incorporated in Ann Arbor, Michigan. The paper is Glatfelter Thor 60# Antique, which is made from 50 percent recycled materials, including 30 percent postconsumer content. The book uses a RepKover binding, which allows it to lay flat when open.

UPDATES

Visit **http://www.nostarch.com/sayno.htm** for updates, errata, and other information.